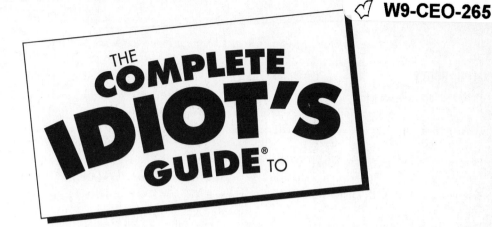

THE COMPLETE IDIOT'S GUIDE® TO

Teaching College

by Anthony D. Fredericks, Ed.D.

ALPHA

A member of Penguin Group (USA) Inc.

To the memory of my parents, Jim and Virginia Fredericks—my first teachers.

ALPHA BOOKS

Published by the Penguin Group

Penguin Group (USA) Inc., 375 Hudson Street, New York, New York 10014, USA

Penguin Group (Canada), 90 Eglinton Avenue East, Suite 700, Toronto, Ontario M4P 2Y3, Canada (a division of Pearson Penguin Canada Inc.)

Penguin Books Ltd., 80 Strand, London WC2R 0RL, England

Penguin Ireland, 25 St. Stephen's Green, Dublin 2, Ireland (a division of Penguin Books Ltd.)

Penguin Group (Australia), 250 Camberwell Road, Camberwell, Victoria 3124, Australia (a division of Pearson Australia Group Pty. Ltd.)

Penguin Books India Pvt. Ltd., 11 Community Centre, Panchsheel Park, New Delhi[md]110 017, India

Penguin Group (NZ), 67 Apollo Drive, Rosedale, North Shore, Auckland 1311, New Zealand (a division of Pearson New Zealand Ltd.)

Penguin Books (South Africa) (Pty.) Ltd., 24 Sturdee Avenue, Rosebank, Johannesburg 2196, South Africa

Penguin Books Ltd., Registered Offices: 80 Strand, London WC2R 0RL, England

International Standard Book Number: 978-159-257-600-5
Library of Congress Catalog Card Number: 2006940218

09 08 07   8 7 6 5 4 3 2 1

Interpretation of the printing code: The rightmost number of the first series of numbers is the year of the book's printing; the rightmost number of the second series of numbers is the number of the book's printing. For example, a printing code of 07-1 shows that the first printing occurred in 2007.

Printed in the United States of America

Note: This publication contains the opinions and ideas of its author. It is intended to provide helpful and informative material on the subject matter covered. It is sold with the understanding that the author and publisher are not engaged in rendering professional services in the book. If the reader requires personal assistance or advice, a competent professional should be consulted.

The author and publisher specifically disclaim any responsibility for any liability, loss, or risk, personal or otherwise, which is incurred as a consequence, directly or indirectly, of the use and application of any of the contents of this book.

Most Alpha books are available at special quantity discounts for bulk purchases for sales promotions, premiums, fund-raising, or educational use. Special books, or book excerpts, can also be created to fit specific needs.

For details, write: Special Markets, Alpha Books, 375 Hudson Street, New York, NY 10014.

Publisher: *Marie Butler-Knight*
Editorial Director: *Mike Sanders*
Managing Editor: *Billy Fields*
Senior Acquisitions Editor: *Paul Dinas*
Senior Development Editor: *Phil Kitchel*
Senior Production Editor: *Janette Lynn*
Copy Editor: *Amy Borrelli*

Cartoonist: *Richard King*
Cover Designer: *Kurt Owens*
Book Designer: *Trina Wurst*
Indexer: *Angie Bess*
Layout: *Ayanna Lacey*
Proofreader: *Terri Edwards*

Contents at a Glance

Contents

Introduction

After more than two decades of teaching college students, I've come to one inescapable conclusion—no two students and no two courses are ever alike. There is as much variety in classes and students as you'll find in a bag of Halloween candy. And I love it! Each new class has its own personality, just as each student brings a distinctive set of expectations and learning behaviors to the classroom. That's both scary and exciting, and no two days or two semesters are ever the same! For me, teaching college students is one of the most incredible, challenging, and satisfying experiences of my life—and I love it!

I wrote this book for several reasons. The most important was simply because there was a need for a down-to-earth, practical guide that would cut through all the theory and get down to the essential ingredients of effective teaching and effective learning. This is not a textbook overflowing with citations and research, it's a guidebook based on the best thinking of the best college teachers in North America. What you have in your hands is an all-inclusive guide that brings together cutting-edge teaching strategies that guarantee your success as a college teacher. (Sorry, but I can't guarantee promotions or tenure.) There are no long-winded harangues, no boring presentations, and no faded lecture notes. This book was guided by three essential words: *practical, practical, practical!*

Teaching college is filled with unique challenges, unique opportunities, and unique possibilities. My educational philosophy has always been that the best teachers are those who know they have as much to learn as they have to teach. I sincerely hope this guide will provide you with a lifetime of teaching success—now and well into the future. It truly is a most exciting journey!

How to Use This Book

Becoming a good college teacher is more about process than it is about product. It's about the practical strategies and powerful techniques that engage students in the dynamics of any subject or any topic. It's what works with real students in real classrooms. I've organized this book into six sections to tell you exactly what you need to know. Teaching is always challenging, but learning to be an outstanding college professor doesn't have to be.

Part 1, "Teaching Undergraduates," provides you with an inside look into the nature of college students. You'll discover how they learn and how you can make that learning both effective and memorable.

Part 2, "Preparing to Teach," shows you how to put a course together, how to select the best possible textbook, and how to write a course syllabus that is both detailed and flexible.

Part 3, "Teaching College: The Nitty Gritty," is chock-full of practical ideas and sensible solutions. You'll discover how to open a course with a bang, how to conduct an effective class, what a good lectures needs, how to engage students in discussions and group work, and how to enhance their thinking abilities.

Part 4, "Connecting with Students," details the specific features students expect from a good learning experience, how you can meet the needs of the diversity of students in your courses, how to effectively teach large classes, and how to deal with the inevitable "problem students" that show up in your courses.

Part 5, "Challenges and Possibilities," discusses how you can effectively evaluate your students, how to plan for meaningful internships and distance learning endeavors, and how to deal with some of the little things (attendance, tardiness, cheating, late papers) that will have an impact on your teaching.

Part 6, "Life as a College Teacher," details how adjunct professors can be successful, the strategies teaching assistants need to know, how to effectively manage an adult education course, and the instructional benefits of course evaluations. You'll also discover tips and strategies to reduce the stress in your life and plan for a long-term teaching career.

I've also provided you with lots and lots of practical resources you can use every day. There's a glossary of terms used in college teaching, a list of valuable resources and websites, and some sample course syllabi for you to review and emulate. You'll find all these in the appendixes.

... And There's More

In addition to all the practical tips, innovative ideas, and creative strategies throughout this book, I've included several sidebars that provide you with even more stuff to help you succeed.

From the Field

These are the tips, ideas, and advice I've collected from college professors all over North America. They represent a wide range of disciplines and a wide range of experiences, but their words of advice are clear, direct, and thought-provoking.

"Research Says"

Here you'll discover some of the latest cutting-edge research from some of the leading investigators in the country. The principles of good teaching (and learning) are empirically documented in these boxes.

Red Flag

There are some things you'll need to be careful with or events you'll need to watch out for. Here you'll learn about some of the cautions of college teaching.

def•i•ni•tion

Just like any other field, college teaching has its own unique set of terminology and vocabulary. I define some of that lingo for you in clear and simple language in these boxes.

Acknowledgments

College professors are fortunate to work in a fraternity that supports, encourages, and stimulates its members to achieve and succeed. Authors are no different. In fact, any book (this one included) is never really the sole effort of the author whose name appears on the cover. I have been most fortunate to enjoy the contributions and counsel of an incredible battalion of advisers, colleagues, and friends—all of whom have made this book far better than I could have ever done on my own.

First of all, I would like to salute a coterie of great thinkers and thoughtful practitioners who over the years, and specifically during the research for this book, offered incredible insights, wonderful support, and magnificent ideas—all of which are liberally sprinkled throughout these pages. I celebrate Brian Furio, Michael McGough, Dominic Delli Carpini, Kay McAdams, Jessica Nolan, Mel Kulbicki, and Tim Newman at York College of Pennsylvania for inviting me into their classrooms, their offices, and their philosophies. I am forever indebted for the continuing counsel of Walt Dudley at the University of Hawaii at Hilo. I am deeply honored by the contributions of Kim West, Ed Ransford, Mike Messner, Richard Fliegel, Terry Seip, and Hernan Ramirez at the University of Southern California. Sincere appreciation is extended to Chris Fredericks at the University of California, Irvine, for setting up some incredible interviews. I am deeply touched by the work and advice of Anita Meinbach and Susan Massey at the University of Miami (FL). Molly Roll at Sinclair Community College in Dayton, Ohio, gave me perceptive comments and detailed information about the role of adjunct professors. I also extend my sincere appreciation to any individuals I may have inadvertently omitted (alas, the plight of the "absent-minded professor"), but whose unselfish contributions pepper this book.

I was equally privileged and honored to visit colleges and universities across the United States to talk with fellow professors, share philosophies and designs, and unabashedly borrow their successes and practical ideas. Educators in California, Arizona, New Mexico, Hawaii, Colorado, Wisconsin, Illinois, Florida, South Carolina, North Carolina, Virginia, Maryland, New Jersey, Delaware, Pennsylvania, New York, New Hampshire, and Maine opened their offices, classrooms, and minds to share their sage advice and delightful wisdom. I am forever indebted to their spirit, creativity, and dedication to the highest ideals of "professorism."

Each page of this book reflects a plethora of conversations, deliberations, and discussions with undergraduate students and their instructors over the years. I am fortunate to be able to work in an environment that nurtures good teaching and supports my efforts to seek the wisdom and counsel of others—irrespective of discipline or institution. I have learned much from these interactions as I hope you will in these pages.

I am equally indebted to Kim Lionetti for her continuing support of my writing career. So, too, does Randy Ladenheim-Gil deserve a standing ovation for guiding this manuscript through the "roaring rapids" of the production process.

Once again, my wife, Phyllis, has endured the trials and tribulations of another Complete Idiot's Guide. She certainly deserves long vacations away from the constant hum of the hard drive. So, too, does she deserve my passionate pursuit of all household matters left undone during the writing of this book. As is my love for her, both are now a certainty!

Trademarks

All terms mentioned in this book that are known to be or are suspected of being trademarks or service marks have been appropriately capitalized. Alpha Books and Penguin Group (USA) Inc. cannot attest to the accuracy of this information. Use of a term in this book should not be regarded as affecting the validity of any trademark or service mark.

Part 1

Teaching Undergraduates

Think about your days as an undergraduate. Do you recall the classes you sat through, the lectures you listened to, and the textbook assignments you read? Maybe your undergraduate experiences could be summed up in three words—the good, the bad, and the ugly.

Well, now you're a teacher of undergraduate students! Perhaps you're just starting your first college position. Or, maybe you've been around the block a few times and are looking for some new ideas and new strategies. Either way, it's safe to say that the journey ahead can be scary, thrilling, and invigorating—all at the same time! Part 1 reintroduces you to those creatures we call "college students"—how they think, how they behave, what they want, what they don't want, and how we can make the next few years of their lives educationally productive. It's a challenging trip—but you're bound to have some fantastic experiences (as will your students)!

Starting Out

In This Chapter

- ◆ Who is this book for?
- ◆ All the "hats" you will wear
- ◆ What are the challenges you will face?
- ◆ What they never told you in the interview
- ◆ What this book can do for you

Each year in the United States, as a new academic year begins, more than 16 million full- and part-time undergraduate college students fill classrooms, lecture halls, laboratories, seminar rooms, and auditoriums. Waiting for them are nearly 1.6 million college teachers—rookies and veterans—ready to share their specific disciplines, philosophies, concerns, ideals, and subjects with a (hopefully) eager and willing audience. Most of these postsecondary instructors are employed in public and private 4-year colleges and universities as well as 2-year community colleges.

Although your reasons for becoming a college teacher may be personal and unique, you are part of a select group of individuals—a tradition and a profession that has endured for thousands of years. From the ancient Greeks to the present day, teaching college students engages individuals in a process that furthers insight, inquiry, and personal achievement.

From the Beginning—Who Is This Book For?

So, you've gotten your first full-time college teaching job, or maybe secured an adjunct position—teaching one or more college courses on a part-time basis. You might even be a graduate assistant or teaching assistant in charge of a seminar class or discussion group for your major professor. Or perhaps you've been teaching for a while and are looking to modify and adjust your teaching style to keep up with a new generation of college students. Well, this book is full of practical information, advice, resources, and ideas for new (and not-so-new) college professors at all levels and in all disciplines.

Just Hired: Full-Time College/University Teacher

Maybe you've successfully negotiated the complicated (and long) hiring process and secured your first job as a full-time college teacher. Besides moving to a new area, securing a place to live, and learning everything there is to know about your new institution, you may be wondering how to design courses that will be effective, memorable, and intellectually stimulating. I've designed this book to provide you with a complete and thorough overview of effective college teaching and what good college teachers need to be successful. Use this book as an introduction to the skills and talents necessary for a successful career in academia.

Just Hired: Adjunct Instructor Needs Answers

Perhaps you've been hired as an *adjunct professor/instructor* to teach one or two evening courses at the nearby university or college. You know everything about your profession or discipline and now you have the opportunity to share that knowledge with college students on a part-time basis. Although you're not a full-time faculty member, you're wondering if you have everything you need to be successful as a college teacher. You might be asking yourself the following questions:

◆ Do I have the skills to be a good college teacher?

◆ What do I really need to know to design an effective college course?

◆ I don't have time for theories—are there any practical teaching strategies I need to know?

◆ I want to be successful and I want my students to be successful. What do I do?

def•i•ni•tion

An **adjunct professor/ instructor** is hired to teach college courses on a part-time basis. He or she teaches one, two, or three courses during a semester, but does not receive any full-time benefits (health insurance, workers' compensation, preferred parking, and so on).

Those are all important and relevant questions. I'll help you find the answers to each one so you can and will succeed!

Just Hired: Graduate Assistant or Teaching Assistant

You've worked long and hard to get to this point. You've impressed the professors in your major department and they've agreed to give you one or more sections to teach. Now you're probably asking yourself lots of questions. Your anxiety level is building and your stressors are escalating, because now you have to put everything you learned into practice.

Don't be too hard on yourself—your feelings are the same as every other beginning GA or TA. Thousands of other graduate students (including me) felt the same way just prior to that all-important first day of the semester. This book will offer you down-to-earth suggestions that will ease your transition into teaching college, deal with the challenges that face you, and ensure your success from day one.

Veteran College Teacher Wants to Improve

Congratulations! One of the most important characteristics of a good college or university teacher is the realization that you can never know everything about teaching—or anything! One reason I've been in this profession for more than 3 decades is the anticipation that there is always something new to learn.

As a practiced college teacher, you may be looking for some new perspectives, new information, or new solutions to common challenges. Rest assured that this book will provide you with practical ideas garnered from experienced college teachers in large and small private and public institutions—settings just like yours. Tap into their expertise and take advantage of their insights.

A Few Facts and Figures

Here are some interesting facts and figures about teaching *postsecondary students* and the profession of college teaching. You might wish to consider these if you are thinking about a career as a full- or part-time college instructor or professor.

def•i•ni•tion

Postsecondary students are students beyond the high school level who are pursuing a degree or attempting to enhance their knowledge or career skills.

Employment Demand

Data released by the United States Department of Labor (Bureau of Labor Statistics) shows that the following academic fields typically have the highest demand for college teachers (rated from high to low):

- Health specialties
- Graduate teaching assistants
- Vocational education
- Business
- Art, drama, and music
- Biological sciences
- English language and literature
- Education
- Mathematical sciences

- Computer science
- Engineering
- Nursing
- Psychology
- Foreign language and literature
- Communication
- History
- Chemistry
- Philosophy and religion

def•i•ni•tion

Being on the **tenure-track** means having a full-time teaching position which, after a trial period (typically 6 years), converts to a status that gives protection from summary dismissal.

The Bureau of Labor Statistics also reports that future opportunities for postsecondary teachers are expected to be good through 2014, but that many new openings will be for part-time or non-*tenure-track* positions. Overall, the employment of postsecondary teachers is expected to grow much faster than all other occupations over the next decade.

Average Salaries

According to the American Association of University Professors, the average salary for full-time faculty members in 2004-2005 was $68,505. That same report indicated that the median annual earnings of all college teachers in 2004-2005 were $51,800. The middle 50 percent earned between $36,590 and $72,490.

There is a lot of variation in the earnings of college professors relative to rank, type of institution, geographic area, and field. In 2004-2005 the average full-time faculty member salaries were as follows:

- $91,548 for full professors
- $65,113 for *associate professors*

◆ $54,571 for *assistant professors*

◆ $45,647 for *lecturers*

◆ $39,899 for *instructors*

def•i•ni•tion

Instructors and **lecturers** are non-tenure-track faculty who teach part-time or conduct laboratory courses or seminars. They often lack the terminal degree in their respective field.

An **assistant professor** is an entry-level full-time college professor.

Associate professor is a rank higher than assistant professor, typically achieved after 6 years of full-time teaching.

The highest rank is **full professor**, typically obtained after 5 or 6 years at the associate level.

In 2004–2005, faculty salaries averaged $79,342 in private independent institutions, $66,851 in public institutions, and $61,103 in religiously affiliated private colleges and universities.

It's also important to note that faculty in 4-year institutions earn more than their colleagues at 2-year colleges. The highest-paying disciplines are usually law, medicine, financial management, chemical and electrical engineering, and business administration. In other fields, such as education and the humanities, the average salaries are lower.

> **"Research Says"**
>
> In 2005, adjunct professor salaries ranged from a low of $800 per course at some 2-year institutions to over $4,000 per course at some 4-year institutions with graduate programs. The average salary range for adjunct instructors is $2,400-$3,500 per course.

Your Many Roles as a College Instructor

As a college teacher, you don't just teach a couple courses and go home. You'll be fulfilling many roles in the lives of your students and in the life of the institution. Let's take a look at some of the responsibilities you will assume:

◆ Preparing course materials and syllabi

◆ Conducting classes

◆ Attending department meetings

◆ Attending faculty senate meetings

From the Field

Thomas Cronin, in his article "On Celebrating College Teaching" (Political Science and Politics [American Political Science Association], 1991, p. 482-491) states:

Great teachers give us a sense not only of who they are, but more important, of who we are, and who we might become. They unlock our energies, our imaginations, and our minds. Effective teachers pose compelling questions, explain options, teach us to reason, suggest possible directions, and urge us on.

- Administering and grading exams
- Supervising teaching assistants
- Monitoring student research
- Serving on faculty committees
- Traveling to professional meetings and conferences
- Presenting papers, leading workshops
- Networking with colleagues from other institutions
- Conducting research
- Writing papers, monographs, articles, and books, and submitting them for presentation and publication
- Consulting services
- Advising students

Some Challenges of Undergraduate Education

No matter what level of collegiate instruction you're working at, you undoubtedly have many questions right now. Here are some of the major concerns of new college teachers everywhere:

- How can I get students excited on **the first day** of a new class?
- How can I maintain and promote their **enthusiasm** for learning throughout the semester?
- How can I design a course **syllabus** that covers all the relevant and necessary principals?
- How can I get to know my **students** as individuals?
- How can I design dynamic and interesting **lectures** that will inform and engage my students?
- What kinds of out-of-class **assignments** should students do that will extend and promote learning?

◆ How can I lead classroom **discussions** that will promote learning and foster higher level thinking?

◆ How do I **evaluate** students fairly and equitably?

◆ How do I promote or enforce the institution's **academic integrity** with policies on honesty, plagiarism, and cheating?

Does that sound like a lot? Don't worry! We'll discuss each of those concerns in the pages of this book. I aim to provide you with practical, down-to-earth ideas and suggestions to help you become the best college teacher possible.

What Your Students Will Say

Several research studies with college students have sought to define the teaching behaviors or techniques that promote learning, engage students, and foster positive communication between professors and undergraduates. Among the top college teacher behaviors were ...

◆ Approachability.

◆ Helpfulness in and out of class.

◆ Showing respect for students and not talking down to them.

◆ A positive and welcoming classroom atmosphere.

◆ An instructor who demonstrates enthusiasm about the discipline and about teaching.

◆ Someone with a sense of humor.

◆ Someone who values opinions different from his/her own.

◆ An individual willing to share some of who they are outside the teacher role.

> **"Research Says"**
>
> In study after study, the single most important college teacher criteria expressed by undergraduate students nationwide was "instructors who show enthusiasm about their discipline and about teaching."

What They Never Told You in the Interview

Let's assume that you're about to begin your first year of teaching college. You've completed all your graduate work, received your degree, and now have what you've always wanted—a position teaching and inspiring young scholars in your chosen field.

You're anticipating that first day of classes, but soon begin to realize that teaching at the collegiate level is much more than providing a couple of stimulating lectures and grading a stack of essays. Here are some of the other discoveries you are also about to make:

- This is not a 9-to-5 job. There will be all sorts of demands on your time, from advising students about the courses they need for the following semester to endless committee meetings on endless topics to department meetings that can go on for hours and hours.

- You may be asked to teach sections, courses, and classes that are in conflict with your personal schedule—Saturday morning classes (ugh), evening courses, or late-afternoon seminars. As the "new kid on the block" you'll get the courses and sections no one else wants.

- Students will say things about you that you wouldn't want your mother to hear. They'll talk about your attire, your mannerisms, your sense of humor (or lack thereof), the car you drive, and a thousand other things that have nothing to do with your role as a college teacher. You will be rated and evaluated in ways that your department chair or the administration never intended. (But don't act surprised—weren't you a student once?)

Red Flag _____

One of the most popular websites used by college students to rate, evaluate, and share "inside information" about their college professors is www.ratemyprofessors.com. This site allows students at almost every collegiate institution to provide comments about specific instructors and the courses they teach. The reviews are not always flattering.

- Students will blame you if they fail a course or receive an unsatisfactory grade. You may hear, "This is the first time I've ever taken a course and not gotten an A," or, "I have to get an A in your course or I'll lose my scholarship."

- Not only will you have teaching responsibilities, but you will also spend lots of time advising and counseling students. You will help them through their love lives, conflicts with their parents or roommates, career choices, money problems, part-time jobs, sinking G.P.A.'s, and a host of other personal issues. You'll also be asked to write dozens of letters of recommendation.

- Students will ask, "I can't be in class on Thursday. Are you going to talk about anything important?"

What This Book Can Do For You

Suffice it to say, teaching college is much more than standing in front of an auditorium full of students and giving a stimulating lecture.

Experience Pays

The information in this book is not a collection of pedagogical theories or dull, dry research. What you will get is my own experiences as a college teacher for more than 2 decades. You'll also get the experiences of scores of other college teachers from around the country who have been where you are now. I've interviewed them, visited them, and borrowed their ideas to share with you. Their wisdom and suggestions are liberally sprinkled throughout this book. Most important, this book is a guide based on what actually works in college classrooms irrespective of discipline or institution.

The emphasis in this book is on practicality. You want information and ideas that work. You want suggestions that can be used *right now!* You want support and encouragement from college teachers who know what works and what doesn't. Every idea in this book has been test-driven by college teachers in every type of institution. There are no long boring theories here—simply what works based on the day-in and day-out experiences of seasoned professionals.

Your Single Source of Information

There are lots of journals, books, monographs, and websites you could consult. There are hundreds of outstanding college professors across the country (each honored with one or more teaching awards) whom you could contact. There are thousands of outstanding students in a variety of fields who would be willing to give you inside information about effective collegiate teaching. You could check them all yourself. To do so, however, would take more time than you have right now. I've checked them out and provided you with the most useful, most relevant, and most necessary information. You can consider this book as your one-stop-shopping guide to effective college teaching.

Your Personal Companion

Please use this book as your companion and as your guide. It's not important that you read it from cover to cover. Pick a chapter, any chapter, read it, and implement its practical ideas into your own college classes. Do the same for other chapters—in fact,

I would suggest that you dip in and out of this book on a regular basis. Read the chapters in any sequence that makes sense to you and that provides you with the immediate answers you need to answer your unique and personal questions. Keep this book on your desk or in your bookcase and read a section every other day or so. In short, make this book your book, your companion. Use what you need when you need it.

Not a Panacea

Looking for guidance on becoming a successful and effective college teacher? I'll give you the basics—the strategies and methods that can create a course where students are learning with enthusiasm and you are teaching with passion and energy. But every course and every class is different, just like every student and every instructor is different. I don't pretend to know every student in your courses, the policies of your institution, or the dynamics of your specific field. I don't have an answer for every single problem, situation, or concern that may pop up in your unique situation. But what I can give you is a set of practices and procedures that will make your job less stressful and your undergraduate students more engaged in the learning process. I can't offer you guarantees, but I can offer you practices that have worked in colleges, courses, and classes by undergraduate instructors just like you.

I sincerely hope you enjoy your journey through this book. It is a compilation of the best thinking, the latest research, and the finest college teachers' advice from around the country. I'm here to help you choose the strategies and procedures that will make you an unforgettable college teacher—one who inspires students and has a long and productive career. I know your time is valuable, so let's get started.

The Least You Need to Know

- Teaching college is demanding and challenging; but is also filled with incredible possibilities.

- The demand for new college teachers is great, as are the demands on their time.

- College teachers assume many different roles besides that of an instructional leader.

- Use this book as your personal guide and companion—I'll help you find answers to your most pressing questions and immediate concerns.

Chapter 2

How College Students Learn

In This Chapter

- ◆ The "transmission" model of teaching
- ◆ Constructivism in college classrooms
- ◆ Laws of learning
- ◆ Learning is questioning
- ◆ Motivating students to learn

The human brain is a marvelous organ. This 3-pound mass of gray matter is 78 percent water, 10 percent fat, and 8 percent protein. The remainder is a combination of other substances. This organ keeps us alive and functioning. It also has the capacity to learn a wide variety of new information.

But learning—particularly for college students—is not simply the memorization of new information in a particular discipline. It's much more than the attainment of high scores on midterm exams or the submission of lengthy papers with extensive bibliographies. Learning, as we will discover, is a multidimensional process—one that goes far beyond lectures, labs, assignments, or grades.

Psychology of Learning 101 (a Very Short Course)

In numerous studies over the last two decades, college students consistently define learning as "the accumulation of knowledge." Or, to put it another way, the more knowledge you accumulate, the smarter you get. Traditionally, college professors dispense vast amounts of information, students dutifully record that information in their notebooks, and the ability to retain (memorize) that information is assessed periodically via exams or written papers. Those who remember the most information get the highest grades; those who don't get much lower grades. As a result, students often envision learning as the simple transference of information from one head to another.

The sequence described above is referred to as the *transmission* model of learning (and teaching). The instructor's responsibility is to dole out a body of knowledge. The student's responsibility is to commit that knowledge to memory. Knowledge is transmitted by an expert and passively absorbed by a novice.

def•i•ni•tion

In a **transmission** model of learning, students commit large amounts of factual information (as presented by an instructor) to memory (or their notes). In a **transactional** or **constructivist** model, students process the material using a variety of interactive learning activities.

New research on how college students learn turns that traditional model on its head. Educators now subscribe to the notion that learning involves an active and energetic relationship between the learner and the material. That is, the learner-material relationship is reciprocal and involves characteristics of the learner as well as the nature of the materials. This research, often referred to as a *transactional* or *constructivist* approach to learning, has particular applications for college professors.

Here are two principles of transactional learning that will be particularly useful to you as you begin designing your college courses:

◆ Learning is a lived-through experience or event. The learner "evokes" the material, bringing a network of past experiences with the world and with other information.

◆ Learning occurs best when there are opportunities for a reciprocal transaction between the learner and the material.

In brief, this suggests that learning is less about the *products* of a subject and more about the *processes* that engage students in using those products.

Changing Paradigms

There is an interesting shift taking place in undergraduate education. We are now seeing less of an emphasis on *what* to learn and more of an emphasis on *how* to learn. This paradigm shift places a greater emphasis on *producing* learning as opposed to *providing* instruction. The chart below illustrates this shift.

Transmission (Traditional)	Transactional/Constructivist (Current)
Information is transferred from instructor to students	Knowledge is constructed by instructor and students
Competitive	Cooperative
Instructor directed	Student centered
Focus on memorization	Focus on developing conceptual relationships
Evaluation is standardized	Student self-assessment
Instructor talk predominates	Inter- and intraclass discussions
Focus on the products of thinking	Focus on the processes of thinking
Students answer questions with predetermined answers	Students generate (and seek answers to) self-generated queries
Course completion	Lifelong learning
Authoritative	Power is shared; students are empowered
Prior knowledge is disregarded	Prior knowledge is respected and built upon

Learning as Narrative (an Anecdote)

Since 1980, Dr. Walt Dudley has been a professor of oceanography at the University of Hawaii at Hilo. He is also the recipient of the Board of Regents Award for Excellence in Teaching. Dudley teaches courses on the chemical, geological, and biological components of the world's ocean. His area of expertise is in tsunami research, primarily tsunami mitigation. In developing his courses he began talking to survivors of the disastrous tsunamis that hit Hilo in 1946 and 1960. He believed that their stories would add an important human dimension to the scientific data he shared with students.

Dudley discovered that when he wrapped the scientific data about tsunamis around stories of how people survived (or didn't survive) past tsunamis in the Hilo area the scientific information became more meaningful. "It's the stories about real people that make science come alive," Dudley says. "Stories get everyone's attention. Students are motivated to learn science because it's personal; it's real. With stories, students say, 'Wow, science is really neat!'" His students are involved in a transactional learning experience—one they will remember long after the course is over.

Laws of Learning

From my conversations with college professors around the country about how students learn and how professors teach, I have discovered that there are certain laws that govern the learning process. These laws apply to any student in any course or at any level. Just as important, they also support what we know about how learning takes place and how we can facilitate that learning.

- **Law of Readiness:** Students learn more easily when they have a desire to learn. Conversely, students learn with difficulty if they are not interested in the topic.

- **Law of Effect:** Learning will always be much more effective when a feeling of satisfaction, enjoyment, or reward is part of the process.

- **Law of Relaxation:** Students learn best and remember longest when they are relaxed. Reducing stress increases learning and retention.

- **Law of Association:** Learning is best comprehended when the mind compares a new idea with something already known.

- **Law of Involvement:** Students learn best when they take an active part in what they're learning.

- **Law of Relevance:** Effective learning is relevant to the student's life.

- **Law of Intensity:** A vivid, exciting, enthusiastic, enjoyable learning experience is more likely to be remembered than a boring, unpleasant one.

- **Law of Challenge:** Students learn best when they are challenged with novelty, a variety of materials, and a range of instructional strategies.

- **Law of Feedback:** Effective learning takes place when students receive immediate and specific feedback on their performance.

- **Law of Expectations:** Learners' reaction to instruction is shaped by their expectations related to the material. (How successful will I be?)

- **Law of Emotions:** The emotional state (and involvement) of students will shape how well and how much they learn.

Constructivism

One of the most exciting developments in undergraduate education is a shift away from a delivery system of teaching to a constructivist model of education. Psychologists have helped us look at the teaching-learning partnership in a new way. Through intensive research, we have learned that learning is not simply the passive accumulation of knowledge, but rather how we make sense of the knowledge we gain. This is referred to as a constructivist theory of learning.

Constructivism recognizes that knowledge is created in the mind of the learner. Professors help students relate new content to the knowledge they already know. In addition, students have opportunities to process and apply that knowledge in meaningful situations. Rather than being a passive transfer of knowledge from professor to student, it is how knowledge is constructed in the mind of each student. This is active teaching and also active learning.

> **"Research Says"**
>
> Research from a number of cognitive scientists has demonstrated that when students think about material in more meaningful ways (as opposed to simply memorizing it), their underlying brain structures are changed in such a way that more lasting learning is promoted.

Red Flag

"The mind is not a vessel to be filled, but a fire to be kindled."

—Plutarch

Learning in a Postsecondary Environment

Regardless of the subject you teach, the concept of constructivism will provide you with innumerable opportunities to design lessons in concert with how undergraduate students learn. To do so, you need to be aware of and address the following elements of learning.

Knowledge Is Constructed

We now know that people learn because they construct knowledge, using what they already know as a foundation for a new topic and then relating the new information to it. In other words, we are all trying to make "mental connections" whenever we encounter new information. For new information to make sense, it must be related (or connected) to other information.

Look at it this way: when a carpenter remodels your kitchen, she is using new materials in combination with previous materials to form something new and more beautiful. This is constructivism at its best. Here are some suggested practices:

Assess what your students know and allow them to vocalize their past experiences, readings, or backgrounds of experience. Knowing what your students know and using that knowledge to construct a lesson is a powerful teaching tool.

Provide students with opportunities to challenge their own preconceived notions or concepts. This can be accomplished through a systematic ordering of questions such as these:

◆ Is this idea similar to anything you may have read before?

◆ What were you thinking when you read this part of the chapter?

◆ What have we learned so far?

◆ Did you change your mind about anything after our discussion?

◆ Do you have any personal questions about this material that have not been answered so far?

◆ What did you do when you didn't understand something in the text?

◆ What makes you feel your interpretation is most appropriate?

◆ What new information are you learning?

◆ How did you arrive at your interpretation?

From the Field

Richard Fliegal, assistant dean of academic programs at the University of Southern California, shares two valuable pieces of advice for new professors: "First, it's critical that you know [early in the semester] who your students are, why they are there, and what they know. Second, always remember that their engagement is more important than your performance.

Challenge their misinterpretations, preconceptions, misperceptions through dynamic problem solving (see Chapter 12). Provide supportive opportunities for students to wrestle with real-life challenges in your respective field. This should be done in a "safe" environment—one which encourages students to try something, fail, receive encouraging feedback, and then be encouraged to try again.

Always focus on the utility of the information presented; in short, why do students need to know this stuff? The universal question in the mind of every learner is, "Why do I have to know this stuff?" By providing opportunities for students to use information in practical situations, they will not only learn the essential facts, but also understand the reasons why they need that data. Be sure students have opportunities to respond to the following questions:

- How is the information used by practitioners?

- How can it be used to solve problems both in and out of class?

- What are some of the clinical implications of the data or research?

- How have others struggled or wrestled with this information?

- And, most important, what has this information got to do with real life?

Learning Is Questioning

Young students often come to college with limited backgrounds, limited life experiences, and limited exposure to a field of study. Their learning has frequently been narrowly defined. However, you can considerably expand and enhance that learning just by asking your students some questions.

Questions help us begin to make sense of a topic—a topic like your students' own personal and academic background, something they've probably never stepped back and considered objectively. Questions help us categorize and "file" information in our memory for later retrieval.

Most important, questions are essential in helping students construct knowledge, simply because they help students think about what they're learning, its importance, and its relevance to what they already know.

Use penetrating, critical, and higher-level questions (see Chapter 12) to help students look deeper into a topic or subject. Challenge students' thinking, but challenge conventional thinking, as well. A judicious use of "higher-level" questions can help students see some of the inconsistencies in their own thinking in addition to the strengths (or fallacies) of principles, issues, and concerns in your field. Here are some examples:

- **Comparing:** How are these things alike?

- **Classification:** Into what groups could you organize these things?

- **Induction:** Based on this information, what is the likely conclusion?

- **Deduction:** What predictions can you make or what conclusions can you draw?

- **Error analysis:** How is this information misleading?

◆ **Constructing support:** What is an argument that will support this claim?

◆ **Abstraction:** What is the general pattern underlying this information?

◆ **Analyzing perspectives:** What is the reasoning behind this perspective?

Provide multiple opportunities for students to generate their own questions. Learning occurs when we obtain answers to questions that really matter to us. When students begin asking questions about what they are learning, they are beginning to assume one of the major roles of an accomplished, active learner: *they care.*

From the Field

Kay McAdams, an associate professor of history, says, "Content is merely the vehicle for learning. The real challenge is to get students to question the content—to interpret it from a variety of viewpoints. That's when learning occurs."

Learners are motivated to learn when they have a personal stake in the information, research, or concepts. In short, they become "constructors" of knowledge. Consider the following possibilities:

◆ Write one question about the title of the next chapter.

◆ Turn to a partner. What is one question you have about today's reading?

◆ So far we have talked about X; what about Y?

◆ (at the end of class) What is one question that is unanswered for you?

Learning Is a Psychological Endeavor

For years psychologists have told us that knowledge is socially constructed and that a student's perception of self is critical to the construction of that knowledge. To look at it another way, undergraduate students become more knowledgeable (about a subject or discipline) when it is linked with their self-concept or with their interactions with others.

Equally important is the fact that postsecondary students learn something best when they care about the material on a personal or emotional level. As faculty members we often say that we want our students to "be excited," "be curious," "be interested," "be stimulated." We want our students to put a value on what they are learning. Students, too, want to know about the value of their educational experiences. Again, it comes back to a previous question: "Why do I have to know this stuff?"

From the Field _____

L. Dee Fink, recipient of the Outstanding Faculty Award from the College of Liberal Studies at the University of Oklahoma, asks an intriguing question: "If we include lots of content but students end up neither caring about the subject nor learning how to keep on learning, what are the chances that students will either retain what they have learned or make the effort to keep on learning?"

The key is in how students are motivated to learn. There are two types of motivation. *Extrinsic* motivation is when one person allows or relies on others to provide his goals and rewards. *Intrinsic* motivation, by contrast, is when drive and ambition come from within, when an individual sets her or his own goals and feels empowered to pursue them.

def•i•ni•tion _____

Extrinsic individuals are strongly influenced by others (parents, teachers, peers). **Intrinsic** individuals take primary responsiblility for what happens to them.

As you might expect, logic and research support the notion that intrinsically motivated students do better academically than extrinsically motivated students. Here are some common characteristics of externally motivated students:

- They are engaged in a competitive atmosphere that becomes self-defeating in the long run.

- They work only for rewards, asking, "How long should this paper be?" and "What grade did I get?" Motivation to learn is secondary to reward accumulation (grades), the relationship between effort and achievement is not apparent, and the learning process is not valued.

- They avoid creative and problem-solving activities in favor of low-level thinking (memorizing).

- Their goals (if any) are short-term and immediate. They avoid long-range plans and projects.

- They take no personal responsibility for their learning, but rather see the things that happen to them as matters of luck, chance, or conspiracies.

- They fall into a self-perpetuating cycle in which a lack of success substantiates a belief that they will never be successful.

Because there is a strong relationship between motivation and learning, be mindful of the behaviors you exercise in the classroom that can lead to heightened levels of intrinsic motivation and, in turn, heightened levels of achievement.

Remember that learning happens best in a social context. The use of cooperative learning opportunities (see Chapter 11) allows students to process material and entertain a variety of viewpoints. Participation is valued and celebrated in group work. Students see a host of perspectives on a topic, rather than a single teacher-oriented view.

Offer regular and consistent encouragement that recognizes a student's effort ("You worked really hard on this project); promotes self-evaluation ("How do you feel about your work so far?"); and emphasizes effort and progress of a task ("You've certainly made quite a bit of improvement on this project, don't you think?"). Encouragement places a value on the development of intrinsic students—those who begin to assume responsibility for their own learning.

Establish an "invitational classroom" in which you give students some say in the focus or direction of the coursework. Give students opportunities to establish their own goals for a course. What would they like to learn? How can this course be made relevant to their personal life? What would they like to get out of it? Invite students to suggest alternate or additional readings (from their own experiences) for a specific topic. Provide them with different viewpoints on a specific topic and ask them to select the one they are most interested in pursuing for an assigned paper.

From the Field

Richard Fliegal says, "The primary relationship in a college classroom is between the teacher and the student, not the teacher and the subject."

Finally, I always extend a challenge to students in every course I teach. At any time during a class or at any point in the semester, they are invited to raise their hand and ask, "Why do we need to know this?" That's often a signal to me that I've gotten too wrapped up in what is important to me, rather than what is necessary for students. It's the time when I need to stop and share with my students why the material is important to their lives or careers and how it relates to the overall course in general.

Caution!

A constructivist philosophy of teaching and learning can reinvigorate any college subject and promote learning as an active process. But if you are more familiar with traditional forms of teaching where the teacher delivers instruction, you may find this approach challenging.

There's a saying that has been around for a long time: we tend to teach as we were taught. If we have been taught with more traditional forms of instruction (such as lecture), we have a tendency to teach in roughly the same way. Yes, we are products of our experiences.

Moving your philosophy to a more constructivist view may be a challenge. I suggest that you talk with colleagues, read current educational periodicals, and observe constructivist teaching (and learning) in action. Observe how students behave in a constructivist classroom—especially how they are actively engaged in the learning process. You may discover, as did I, that this shift in philosophy can result in some exciting and dynamic lessons no matter what course or discipline you teach.

The Least You Need to Know

- Learning occurs when there is a dynamic relationship between students and the material.
- Constructivism recognizes the importance of process over product.
- Good questioning facilitates good learning.
- Intrinsic motivation stimulates higher levels of learning.

Chapter 3

Best Practices: Seven Principles

In This Chapter

- Developing student relationships
- Making active learning a reality
- It's all about feedback
- The importance of time on task
- The value of high expectations
- How to work with diverse learners

The custodian in my building has a master key that she uses to open all the offices and classrooms. Each morning, long before I arrive on campus, she comes in to each faculty member's office and attends to her various chores. She enters each of the classrooms in our wing and gets them ready for the 8:00 classes that will begin later in the morning. She can do all this with just one key, which opens more than 40 different locks in a single building.

Wouldn't it be interesting if there was just one key that would open up the minds of all our college students? Guess what? It isn't going to happen.

However, researchers have discovered several keys that are critical to the success of college students as well as to the success you can enjoy in all your courses. Sometimes known as "best practices," these keys can help you teach more effectively and your students learn more positively. Let's take a look at them in a little more detail.

The "Best Practices" Study

In the late 1980s, the American Association for Higher Education (AAHE) Task Force on Best Practices in Higher Education began looking at all the research on the factors leading to undergraduate student success. They reviewed scores of longitudinal studies, examined reams of empirical research papers, and interviewed numerous individuals in institutions across the United States.

The results of this extensive review were published in the *AAHE Bulletin* in 1987. The report addresses seven conclusions or principles that have a significant impact on how well college students learn, irrespective of the course or discipline. These seven principles provide college professors, both experienced and novice, with important considerations in the development of any course. They are ...

From the Field

Mike McGough, an associate professor of education, offers this advice: "When I began teaching college I did it based on what I knew (or thought I knew). I'm now building on that knowledge by integrating it with what I read and hear from the experts. That research helps me shorten any distance between my courses and my students."

- ◆ Encouraging student-faculty contact.

- ◆ Encouraging cooperation among students.

- ◆ Encouraging active learning.

- ◆ Giving prompt feedback.

- ◆ Emphasizing time on task.

- ◆ Communicating high expectations.

- ◆ Respecting diverse talents and ways of learning.

Student-Faculty Contact

One of the most interesting results to surface from this intensive, multistudy research project was the finding that "frequent student-faculty contact in and out of classes is the most important factor in student motivation and involvement." That is to say, as faculty members our job does not begin and end at the threshold to the classroom.

It extends into our offices, the student union, administrative offices, sports fields, the gymnasium, dormitories, and out in the larger community. In short, the more face-to-face time we have with students outside the classroom, the more they'll care about learning inside the classroom.

> **"Research Says"**
>
> One study conducted in 1975 found that relationships developed outside the classroom between faculty and students are the part of teaching that may have the greatest impact.

Suggestions

Here are some suggestions you can consider to effect and sustain student-faculty contacts:

◆ If you teach large classes, schedule some smaller, seminar-type classes where students can interact in small groups. These need not be formal affairs, but can be done on an ad hoc basis.

◆ Provide opportunities for students to meet informally in your office in small groups. Discuss elements of the course or college life in general.

◆ In one introductory course I teach, I make a point during the first three weeks of the semester to have each individual student come to my office for a cup of coffee and some casual conversation. I use this time (15–20 minutes) to get to know them on a personal basis.

◆ If practical, set up a time in the cafeteria, student union, or a vacant library room to meet with students to chat about the course or other items of interest.

◆ Set up a "brown bag" lunch with students once a month. Schedule a day and time when you can meet with students over some pizza or sandwiches for some informal conversation.

Cooperation Among Students

Another finding from the AAHE study was that "learning is enhanced when it is more like a team effort than a solo race. Good learning … is collaborative and social, not competitive and isolated. Sharing one's ideas and responding to others' actions sharpens thinking and deepens understanding." Most employers will state that one of the most valuable skills any prospective employee can bring to an organization is the ability to work with others and contribute to the welfare of a group.

Suggestions

The elements of cooperative work are woven throughout this book and are specifically addressed in Chapter 11. However, here are some specific suggestions that will help students develop the skills they need for working together effectively:

 Red Flag _____

Don't make the mistake of assuming that college students know how to work in groups. They may come from academic backgrounds in which individual achievement was more highly prized than cooperative ventures. It's critical that students be trained in the dynamics of group work if it is to having a significant impact on their learning.

- Invite students to discuss and record the factors and elements that contribute to effective group functioning. Consider editing and refining these suggestions and distributing them as a class handout.

- Emphasize the value of everyone contributing to a group discussion. There is no hierarchy in group work—everyone has an equal role.

- Groups should have a specific task. Make sure everyone within a group knows the final product or the ultimate goal of the group's work.

- Keep group sizes manageable. Large groups seldom give everyone a chance to contribute and develop positive social relationships.

- Groups should be heterogeneous in their composition. A variety of abilities, perspectives, viewpoints, gender, age, and other factors should be used to formulate groups.

- Consider using a combination of three different cooperative grouping patterns: informal (ad hoc groups lasting from a few minutes to an entire class period), formal (groups organized to tackle a specific assignment, lasting a few days to several weeks), and base groups (groups that stay together for the entire semester).

- Monitor group progress on a regular basis. Move around the classroom and listen in as students tackle a problem. Check to see that they are on track and on schedule.

"Research Says"

A research study in 1996 examined the work produced by cooperative groups of various sizes. These included groups of two, three or four, and five to seven. The report concluded that teams of three or four members were significantly more effective (in terms of what was learned) than groups of any other size.

Active Learning

The AAHE task force states, "Students do not learn much just by sitting in classes and listening to teachers, memorizing prepackaged assignments, and spitting out answers. They must talk about what they are learning, write about it, relate it to experience, and apply it to their daily lives." In short, this means that students must not merely *accumulate* knowledge; they must have opportunities to *process* that knowledge. This is what is known as *active learning*.

The principles of active learning are sprinkled throughout this book. Specific classroom strategies such as teaching methodologies (Chapter 8), discussion (Chapter 10), and questioning techniques (Chapter 12) focus on specific skills that will make active learning a significant element in each of your courses. The emphasis is on providing opportunities for students to *think* about what they are learning by manipulating (or "playing around with") the concepts you share with them.

def•i•ni•tion

Active learning is when students process, rather than just memorize, new information. Based on research in cognitive psychology, information is stored more deeply when it is manipulated through explaining, summarizing, or questioning. Discussion is the vehicle that helps students engage in active learning.

Suggestions

Here are a few suggestions you can consider in designing courses in which active learning has a significant role:

◆ Provide regular opportunities for students to engage in formal discussion sessions.

◆ Frequently pose questions for which there are no clear-cut right or wrong answers. Inform students that you are not looking for a "right answer," but rather want them to intellectually wrestle with a concept or problem.

◆ Design your course so that students have opportunities for self-initiated learning—tasks that let them pursue the answers to their own questions.

◆ Invite students to share their learning experiences with each other. Consider small-group, large-group, or whole-class experiences in which successes and challenges are shared.

◆ Offer students opportunities to apply their knowledge in practical situations. Simulations, problem-solving exercises, case studies, debates, panel discussions, and the like are wonderful examples of active learning.

Prompt Feedback

The AAHE task force stated, "Students need appropriate feedback on performance to benefit from courses .... Students need frequent opportunities to perform and receive suggestions for improvement .... Students need chances to reflect on what they have learned, what they still need to know, and how to assess themselves."

> **"Research Says"**
>
> One exhaustive review (1992) of over 8,000 studies concluded, "The most powerful single modification that enhances achievement is feedback."

Many new professors (and a couple of "old" ones, too) make the mistake of assuming that feedback is simply providing students with test scores in a timely fashion. True, returning tests within a week is important to student motivation, but feedback is a continuous process of informing students about the quality of their learning. That may include test scores; but it is certainly much more than that.

Consider all the forms of feedback at your disposal. These may include but certainly aren't limited to test scores, personal conversations, interviews, verbal remarks in class, body language, whole class comments, written remarks on papers, and so on. Here are some suggestions you can easily incorporate into your course to help students get the feedback they need:

◆ **Feedback should come early and often.** Two quizzes and a final exam are not sufficient to provide students with consistent and regular feedback.

◆ **The feedback should be constructive and corrective in nature.** The best feedback explains what is accurate and what is inaccurate in terms of student responses.

◆ **Feedback should be timely.** The greater the delay between completion and evaluation of an assignment, the lower the achievement (for individuals and the whole class). My working policy is to return exams and papers within one week of submission. If I can't adhere to that one week policy, then I need to examine the length or complexity of the assignments I make.

◆ **Feedback should be specific.** Telling a student that she did "poor work" is ineffective. Telling her that (in response to an exam question, for example) she didn't provide a rationale or substantial argument for the role of information technology in a global economy is more specific and more meaningful.

- **Feedback should be constructive.** Eliminate personal statements and emphasize improvement and learning: "How do the results of this research study compare with your position on the juvenile justice system?"

- **Feedback should be individual, not group-oriented.** The best feedback a student receives is specific to his performance. When students just hear how they compare to others, this tells them nothing about their learning.

- **A growing body of research supports self-evaluation as a positive factor in student achievement.** When practical, provide opportunities for students to maintain a journal, notebook, spreadsheet, or chart of the knowledge and skills they're acquiring.

Time on Task

The AAHE report suggested that college professors need to consider the effect of "time on task" on learning. The task force states, "Learning to use one's time well is critical for students .... Students need help in learning effective time management. Allocating realistic amounts of time means effective learning for students and effective teaching for faculty."

It's a given that many students arrive at college with little or no experience in time management. If we want students to become active learners in our courses, then we need to help them learn to manage their time effectively. This is an institutionwide mandate, not just a job for those who teach freshmen-level courses.

Here are some time-on-task suggestions you can incorporate into your courses:

- Encourage students to maintain a formalized journal to record their thoughts, questions, and perceptions as they read various chapters in the textbook. These journals can become vehicles for class discussions.

def•i•ni•tion

Time on task is the time necessary to satisfactorily complete an assignment. The assignment must be relevant to what students are learning (as opposed to "busy work").

Red Flag

Time on task does not mean assigning students additional pages to read in the course textbook (or even adding more textbooks to the course). In short, more assignments does not necessarily equal greater learning.

◆ Provide students with a variety of out-of-class assignments above and beyond the typical "read the chapter and answer the questions." Offer projects in which students can apply their newfound knowledge in various venues.

◆ Give students choices: "Here are three different projects (written paper, PowerPoint presentation, speech) related to our discussion of sacred texts. Choose any one to complete."

◆ You may wish to provide students with study questions to consider as they read outside material. Invite them to discuss their responses in a follow-up class.

◆ The long-standing rule of thumb is that college students should prepare for two hours outside of class for every hour spent in class. If you subscribe to this maxim, plan your "outside" assignments accordingly.

◆ Most college campuses have learning resource centers that offer students tutoring assistance, study techniques, and instruction in time-management. Make sure your students are aware of the services available and mention them frequently throughout a course.

High Expectations

Another significant factor that surfaced from the AAHE report relates to the academic expectations we have for our students. The task force stated, "Expecting students to perform well becomes a self-fulfilling prophecy when teachers and institutions hold high expectations of them and make extra efforts."

Simply put, students will achieve in accordance with how we expect them to achieve. Or, to use an old track-and-field metaphor, the higher we set the bar, the more students will work to get over that bar.

From the Field

Dominic Delli Carpini, an associate professor of English, says, "I'm serious about students' learning. I'm always challenging them to do more and I get upset when they do bad work. However, one of my greatest challenges is to motivate them to learn outside of class and outside of any single course."

Here are some suggestions you can incorporate into your courses that will help you emphasize the high expectations you have for students:

◆ In preparing your course syllabus try to keep the emphasis on learning rather than the simple memorization of information. The syllabus should reflect your concern about the value of *process* over *product*.

◆ From the first day of class, provide students with higher-level thinking questions (see Chapter 12). Eliminate or significantly reduce the number of low-level questions and focus more on application, analysis, synthesis, and evaluation questions. This holds true for all your verbal interactions with students.

◆ Share your goals for the course on the first day. Let them know what will be covered, how it will be covered, and, most important, what they will be able to do with that knowledge at the end of the course. It would be important to share these goals with students verbally, on the syllabus, and consistently throughout the semester.

◆ Interestingly, a significant body of research has demonstrated that many students are unaware that the effort they put into a learning task has a direct effect on their success relative to that task. It's important, therefore, to regularly emphasize the effort necessary to master the concepts and principles of any course.

◆ After the first two weeks of a course, invite students to list their specific learning goals for the course. What do they want to learn? How will they accomplish that learning? You may wish to do this as a whole-class activity or by inviting each individual student to list her or his personal goals.

◆ Plan to list your goals for the course on the chalkboard sometime during the first week of class. Let students know what they should have accomplished by the end of the course as well as what you will do to help them reach those goals.

Diverse Talents and Ways of Learning

The seventh and final principle promulgated by the AAHE refers to the incredible diversity of students you may have in your classroom. The task force stated, "People bring different talents and styles of learning to college. Students need an opportunity to show their talents and learn in ways that work for them." It's easy to look out over a sea of faces at the beginning of a semester and see a mass of students without form, features, or personality. "Teach to the mass and let the chips fall where they may," I was told early in my career. Unfortunately, we now know that statement is totally erroneous—it inhibits learning more than enhances it.

It should go without saying that in any course you will have students with a variety of educational backgrounds, political inclinations, learning objectives, career goals, attitudes, and interests. Students will vary in a plethora of other ways, making each one unique and distinctive. There is no such thing as an "average student"—in fact, one of the most exciting challenges of higher education is to provide for the diversity of students in a fair and equitable manner.

From the Field

Ed Ransford, a professor of sociology at the University of Southern California, says, "One of the most critical factors in any class is the creation of a safe, respectful environment. This is an environment where people hear each other, where everyone is respected, and where nobody is put down. It's an environment where differences are celebrated and enjoyed."

Considerable attention is spent on the diversity of students you will discover in your classes in several chapters of this book. Here are a few additional suggestions to consider:

◆ As you will learn later in the book, the most significant factor in getting a course off on the right foot is to learn the names (and correct pronunciation!) of all your students. Make this effort early, and you'll be able to celebrate each person's individuality throughout the length of the course.

◆ As appropriate, learn about the cultures, religions, beliefs, and customs of individuals from countries other than the United States. It may be appropriate to spend a few moments each week to discuss these with the respective individuals.

◆ Learn as much as you can about the various learning styles in your class. Some will be visual learners; others will be auditory learners. Some will be right-brained; others will be left-brained. Provide students with a brief self-evaluation form on which they can indicate their preferred learning styles. Consider these as you plan your presentations throughout the semester.

◆ Be aware that some students may have learning disabilities that may affect their in- or out-of-class performance. Be prepared to provide alternate teaching or learning strategies.

◆ Check with your campus library or log on to selected websites and learn as much as you can about multiple intelligences. Become knowledgeable about the eight different types of intelligence and how you might be able to provide learning opportunities that respects each of these in your classroom.

Some Final Words

What becomes clear from all this research is that teaching is a complex interrelationship of various perspectives and practices. Learning, too, is a complicated arrangement of factors and events that vary from course to course and professor to professor. It is, in a way, an amazing juggling act—one that never stops and one you'll keep modifying and refining throughout your professional career.

One important point here—don't expect to master these seven constructs in your first year. No dean or department chair will ever evaluate you based on your total mastery of all seven principles. A good cabernet takes a few years to achieve the peak of flavor. And like a good wine, you can, too.

The Least You Need to Know

- There are seven principles that have a major impact on how well college students learn.

- The nature of the student-teacher interaction is significant.

- Students should be involved in a variety of active learning experiences.

- Feedback is a critical element in the teaching/learning cycle.

- Students need to be in learning environments rich with high expectations.

Part 2

Preparing to Teach

"OK," you say to yourself, "I got the job I always wanted. Now, what do I do?" Now, you're faced with a thousand decisions, a million possible resources, and a billion facts, concepts, and principles to include in a course. Oh, and you've got a couple hundred students to teach as well. It seems like your cup is truly overflowing with challenges and possibilities.

Part 2 provides you with practical ideas on course design, textbook use, and how to assemble a fully functioning course syllabus. This section is the foundation for the educational house you are about to construct. I provide you with all (well, almost all) the tools you need, as well as the resources that will make those initial steps successful. Grab some coffee—we're about to begin a magical journey full of wonder and adventure!

"No late papers. I said none. Zero. Not ever. Not even one."

Chapter 4

Designing a Course

In This Chapter

◆ Two very important questions

◆ Developing an action plan

◆ Formulating goals and outcomes

◆ A taxonomy of significant learning

◆ Five critical factors you need to know

My wife and I love to travel to Hawaii. Each time we go, we spend considerable time in advance poring over maps, guidebooks, Internet sites, travel brochures, back issues of *Hawaii Magazine*, and other resources to determine the places we want to see and the adventures we want to experience. Each journey is different because we always try to enjoy new things, knowing that we can't include every aspect of the eight islands in a single trip.

Designing a college course is much the same thing. As a new professor, you may want to include everything about your discipline in your course, but you have a limited amount of time or resources to do so. When we go to Hawaii we establish very specific "must-do's." Designing a course also means designing specific (manageable) goals and outcomes that give both you and your students a sense of direction and accomplishment. The result can be a learning adventure full of great memories.

Two Critical Questions

Two critical questions confront every college teacher, whether novice or experienced. Your response to these two queries will determine, in large measure, the success you enjoy as a professor and the academic success students will enjoy in your courses. They are crucial in the design of every effective course—from introductory freshmen courses to graduate seminars. They are …

1. What will I teach? *(Goals)*

2. What will students learn? *(Outcomes)*

def•i•ni•tion

Goals are the ideas, principles, concepts, or questions that you want to include in a course or that you want to teach. They are the end products of a course.

Outcomes are what students will learn as a result of their exposure to those course goals. They are the skills that students develop throughout a course.

From the Field

Peter Filene, professor of history at the University of North Carolina at Chapel Hill, says that "professors have difficulty focusing on outcomes. They prefer to talk about what they themselves will do instead of what their students will do."

One of the classic errors many new professors make is that they tend to concentrate on the first question almost to the exclusion of the second question. They spend a lot of time planning what they will teach in their courses, but insufficient time on what they plan to have students learn in those courses. Many new professors, fresh from graduate school, have all the latest theories, statistics, research, and content about a particular subject. They often spend an inordinate amount of time trying to fit that content into the parameters of a 15-week semester. Little thought is given to the "learning" they want students to have at the close of that course.

Reframing the Questions

One way to begin designing your courses is to reframe the questions. Instead of asking yourself, "What will I teach?" consider these two modifications:

1. What do students need to know?

2. What will they be able to do with that knowledge?

This provides you with two critical focal points. It helps you to zero in on the necessary content while keeping in mind the utility of the content in students' lives. If your sole goal is to have students memorize the content (the traditional approach) then you are eliminating a critical component of the teaching/learning paradigm. That is, what do you want them to do with their newfound knowledge?

In short, teaching is about changing—changing students' minds, changing their perceptions and outlooks, and changing their interpretations of the world. Giving them knowledge is one thing; giving them opportunities to use that knowledge is the sine qua non of a good college course.

Course Introduction

In Chapter 6, we will discuss the components of a good course syllabus. Before you write that syllabus, however, give some thought to constructing a course introduction—frequently the initial paragraph in many course syllabi. By focusing on the goals and outcomes of a course, you will be able to address the two critical elements of any subject—what will you teach, what will they learn? Everything else in the course can stem from the answers to these two initial queries.

Following is a course introduction for a course I teach every semester, Teaching Elementary Social Studies, for preservice teachers in their junior or senior year. Note how both the goals and outcomes of the course are embedded in the introduction.

> This course is an introduction to the processes, practices, and procedures that encompass the elementary social studies curriculum. It is a course dealing with human interrelationships and interdependencies. The course is an examination of the issues, concerns, and connections that affect us everyday and are woven into the fabric of our culture and society.
>
> By the end of this course, you will be able to effect a "process-driven" social studies curriculum that provides "hands-on, minds-on" experiences to teach youngsters to deal with those concepts. You will be able to make critical decisions that will help students explore the specifics of the six social studies disciplines. And you will be able to demonstrate the methods and materials of effective instruction throughout the social studies program.

Dominic Delli Carpini, a colleague of mine in the English Department, shares this course introduction for a senior-level course on Advanced Composition:

> Advanced Composition has one major goal: to help you to develop your repertoire of stylistic techniques. Learning to develop your "style," the third canon of rhetoric, means

practicing writing at the micro-level: learning more about syntax—the way sentences function—and the ways that sentences are composed of carefully chosen words (in carefully chosen forms). We will also discuss the ways that all those carefully crafted sentences can be combined into paragraphs that are coherent, cohesive, and hence effective in given rhetorical situations. Writing is a craft; this course can make you a craftsperson.

The previous examples encompass both goals and outcomes. They provide students with a blueprint for the semester: what they will learn and what they'll be able to do as a result of that learning. Just as important, they provide you with a forum through which you can answer the two critical questions of any course.

Three, Two, One

Let's say you're designing a course titled Survey of the Music Industry. There's a course chock-full of information and details! Potential topics include: career planning, creative careers, producing/directing, performing, teaching, songwriting, music publishing, copyright registration, sources of royalty income, performance rights, music licensing, the role of unions, music associations, arts administration, talent agencies, and artistic management.

That's a lot of stuff for one course! How do you get it all in? My suggestion—don't try to. In trying to fit all that information into a single course, you risk ignoring or eliminating student outcomes for the sake of (or at the expense of) all your planned goals.

Here's a sequence of activities that will help you respond to the two critical questions above while maintaining your sanity: make a list of all the goals, concepts, or principles that are part of the course. These can be obtained from your own experiences, a planned course textbook, suggestions from colleagues, or research. You can begin drafting your list of goals by providing answers to some of the following self-directed queries:

- What is important for students to know?
- What topics interest me the most?
- What concepts should I emphasize?
- What is the main idea of this course?

Identify the *three* most critical goals. These should be more general than specific. For example, "planning for careers in the music industry," rather than "the ABC Talent Agency."

Make a list of all the outcomes you want for your students. You can begin drafting your list by providing answers to some of the following self-directed queries:

◆ What do I want students to be able to do by the end of the course?

◆ What new skills will students have after this course?

◆ How will students' thinking be changed by this course?

◆ What student perceptions or misperceptions do I want to challenge?

Select the *two* most critical outcomes. Be sure these are framed in terms of what students will be able to do with the information you provide them. For example, "Students will be able to use standard methods of solving ordinary differential equations and apply them to physics."

Design a *one*-paragraph introduction to the course, incorporating the three goals and two outcomes. You may wish to direct this introduction to students ("By the end of the course, you will be able to ...") or you may wish to keep it impersonal ("This course is an introduction to the principles of ..."). Make this introduction the opening paragraph of your course syllabus (see Chapter 6).

You may argue that three goals and two outcomes are insufficient for your subject or course. I realize that most courses involve an overwhelming plethora of principles, concepts, factual information, and issues. However, the key here, especially in initial course design, is simplicity. It's also to provide you with a manageable plan that helps you focus. Inevitably, you will deal with many issues and concerns throughout the semester, but the 3-2-1 plan will provide you with a reliable compass as you begin to design that course.

Know, too, that as you progress through your teaching career, you will refine and sharpen your course design. Suggestions from colleagues, ideas from periodicals and journals, research, conference proceedings, and other information sources will all become part of your courses. For now, you just need a solid platform. Don't try to do everything the first time out. Keep the plan manageable, simple, and straightforward. Remember that good courses and good instructors are always evolving. Start with a simple plan and then, as the class progresses and you add to your experience base, adjust and modify the course accordingly.

A Taxonomy of Significant Learning

L. Dee Fink, professor of geography at the University of Oklahoma, has examined the research on quality teaching and learning and has developed a taxonomy that leads to significant learning (and effective teaching) in any type of college course.

Fink's taxonomy is significant in that it can help you design a course that addresses all the major factors that help students learn—not just for the length of the semester, but long after the semester is over. Here are the six elements of this taxonomy:

- Foundational knowledge
- Application
- Integration
- Human dimension
- Caring
- Learning how to learn

Foundational knowledge represents the major ideas and concepts of a subject—the facts, information, and ideas that are the underpinnings of a topic or course. These may include dates, terminology, basic research, significant events, definitions, people, or places.

Application is the opportunity for students to engage in various types of thinking. The thinking may be critical, creative, or practical (see Chapter 12). It also includes the ability to manage complex projects or develop performance skills.

Integration describes students' ability to connect ideas, people, and different realms of life (for example, between school life and occupational life). It also involves the ability to make connections between different disciplines (for example, between English and physics or between Spanish literature and the colonial history of Latin America).

The *human dimension* involves learning more about oneself as well as about others. It is the personal and social implications of learning—including citizenship, leadership, teamwork, and character building.

Caring refers to the affective value of a topic or subject. It's the degree to which students care about something and their willingness to make it part of their lives.

Learning how to learn focuses on helping students become better students—throughout the course and afterwards. Learning *how* to learn is just as critical as learning *what* to learn. Continuing the learning process after the course is a significant factor in the success of the course.

Fink is quick to point out that this taxonomy is not hierarchical but rather is interactive and relational. It demonstrates the combination of components necessary for any course. This is a synergistic relationship— emphasis on any single component influences the development of other components.

For example, if you include several opportunities for students to critically think and analyze a particular concept in your course, you will also be assisting them in caring about that concept. Why? Because now they have an active role in the learning process. They are beginning to *construct* knowledge.

> **"Research Says"**
>
> According to Professor Fink, "For learning to occur, there has to be some kind of change in the learner. No change, no learning. And significant learning requires that there be some kind of lasting change that is important in terms of the learner's life."

Significant Learning and Course Design

I like the previous model because it helps me when I'm building a brand new course. I know that I need to incorporate all six elements of significant learning so that students will achieve the maximum learning benefits. Beginning with these six elements gives me a blueprint and a structural outline that shapes and guides my overall course design.

Here's how I used this taxonomy to design an Introduction to American Education course:

"By the end of this course, students will ..."

Foundational knowledge:

- ◆ Understand the history of the American education system.
- ◆ Identify significant individuals (Dewey, Piaget, Bruner) in American education.

Application:

- ◆ Be able to identify and critique significant issues in American education.
- ◆ Be able to analyze the work of a local school board.

Integration:

- ◆ Identify the relationship between American education and European education.
- ◆ Identify the role of education in the lives of people from varying socioeconomic groups.

Human dimension:

- Identify the role of education in one's personal life—for better or worse.

- Learn the responsibilities of educators outside the classroom.

Caring:

- Understand and apply ethical behaviors in everyday teaching situations.

- Develop a keen interest in the concept of "teacher as researcher."

Learning how to learn:

- Realize the importance of the teacher as a lifelong learner.

- Develop a personal agenda for graduate work and long-term professional training.

The items listed in each of the six categories became my working list of goals for the course. Obviously, your goals will look quite different from mine and will vary from course to course. What is significant is the emphasis on both *content* and *process*. That is, what students will learn is valued just as much as what you will teach.

In the "Old Days ..."

College courses have traditionally been put together topically: college professors would compile a list of topics, subjects, issues, and principles (in 1, 2, 3 or A, B, C order) and divided it over the length of the course. The basic intent was to cram in as much information as could be covered in a 15-week semester. The thinking was that the more knowledge students were exposed to, the more they would learn.

We know from decades of research (see Chapter 2) that that kind of thinking is both erroneous and fallacious. More content does not equal more learning. As we have seen earlier, learning is more complex than that. Learning *involves* the learner; it is not something done *to* the learner. This fact alone should be a significant element in the design of any college course. This requires a shift from the traditional brand of content-centered teaching (which focuses almost exclusively on foundational knowledge) to a more learning-centered model in which students are intimately involved in the dynamics of learning.

From the Field _____

According to associate professor of communication, Brian Furio, "It's a learning environment rather than a 'classroom.' I want to make learning interesting and appealing. I want students to learn because it relates to their lives. It's important that I make the content something the audience can use. In short, the process is more important than the product!"

Five Factors That Make a Difference

How can you use learner-centered learning to design an effective and successful course? Here are some factors you may wish to keep in mind—before you make a list of course topics:

Don't worry about trying to cover all the content in your discipline or subject area. Think about how many years of graduate work it took you to master all that content. You will only have these undergraduate students for 15 weeks; it would be impractical to expect that they should (or could) master all the essential information in that short time frame. Instead, identify a _few key concepts_ to emphasize.

> **"Research Says"**
>
> A significant and overwhelming body of research has shown that students typically retain 20 percent or less of the content of their college courses. A few studies have found rare high values of 50 percent.

Keep in mind that the content (or foundational knowledge) is only one element in the design of a course. Other kinds of learning need to be woven into the fabric of a course so that students understand its value in their lives and its relationship to the rest of the world. The content provides you with a launching pad from which students can begin to explore and analyze course elements in a variety of dimensions. Admittedly, achieving a balance between goals and outcomes is a tricky endeavor, but the rewards for both you and your students will be enormous.

Be cautious when using the textbook as an outline for your course design. The authors of the text do not know your students or your specific teaching situation. They are not aware of the dynamics of your institution or the experiences you bring to that institution. Therefore, you should use the textbook as a guide rather than as a "bible" in the design of a course. Feel free to eliminate sections, chapters, units, or resources if they are not appropriate. Additionally, consider rearranging the chapters or topics to suit your specific emphases in a course. (Although you should minimize skipping around, and always tell students your reasons for doing so). Always consider additional

Red Flag

According to Mike Messner, chair of the sociology department at the University of Southern California, "Early in my teaching career I wanted to convert students .... I wanted them to be leftists and feminists. I used my class as a bully pulpit. I've since learned that that thinking shows disrespect and it's not good pedagogy—it's religion."

resources, research, and documents to augment your course design. Providing students with multiple perspectives will enhance their engagement in any subject.

In my interviews with successful college teachers across the country, no one said that they wanted students to know all the facts about a specific topic or course. They all indicated that they wanted students to use information in real-life situations, become lifelong learners, be able to think critically and creatively, make connections between a topic in the class and events outside the classroom, understand interrelationships, and become active problem solvers (among other topics). Almost to a person, these outstanding teachers said that a focus on outcomes was just as important as goals—many argued that it was even more important. In designing your course, therefore, you may wish to think about the outcomes first—prior to addressing the goals. Use the 3-2-1 model, but consider addressing the "2" section first. Afterwards, you can identify the goals that will help you promote those outcomes.

Remember that a course—any course—needs to be flexible. A course will evolve over several semesters, even during a single semester. You'll discover new resources, a potential guest speaker will unexpectedly arrive in town, a new video will be released, students will take a discussion in a new and unplanned direction. It's important to remember that the design of a course needs to be flexible and malleable.

Learning (and teaching) is never in a straight line. Be willing to modify, adjust, and make needed corrections—just as you would want your students to do as they embark on the educational journey you've prepared for them.

The Least You Need to Know

- ◆ Goals and outcomes are both necessary for a successful course.
- ◆ There are several critical steps to be followed in developing a well-structured course.
- ◆ Significant learning can be accomplished with a six-stage taxonomy.
- ◆ Five factors are necessary in the design of a learner-centered course.

Chapter 5

Selecting and Using Textbooks

In This Chapter

- ◆ Textbook organization and design
- ◆ Finding and selecting an appropriate text
- ◆ Using textbooks in class

Several years ago I wrote a college textbook on teaching language arts. In the preface I stated that if any topic, subject, or course is to be exciting and dynamic, then that excitement has to be woven throughout the textbook. As both an author and college instructor, it is my fervent belief that the use of a textbook has the potential to make or break a course—not just by its material or organization but more importantly by how it is used.

This chapter provides you with an overview of the attributes of quality college textbooks, how to integrate textbooks into the design and delivery of course concepts, and some of the tips and suggestions regarding textbooks used by some of the best college instructors. Consider these ideas as possibilities, not absolutes, for the design of your courses.

Textbooks: What's Inside?

Textbooks come in all shapes and sizes depending on the nature of the discipline, the materials to be covered, and the level of a particular course (lower division, upper division, graduate). While there is a great deal of variation among textbooks and textbook publishers, here are typical features which, in varying degrees, are found in an "average" college textbook:

- ◆ **Key questions:** Often at the beginning of a chapter to alert students to key concepts.

- ◆ **Key ideas:** Highlighted sections throughout the chapter or at the end to summarize important points.

- ◆ **Introductions:** A brief overview of chapter content.

- ◆ **Quotations:** Statements from experts in the field that underscore a specific point of view.

- ◆ **Student activities:** Projects or out-of-class investigations that reinforce chapter concepts.

- ◆ **Commentaries:** Specific points of views (either complementary or conflicting) about a specific issue.

- ◆ **Vignettes:** Brief stories or anecdotes that illustrate a specific point of view.

- ◆ **Marginal notes:** Brief notes that highlight key ideas within a chapter.

- ◆ **Chapter summaries:** A short and compact overview of key chapter concepts or ideas.

- ◆ **Suggested readings and resources:** Lists of print and Internet sources (often with annotations) for students to locate additional information on specific topics.

- ◆ **Glossary:** Definitions of key vocabulary.

- ◆ **Resource handbook:** This may be a supplementary publication that contains additional related readings, annotated bibliographies, out-of-class activities, charts and graphs, or practice materials for labs and/or seminars.

- ◆ **Website support:** This may include self-assessments, exams, readings, web links, or a sample syllabus.

def•i•ni•tion

A **textbook** is a collection of the knowledge, concepts and principles of a selected topic or course. It is usually written by one or more college professors, researchers or experts in a particular field or discipline.

Textbooks provide several advantages for any college course. The material to be covered and the sequence of topics are spelled out in detail, with a balanced presentation of up-to-date information research, and principles that are relevant or reflect current opinion and/or practice in a discipline. Textbooks give students a foundation of knowledge—particularly in subject areas where they have no previous experience—as well as a framework for the organization of research or current thinking about a course.

Selecting an Appropriate Textbook

College students expect that there will be outside reading for almost any course. That means that they will need to purchase one or more textbooks in order to obtain the necessary concepts, principles, opinions, background information, and current research. The careful and judicious selection of texts ensures that students will be able to come to class prepared and will be able to leave the course with appropriate levels of comprehension.

From the Field

Professor Robert Rotenberg of DePaul University in Chicago says that professors need to distinguish between "an opportunity to teach the book, rather than looking for a book from which students can learn." In other words, a textbook is not an out line for teaching the course; instead, it is a resource that addresses students' needs relative to course content.

In most disciplines there are many potential textbooks available. In disciplines that are relatively new or for experimental courses, the range of available textbooks may be limited. How do you find out about the textbooks in your field? As soon as you are assigned to teach a specific course, contact colleagues in your department. Ask them for the titles of textbooks they have used in the past or for the names of authors or researchers they admire or respect.

Most textbook publishers have sales representatives assigned to a specific geographical region (a set of colleges). You can locate these reps through each publisher's website. Ask them to provide you with complimentary *desk copies* of relevant textbooks for your review. You can often bypass the sales reps by ordering *examination copies* of selected textbooks directly on each publisher's website.

def•i•ni•tion

A **desk copy** or **examination copy** of a textbook is provided free of charge to any professor who is considering it for a specific course. After the review process, some publishers ask that the books be returned to a central warehouse. Other publishers allow professors to keep these complimentary copies.

Here are just a few of the college textbook publishers in the United States:

- Pearson/Merrill/Prentice-Hall/Allyn & Bacon (www.ablongman.com)

- Houghton-Mifflin/D.C. Heath (http://education.college.hmco.com)

- Jossey-Bass (www.josseybass.com)

- Waveland Press (www.waveland.com)

Whenever you attend a conference or convention in your discipline, visit the textbook display booths in the exhibit area. Here, you will discover the latest texts as well as the newest supplemental materials. Be sure to sign up for their mailing lists. Get the business cards of the sales reps, too. Often, publishers will grant you a conference discount if you would like to take a potential text home immediately.

Also, while at conferences, peruse the listing of scheduled presentations, seminars, workshops, and discussions in the conference program. Plan to talk with some of the presenters about the texts they recommend or use in their courses. Ask to see the syllabi of colleagues in your department. Check out the texts they are using in their courses. You may wish to contact professors at other institutions (via the respective college websites) and ask them for complimentary copies of their syllabi or specific recommendations of potential textbooks for a specific course.

Textbook Evaluation Scale

Suffice it to say, textbooks come in all shapes and sizes. Some are like enormous unabridged encyclopedias, while others treat subjects superficially. Some are chronological in nature; others target specific concepts or principles. However, since textbook publishers tend to have fairly rigid guidelines on textbook authorship, there are many elements which tend to be repeated irrespective of discipline, topic, or course.

The following chart has many of the elements that are essential to a good college textbook. Since each course and each discipline is different, not every element will be part of every textbook (a geometry textbook may not have recommended readings; a poetry text may not have any graphic elements). You can use this scale to evaluate various texts for a particular course. Rate each feature from 5 (high) to 1 (low). If an item is not applicable, circle NA. Upon completion, tally the ratings to determine the best all-around textbook for a course.

Title of textbook: _____

Author(s): _____

Date of publication: _____

Publisher: _____

Sequential table of contents	5	4	3	2	1	NA
Up to date (current)	5	4	3	2	1	NA
Glossary	5	4	3	2	1	NA
Bibliography	5	4	3	2	1	NA
Recommended readings	5	4	3	2	1	NA
Suggested websites	5	4	3	2	1	NA
Index	5	4	3	2	1	NA
Engaging writing style	5	4	3	2	1	NA
Thorough, factual coverage	5	4	3	2	1	NA
Headings and subheadings	5	4	3	2	1	NA
Captions and labels for graphics	5	4	3	2	1	NA
Sidebars with relevant information	5	4	3	2	1	NA
Practice exercises/activities	5	4	3	2	1	NA
Chapter previews	5	4	3	2	1	NA
Chapter summaries	5	4	3	2	1	NA
Extension activities/homework	5	4	3	2	1	NA
Uncrowded page layout	5	4	3	2	1	NA
End-of-chapter questions	5	4	3	2	1	NA
Appropriate font, margins, line length	5	4	3	2	1	NA
Graphic elements (art, photos, charts)	5	4	3	2	1	NA

Use Them Wisely!

A textbook is only as good as the teacher who uses it. It's important to remember that a textbook is just one tool, although a very important one, in your teaching arsenal. Sometimes, teachers lean too heavily on textbooks and don't consider other aids or materials for the classroom. Some teachers reject a textbook approach to learning because the textbook is outdated or insufficiently covers a topic or subject area.

From the Field

Kay McAdams, an assistant professor of history, states, "I often provide my students with material that I don't neces-sarily agree with. I like to provide them with divergent viewpoints—not necessarily my own views. This provides a rich seedbed for in-class discussions."

One of the many decisions you will make as a teacher is how you wish to use the textbook. As good as they may appear on the surface, it's important to realize that there are some limitations to textbooks.

Surveys of college students across the country reveal several issues (read: complaints) about college texts. These negatives have remained constant over the years; you may have even voiced one or more of them in your undergraduate years. However common these negatives may be, they should also be considerations in your selection of appropriate textbooks.

Many students feel that textbooks are overpriced or are another way for the institu-tion to pry more money from their wallets. Many textbooks are poorly written; they're often written by an expert in the field—someone who has a great deal of knowledge, but who may not be a professional author. There's a big difference between know-ing a lot about something and being able to effectively communicate that knowledge. Writing skills are often in short supply in textbooks.

Textbooks are often "over the heads" of students. A great number of textbooks are sophisticated interpretations of relevant research. Those interpretations make sense to other practitioners, but may have little relevance for students just beginning their academic journey. In short, students often find textbooks incomprehensible and/or unreadable.

Textbooks are also often too broad in their scope. It's not unusual for students to reject textbooks simply because of what they are—compendiums of large masses of data for large masses of students. Students often find it difficult to understand the relevance of so much data to their personal lives.

"Research Says"

According to data released by The College Board the average cost for college texts (for one student, one semester) ranged from $801 to $904 (2005–2006). In the *2006 College Store Industry Financial Report* issued by the National Association of College Stores the gross margin (the difference between what a college store pays for a text-book and the amount charged a student) for new textbooks is 22.3 percent. After store expenses have been paid, a college store makes about four cents for every dollar's worth of new textbooks sold.

Using the Textbook in Class

One of the common complaints voiced by college students is "The #&%$*@% textbook cost $100 and we only read a few chapters. What a waste!" With the ever-escalating price of textbooks, it seems reasonable to students that they should get something for their financial investment in the academic materials of a course.

Professors typically designate one or more textbook chapters for each topic in a course. The sequence of chapter readings is outlined on the syllabus. Students are expected to read the assigned chapters (prior to class) and come to class prepared to discuss the content. While this is a traditional way of using a textbook, let's make textbook use more beneficial for your students by examining three critical parts of reading texts:

1. Before reading

2. During reading

3. After reading

This sequence is referred to as guided reading and it can enhance the utility of any textbook in any course. Let's take a look in a little more detail.

Before Reading

At this stage, you want to link students' background knowledge and experiences to the text, establish a reason for reading it, and give specific direction on what you want them to get out of it. In short, you draw connections between the text, students' minds, and the course content. Here are some strategies you can share with students before they read an assigned chapter:

◆ Ask students to talk about what they may already know about the topic of the chapter.

◆ Encourage students to note and write down any questions they may have about the topic.

◆ Invite students to make predictions based on the chapter title or subtitles.

◆ Ask students to develop "links" between the assigned chapter and one previously read.

◆ Present and define potentially difficult vocabulary.

◆ Provide students with a study guide or outline of key concepts they should keep in mind while reading.

During Reading

This stage of textbook reading provides students with information necessary to the comprehension of important ideas and concepts. It is where students add to their storehouse of information while actively processing and interacting with the text. Here are some suggested strategies:

◆ Invite students to find the answers to their prereading questions.

◆ Ask students to verify and/or reformulate predictions.

◆ Encourage students to integrate new data with prior knowledge.

◆ Ask students to generate questions (as they read) for classroom discussion.

◆ Invite students to write brief summaries of selected sections (or of an entire chapter)

◆ Invite students to ask themselves some *metacognitive* questions: Why would this information be important for me to know? How does this information differ from other things I know? Why is this difficult for me to understand? Can I write a summary of this section? What do I know so far?

def•i•ni•tion

Metacognition is defined as "thinking about what you're thinking about." It is a mental process in which we contemplate what we understand, what we don't understand, and the reasons for each.

After Reading

Asking students to read a textbook chapter without any follow-up is self-defeating. Considering the material after reading is critical to your students' comprehension, and a wonderful opportunity for you to help students "build bridges" between what they knew (or didn't know) and what they need to know.

Here are some post-reading ideas for you to consider:

◆ Invite students to evaluate prereading predictions.

◆ Engage students in a selection of problem-solving activities (see Chapter 12).

◆ Provide opportunities for students to share perceptions and understandings in small groups.

◆ Encourage students to consider any questions they still have.

◆ Ask students to participate in debates, panel discussions, simulations, role-playing situations, journaling, interviews, and other extending activities.

◆ Invite students to define selected vocabulary words or summarize significant concepts.

One of the post-reading strategies I use in my college courses is a chapter log. I pass out copies to my students at the start of the semester and ask them to partially complete one for each assigned chapter.

Each one poses a critical thinking question for students to record and respond to for each separate chapter. These logs serve as valuable vehicles for small-group discussions of 10 minutes or so. I listen carefully to the conversations and can correct misconceptions, provide additional explanations, or clarify important points in my follow-up lectures or presentations. Here's an example of a chapter log:

Chapter Log

Name: _____ Date: _____

Chapter Number(s): _____ Pages: _____

Topic(s): _____

Group members: _____ _____

_____

Critical Question for this chapter: _____

_____

My response(s) [to be completed before class]:

Group Consensus:

A significant quote from the reading is [to be completed before class]:

    Page: _____ Column: _____ Line: _____

Group Consensus:

Overall, I think today's experience (chapter reading &/or group discussion) was:

❏ Very stimulating   ❏ Interesting   ❏ Fairly interesting   ❏ Confusing
❏ Boring   ❏ Other: _____

The Textbook as a Tool

How you decide to use textbooks will be dependent on many factors, but let me add a note of caution. Don't make the mistake of basing an entire course on a single textbook. Use any textbook judiciously. A carpenter, for example, doesn't just use a hammer to build a magnificent oak chest. She may use a plane, chisel, saw, sander, or any number of tools to create the masterpiece she wishes to build. A great college course, just like a great piece of furniture, needs many tools in its construction.

When thinking about how you want to use textbooks, consider the following:

- Use the textbook as a primary resource for students, but not the *only* resource.

- Use a textbook as a guide, not a mandate, for instruction.

- Be free to modify, change, eliminate, or add to the material in the textbook.

- Supplement the textbook with outside readings, research, and investigations.

- Feel free to eliminate chapters in order to provide more in-depth coverage of other topics.

- Feel free to rearrange the chapters into the order you prefer to present the material.

Red Flag _____

Course packets are only as good as their currency. Don't use outdated research or "tired" articles. The best course packets are those that are refreshed on a regular basis (annually, for example).

Remember, no textbook is perfect or complete. It is one resource at your disposal—a blueprint, a guidebook, and an outline. However, they do provide students with a ready "anchor point" for a course—a way to make sense of new or complex issues that can lead to higher levels of comprehension.

The Least You Need to Know

- The organization and design of most college textbooks is fairly standardized.

- Selecting an appropriate textbook should be done with care.

- You can help students obtain the most valuable information by focusing on before-, during-, and after-reading strategies.

- Courses can be just as effective without a textbook.

Chapter 6

Designing the Course Syllabus

In This Chapter

- ◆ What a syllabus is and does
- ◆ Preparing to draft a syllabus
- ◆ The basic elements
- ◆ Don't neglect the obvious

If you were planning to go on a safari in Africa, you'd have quite a bit of work to do beforehand. You'd have to get a passport, make airline reservations, obtain appropriate clothing and other supplies, make hotel or lodging reservations, plan transportation, and handle a thousand other details. You might even sketch out a "to-do" list and check off each task as it is completed.

A syllabus is a to-do list for both professors and students. It is the instructional guide for a course—a way to map out what you want students to learn, how you will help them learn, and their responsibilities throughout the semester. Let's take a look at some good syllabus-planning strategies and how you can effectively use syllabi in your courses.

Syllabi—What Are They?

The dictionary defines "syllabus" as an outline for a course of study. It lists the topics covered, the requirements for a course, the expectations of students and other types of basic information such as contact information for the instructor and grading procedures.

But a carefully designed *syllabus* is much more than that. Indeed, many institutions consider the syllabus to be a contract between the student and the professor; it lists the expectations of each in reaching a desired goal—the successful completion of a course.

In Appendix C of this book, you'll find examples of several syllabi (in various disciplines) for your review. A syllabus is a blueprint—one subject to modification and revision from year to year and from course to course. The best way to look at a syllabus is as an evolving document that adapts to the needs of students and the needs of a course or discipline. A good syllabus provides an outline for the accomplishment of specific tasks, while at the same time allowing for a measure of flexibility in terms of course concepts and instructor preferences. Syllabi exist for several reasons:

- To communicate to students what the course is about

- To clarify why the course is taught

- To present the primary and secondary topics covered in the course

- To detail the logistics of the course

- To provide a sequence or schedule of topics covered and required tasks

- To establish the assessment and evaluation schedule and procedures

def•i•ni•tion

A **syllabus** is a document distributed to college students at the start of a course. It outlines contact information, course requirements, grading policy, assignments, topics, and other essential elements of the course.

Preparing to Draft a Syllabus

Three of the biggest questions you will face as a college professor are, "What material do I need to cover?", "How much do I need to cover?", and "In what order should I cover it?"

As a beginning professor you may have an urge to cover *everything*. (Experienced professors fall into this trap, too). You may feel that you need to expose students to a wide range of information, concepts, and facts in order to fully convey the subject matter. But convincing research shows that covering less material, in depth, is more effective than covering more material superficially.

The two biggest demons you will need to wrestle in designing a course syllabus are time and material. Finding the right balance will always be a struggle, especially at the beginning of your teaching career. Here are a few suggestions to make that struggle more manageable.

First, decide how you want to organize your course. Select one of the following designs:

- **Deductive** (general to specific): List all the topics as presented in a standard textbook for the subject (or use several textbooks and look for overlapping ideas). Assign each of the topics to a date on the semester calendar.

- **Inductive** (specific to general): Make a large list of all the topics, ideas, concepts, facts, generalizations, and principles that you want to cover. Assign each of the topics to a date on the semester calendar.

Decide on a sequence for the course. In order to make this step successful you need to answer the following question: What do students need to know, and when do they need to know it? Select from one of the following possibilities:

- From simple concepts to more complex concepts

- Chronologically or historically

- From knowledge to application

- From theoretical to practical

- Hierarchical

- From general to specific

Inevitably, you will have more topics than you will have available dates on the calendar. Pare down! Now is the time to make some difficult decisions:

- Which topics are most important?

- Which topics need lots of time and which need only a little?

- Which topics can you skip without affecting the overall content and goals of the course (as described in the college catalog)?

From the Field

Peter Filene, professor of history at the University of North Carolina at Chapel Hill, cautions, "The first time you teach a course is inevitably a dress rehearsal. You will identify the excesses, omissions, and confusions only as you perform it in dialogue with a live audience."

◆ Which topics are favorites of yours and which ones are necessary, but not particularly engaging (for you)?

◆ Which topics will be confusing for students; which ones will be clear and apparent?

Finally, decide on the various ancillary experiences (both in and out of class) you want your students to engage in. These would include (but are not limited to) reading assignments, written reports, exams, quizzes, seminars, forums, discussions, field trips, films, debates, simulations, interviews, observations, internships, and the like. Now, begin to "slot" those specific events into the developing syllabus.

Inevitably, you will discover that there are probably more things to do and cover than there is time available. Unfortunately, there is no magic formula—every subject, semester, class, and professor is different. Know that a syllabus (and the design of a course) is always evolving. What you create now might be vastly different from what you create for the same course 10 semesters from now. That's OK! In the end, a well-structured syllabus is founded on the answers to four basic questions:

◆ What are your goals for students in this course (cognition)?

◆ How will you involve students in those goals (methodologies)?

◆ How will students accomplish those goals (assignments)?

◆ How will you and your students know they have realized those goals (assessment and evaluation)?

Design It Right—the Basic Elements

The following "ingredients" of a course syllabus are offered as an essential outline for any course or any subject. While the exact order of items is not critical, the inclusion of these basic parts will help ensure that your students are up to speed on the design and delivery of your course from the first day of class.

Course Information

The initial page or section of a course syllabus should include basic course information. The following is essential:

- Course number
- Course title
- Credit hours
- Semester or term (e.g., Spring 2009)
- Location of the classroom
- Days and hours the class meets
- Prerequisites/permission of instructor (as required)

Instructor Information

Be sure to provide basic information about yourself. If there are lab assistants or teaching assistants for the course, be sure to list their contact information as well. Include most or all of the following:

- Your name and title
- Your office location
- Your office hours
- Your e-mail address (office and/or home)
- Your personal (or business) web page
- The course web page (if any)

Some instructors list their home telephone number in order to promote additional lines of communication after class hours. If you do, be sure to include the hours when students may call. For example, "No calls before 8 A.M. and no calls after 10 P.M."

Course Description

This is a basic overview of the course and its objectives. Most instructors will include, at a minimum, the description of the course as included in the college catalog. Be aware, however, that the course may have changed or altered since the publication of the catalog, so make sure this description is up-to-date, accurate, and complete. Consider including the following information:

◆ The general content of the course

◆ Instructional methods (for example, lecture, lab, seminar)

◆ Initial and final goals

◆ Need for the course

◆ Relationship of course to the major

Course Objectives

If the syllabus is the road map for the course, then the *objectives* are the destination you want your students to reach at the end of the course. Objectives spell out what students are expected to know or be able to do when they successfully complete the semester.

def•i•ni•tion

The **objectives** listed in your syllabus describe what students will be able to do upon completion of the course.

One of the easiest ways to design the objectives for a course is to modify the catalog description. You may be able to locate appropriate objectives in the textbook(s) you plan to use, or tap into your colleagues' expertise and solicit their thoughts and ideas, particularly if they've taught the course. Take advantage of the resources available through your professional organizations and associations. Through the Internet you can access the syllabi (and course objectives) of comparable courses at other institutions.

Well-crafted objectives have two components: the audience (the students for whom the objective is intended) and the terminal behavior (the anticipated performance). Here's a sample set of objectives for a course on marine biology (BIO-210) taught by Jessica Nolan, an assistant professor of biology:

Marine biology is an introductory course designed to acquaint students with the diversity and ecology of marine organisms. The main objectives of this course are to understand

◆ *How scientists investigate questions in marine science.*

◆ *Which organisms are found in the ocean.*

◆ *How marine organisms are adapted to the unique physical, chemical, and geological characteristics of various habitats in the ocean.*

◆ *Aspects of ecological theory as they apply to marine environments.*

◆ *How human activities are impacting the ocean.*

Some courses, specifically those that must satisfy the standards of outside accrediting agencies (such as a state department of education or a national licensing board), are required to have syllabi that list specific objectives in line with state or national standards. These guarantee students (and any outside reviewers) that course content is aligned with established and recognized standards.

Course Materials

List all the required texts that students will need for the length of the course. For each text, list the author, date of publication, edition, title, place of publication, publisher, ISBN, and price. Here's an example:

Delli Carpini, Dominic. *Composing a Life's Work: Writing, Citizenship, and Your Occupation*, 1st ed. New York: Pearson/Longman, 2005. [ISBN: 0-321-10528-1]. $64.80.

For many courses you will want your students to read materials in addition to the required textbook(s). It is important that you indicate whether these supplemental materials are required for the course, are strongly recommended, or optional. Inform students if these materials will be on reserve in the library or available for purchase in the campus bookstore.

For some courses, specific materials and equipment will need to be purchased or obtained. Be sure to list those items in the syllabus. These may include the following:

◆ Art courses: paint, brushes, special paper

◆ Science labs: lab coats, microscope slides, tools

◆ Math courses: calculators, graph paper

◆ Nursing courses: medical equipment

◆ Psychology courses: specialized tests

◆ Computer courses: software

Course Procedures

This is typically a separate section or series of subsections in a course syllabus. In essence, this section outlines the rules or behaviors expected of students. It is vitally important that this section be included in any syllabus, but even more so for college freshmen and sophomores who need to be fully aware of your expectations. Be sure to at least include information on the following:

- **Attendance:** Include a brief section about attendance. Is it required for each class meeting? Are points taken off for missed classes? Is the final grade reduced for poor attendance? Will attendance affect a borderline grade?

- **Lateness:** Include a statement about the need to be on time for each class session. Some instructors penalize students for excessive tardiness.

- **Class participation:** If your course is primarily a lecture course, then this section may not be necessary. However, if lively class discussions are part of your expectations, then explain that they'll need to be active participants. If class participation is part of the final grade, state that, too.

- **Missed assignments/exams:** Students should know that any missed assignments or exams will have an impact on their final grade, but be sure to include information on how students can make up course requirements in the event of illness, participation in team sports, field trip with another class, family emergency, and so on.

- **Safety rules:** If the course has any safety issues or is inherently dangerous (chemistry, engineering, biology, etc.), list all safety rules in the syllabus. State the importance of these issues as well as any emergency procedures to follow, such as evacuation procedures, location of a first aid kit, emergency phone number(s), location of infirmary, and contact information for campus security.

 Red Flag

On large campuses it may not always be possible for students to get from one building to the next within the allotted time break between classes. The ever-present issue of securing a parking space for students coming from off-campus apartments or part-time jobs may also affect their timely arrival in class. And, unfortunately, some of your colleagues may delay students with "just one more thing before you leave." Bottom line: Be aware of potential tardiness factors that may be beyond the control of students.

Academic Dishonesty

You should also include a statement on academic dishonesty as part of the course syllabus. Because this is such a serious issue with many college students, I prefer to set aside a separate (and often highlighted) section concerning academic integrity.

Here is a statement required on all syllabi at York College of Pennsylvania. Consider this as an example of one you should include on your course syllabi, too:

> *Academic dishonesty will not be tolerated at York College. Academic dishonesty refers to actions such as, but not limited to, cheating, plagiarism, fabricating research, falsifying academic documents, etc. and includes all situations where students make use of the work of others and claim such work as their own. Thus, it is expected that all assigned work for this course will be entirely original. In cases of academic dishonesty, the student involved may receive a grade of "0" for the course and the matter will be reported to the Department Chairperson and the Dean of Academic Affairs [or other appropriate administrators].*

> **"Research Says"**
>
> In one national study comprising 6,165 respondents, one-third of the college students with A's and B+'s indicated that they had cheated. Two-thirds of 6,000 students at "highly selective" colleges indicated that they had also cheated.

Your own institution may have a specific policy statement about academic integrity. Find out what it is and make it a part of every course syllabus.

Grading Plan

For most students, this may be the most important element of your syllabus, so it's essential that students know from the first day how they will be evaluated and all the components of the final grade. Here are the elements you must consider and share with students:

How many assignments (written papers, lab report, original research, midterm and final exams, etc.) will comprise the course?

What value (points, percentages, letter grades) will you give to each of the course assignments? Here's an example of a point system:

Assignment	Value
Lesson Plan	100 points
Internet Project	150 points
Research Paper	200 points
Quiz #1	100 points
Quiz #2	100 points
Final Exam	250 points
TOTAL:	900 points

Here's an example of a percentage system:

Assignment	Value
Thematic Unit	25%
Outside Interview	10%
Self-Selected Project	20%
Multiple Intelligences Report	20%
Quiz	10%
Final Exam	15%
TOTAL:	100%

If you will be offering "extras" such as class participation, effort, attendance, or improvement to determine students' grades, these need to be clearly stated on the syllabus, too.

You should also clarify the institution's policies regarding incompletes (I), withdrawals (W), or pass/fail (P/F) situations. Be sure to state the last day to withdraw from a course for the semester. In cases of incomplete grades, reiterate the college's policy on when the requirements must be completed (many institutions allow 60 days from the end of the semester to complete any outstanding assignments).

 Red Flag

If you're teaching any freshman or sophomore courses, state the appeals process (your own, your department's, or the institution's) for students who feel they have been unfairly evaluated in a course. This is often presented in the college catalog or as a section in the student handbook, but it never hurts to restate it here.

Course Schedule

This section outlines the basic plan for presenting the material of your course. You may wish to offer students a daily or weekly schedule of lectures, topics, textbook readings, and the like.

Consider this portion of your syllabus as the essential road map through the course—a way for students to discover new sights while following a prescribed route. At the very least this schedule should include the following items:

◆ A daily or weekly schedule

◆ Topics/concepts/material for each of the designated dates

◆ Textbook reading(s) for each date

◆ Designated outside readings

◆ Dates of exams, quizzes, or other assessments

◆ Due dates for assignments, written reports, lab work

◆ Special events (guest speakers, videos, field trips)

Here's a partial course schedule for a course entitled Topics in Children's Literature:

Week of	Topic	Textbook Reading	Outside Reading	Other
Aug. 29	Introductions; course syllabus; course expectations	Ch. 1		
Sept. 5	History of children's literature	Ch. 5		Guest Speaker: Ms. Samantha Pfeffer
Sept. 12	What is a good book?	Chs. 2-3	"WOW, What a Great Story!" (article on reserve)	Quiz #1
Sept. 19	Engaging students in literature	Ch. 4		Author/ Illustrator Unit due

You may be concerned that your class schedule is an inviolable outline. Not true! This schedule, just like any schedule, is always subject to change. Those changes may be due to your illness, unexpected weather problems, your attendance at a last-minute conference, power outages, or a thousand other reasons. For that reason, it is always preferable to title this section as "<u>Tentative</u> Course Schedule. This will also avoid any legal difficulties later on if you need to depart from your presemester plan of action.

Miscellaneous

You may wish to include one or more of the following in your course syllabus. These are optional and not all are appropriate for every course or every instructor. Use the ones you feel will provide students with essential information necessary to their academic success.

One thing I do at the end of each semester is ask one or two of the outstanding students in a course to write an open letter to the students taking the same course the following semester. I ask them to share what they learned, how they grew as students, what they saw as the challenges in the course, and how they dealt with them—as well as any of the instructor's idiosyncrasies (including his penchant for bad jokes and awful puns). Then, on the first day of the new semester I read these letters to the new students as a way of introducing them to the course, letting them know I like to give my students a voice, and inviting them to become active participants. These letters are a great way to kick off the new semester.

You may also just want to offer some pointers, tips, or ideas that will help students succeed. These may include study aids, relevant outside materials, availability of tutors, or information from former students. Here are some other examples:

- ◆ **Privacy issues:** Depending on the nature of the course, you may need to include a statement on student privacy (stating that names, e-mail addresses, and the like will not be shared).

- ◆ **Course or instructor evaluations:** Particularly for untenured faculty, student evaluations of the course or instructor are conducted on a regular basis. You may wish to provide students with information on how this will be accomplished in your course.

- ◆ **Guest speakers, instructors, or observers:** If you plan to have any guest speakers or other types of visitors in the class you may wish to address this here. Protocol, rules of behavior, cultural taboos, and common courtesies should be shared with students.

◆ **Study sheets:** If you will be using study or discussion guides, let students know when and where they will be available (on reserve, on your web page, distributed at the start of each class).

◆ **Permission forms:** Inform students if they'll need any special permission forms. In certain psychology courses, for example, students may work with others as part of a research project. Appropriate permission forms (such as those for human study) will need to be completed ahead of time.

◆ **Support services:** Consider including a section detailing all the support services available to students. Start with the most obvious—the campus library. Let students know about the periodicals, journals, abstracts, collections, and audiovisual resources the library has. If your institution has a learning center or tutoring center, share that information with students, too. Inform students of any resources in the local community (museums, public libraries, galleries, social service agencies, laboratories) that can also serve as instructional resources. Give the location, hours of operation, and availability of the campus computer center.

From the Field

Some instructors create a special section in their syllabi that lists some of their beliefs about the course itself as well as about students who take the course. These statements may outline her or his philosophy about teaching in general or about the course content specifically. They may include a brief overview of the instructor's personal philosophy about teaching (and learning). Or, they may include a sentence or two about the relationship of the course content to the "real world" outside the classroom.

The Bottom Line

I like to think of a syllabus as a road map—one that provides students with signposts, signals, detours, places to rest, sights to see, attractions, noteworthy venues, and a well-paved highway on which they will travel throughout the length of the semester. It is also a written document—an agreement between you and your students about what you will be doing and what they need to do to complete their "trip" successfully. Never keep students guessing about a course. If it's important for them to know, it's important to put it in writing.

That said, don't try to include everything about the course in this single document (the proverbial "kitchen sink" syndrome). Many well-written syllabi come in at two to four pages; other poorly designed ones frequently top 20 pages or more. The bottom line is: what do students need to know at the *beginning* of the course? Trying to include every single detail about the course in the syllabus may result on an over-written document—one that students simply won't read, especially if they're preoccupied with getting to know you and the course you teach.

You may find it both appropriate and necessary to introduce other documents or information later in the course as students become more proficient with the course design, your expectations, and the tools they need to enjoy a measure of success. Again, ask yourself this question: *What is the essential information students need to begin this course?*

One More Thought

As a former college student yourself, you've seen your share of syllabi. If you've taught college courses previously, you may have even constructed a few of your own. As a result, it may be that few of the suggestions in this chapter are unique or novel to you—in fact, they might have seemed quite obvious, merely common sense.

"Research Says"

One collegiate research study discovered (through interviews and examinations of course syllabi) that many college professors did not include "obvious" items such as contact information, course objectives, attendance policy, course schedule, and the like in their syllabi.

But keep in mind that students will rely on you to provide them with a way to "enter" your course, your discipline, and your expertise. A well-written syllabus is the key they need to successfully gain this entry and to enjoy a measure of success throughout the semester.

The Least You Need to Know

- A syllabus is a basic outline of what you will teach and how you will teach it.
- A well-designed syllabus has several elements—all of which work together.
- A syllabus should be carefully crafted to get students started on the right foot at the beginning of a course.
- Don't leave anything obvious out of your syllabus.

Part 3

Teaching College: The Nitty-Gritty

Do you have a memorable college professor from your days as an undergraduate student? What did that person do that made you want to come to class each day, and got you thoroughly engaged in the subject matter or completely engulfed in a specific topic?

In Part 3, I'll introduce you to the techniques, skills, and attributes of outstanding college teachers. You may even recognize one of your old instructors in the pages of this section. You'll be introduced to the creative strategies and engaging ideas that guarantee your success with any college course. Here you'll learn how to start off any course with a bang, conduct a class, create effective lectures and discussions, implement cooperative teaching strategies, and get your students thinking more and thinking better. It's a tall order, but there are some exciting things to learn here. Are you ready for the nitty-gritty of college teaching?

"Keep it simple! Ditch the PowerPoint and whap 'em with just a few concepts. Pound it in and keep hittin' 'em!"

The First Day: First Impressions

In This Chapter

- ◆ How to get off to a great start
- ◆ Effective learning communities
- ◆ How to connect with your students
- ◆ Some food for thought

Remember the first time you ever drove a car? Do you recall the anticipation, the fear, the anxiety, the trepidation? Do you remember the various thoughts bouncing around in your head? *What if it stalls out in the middle of the driveway? What if I crash into something?*

It was exciting, but still a pretty scary time, right? Well, your first day of teaching college is just like that. You may have seen expert professors create magic in a classroom. You've probably also had instructors who, to put it gently, couldn't teach their way out of a paper bag. Now it's you in the front of a classroom full of college students—the harshest critics in the world!

Guess what? You're not alone. Of all the questions that college professors ask, "What do I do on the first day (or week) of my course?" is one of the most common.

Starting Off

Think back to your days as a college student. How did your instructors approach the first day of a new course? Did they spend that initial class covering the demands, requirements, and assignments of the course? Did they tell you about the common difficulties students have with the course or subject matter? Did they spend an inordinate amount of time on a confusing and abstract syllabus? Did you leave frustrated or with a heightened sense of anxiety about your ability to complete the courses successfully?

Every college student, whether they're at an Ivy League institution, a liberal arts institution, a state college, a private institution, or a junior college, approaches each new course with some degree of trepidation and anxiety. If it is true that "first impressions are lasting impressions," then it is equally true that we need to help our students get off on the right foot at the start of each new course or each new semester. Indeed, students' success will often be determined by the impressions they take away from that all-important first class.

> **"Research Says"**
>
> Several studies conducted in the late 1990s demonstrated that one of the most significant factors in whether undergraduate students stay at an institution is whether a sense of community is established in their courses.

You can alleviate many of their fears (as well as most of yours) by focusing on two basic concepts. While these are areas you need to focus on during the first day of class, they are also important areas of concentration throughout the entire semester: building a community among the students, and building rapport between them and you.

Building a Community

One of the most common opening activities of the semester, particularly for novice professors, is to spend the first class period going over the syllabus. All of the requirements for the course are dutifully laid out, the grading of assignments and assessment of students is spelled out in minute detail, and the procedures and practices of the course are systematically explained. Afterwards, the instructor asks, "Are there any questions?" Hearing none, he dismisses the class with a "See you next time!"

The problem is that this sends an inappropriate message to students: "The material is more important than you." Students often walk away dazed, confused, and often upset. They're certainly intimidated. Their first impression is that what they do is much more important than who they are.

On the other hand, professors who take time on that all-important first day to begin establishing a "community of learners" will send a most powerful message to students: *the value of people is to be celebrated as much as the value of the material.*

From the Field

Several years ago I co-authored a textbook in which we devoted an entire chapter to "Creating Classroom Environments for Learning." In the section on "Building a Community of Learners" we stated the following: "Effective group membership is essential to establishing positive learning environments where collaboration, meaningful student interaction, and class cohesion are valued." We went on to say, "Community building is [the] basic ingredient to a successful ... classroom."

Opening Up

Here are some opening day activities, ideas, and icebreakers that will get your semester off to a positive start and establish your own "community of learners."

At the start of each semester, I collect comments from the course evaluations students completed at the end of the previous semester. I take time to share some of these (both positive and negative) on the first day and invite student reactions, comments, and discussion. This sends two powerful messages: *other students have indeed successfully completed the course(!),* and an important "thread" or bond exists between students past and present.

Students build a classroom community most effectively by using each other's names. Invite students to pair up with someone they don't know and ask the students to interview each other about the origin, cultural background, family traditions, and significance of their first name. Then invite them to introduce each other to the entire class, giving the background information about their names. Record each student's name on the chalkboard with a short note (as appropriate) about its background. Plan time to discuss the variety of names in the class and why each is special.

Have your students move their desks into a large circle and tell them, "As a class we share certain similarities that may be cultural, philosophical, historical, or personal. We also have some differences as well. This activity is designed to identify our similarities as well as areas in which we might differ. There are no right or wrong answers, and you will not be forced to respond to anything that makes you uncomfortable. OK, please raise your hand (or stand up) for each of the following that applies to you."

Then run down this list:

Live in another state

Ate a pizza in the last week

Have blue eyes

Are a Republican

Speak another language

Are left-handed

Watch a "reality show" regularly

Are married

Are older than 25

Are Hispanic

Are a middle child

Are naturally blond

Were born outside the United States

Have a three-syllable first name

Have more than two grandparents still living

Hate math

Have divorced parents

Have traveled to Europe

Are an athlete

Haven't selected a major yet

Are an environmentalist

Have broken a bone

Are an only child

Know or are related to someone famous

Would rather be in Bermuda right now

Feel free to design and develop your own list of questions in addition to (or in place of) the ones above. After students have responded to several questions, have them form minigroups of two or three individuals—all of whom responded positively to the same question (they all have at least one thing in common). Invite them to interview each other for 5 minutes to discover at least three other things that they have in common (irrespective of the questions above). Give the groups a chance to share their commonalities with the whole class.

Divide the class into several groups. Provide each group with paper and writing instruments. Invite each group to find five things they all share: cultural, physical, personality, outside interests, family-oriented—anything. They may use words, symbols, phrases, or pictures to describe their similarities. After 5 or 10 minutes, invite each member of a group to introduce herself or himself to the entire class and share one of the common items shared by the other members of the group.

Divide the class into several groups. Provide each group with a sheet of newsprint and several markers. Tell each group that they represent an incredible array of talents and experiences. Invite each group to compose a group resumè, including any information that promotes the group as a whole: educational background, knowledge about the discipline, hobbies, major accomplishments, travel, job experiences, major accomplishments, and so on. After sufficient time, invite each group to share their resumè with the whole class.

Schedule a class meeting or roundtable early in the course. This can be a circle of chairs or everyone sitting cross-legged on the floor (you, too!). Take time to talk about some of your expectations as well as some of the exciting learning opportunities you've planned. Invite students to share some of their fears or anxieties, too.

Quick and Easy Ideas

Here are a few quick and easy ideas you can use on the first day of class:

◆ Invite students to arrange themselves in alphabetical order by their first names. You can set this up as a whole class activity or within smaller groups. This activity forces students to discover other names in the class or group.

◆ Write students' names on index cards. Shuffle the cards and pass them out to the class, then have them find the person whose name they have. Students should circulate until every person has been matched with a card.

◆ Whip around the classroom and ask each student for a short response to a key question. For example, "One thing I expect to learn in this course is …." Invite students to pass if they wish.

Building Rapport

A plethora of research and my own interviews with college students in a variety of institutions has revealed that one of the most significant factors that ensures the success students experience in a course is the rapport they establish with the professor.

In my annual informal assessments of students, the following comments are those that are frequently proffered in response to the question, "What characteristics of an instructor help you learn best?" Here are the eight responses ranked highest over each of the last five years:

- Respectful of students
- Approachable
- Caring
- Willing to help

- Open-minded
- Supportive
- Fair
- Considerate

Red Flag

Professors who are arrogant, elitist, or distant create uncomfortable classroom environments that impede the learning process and inhibit students' participation and engagement in the subject.

It's interesting to note that none of the top eight responses have anything to do with knowledge of subject matter, number of books or articles published, tenure, rank, alma mater, or age. They all center around the interpersonal relationships between students and professors. In short, the rapport we establish with our students has more to do with their academic success than does the number of degrees we hold, the number of years we've been teaching, or our stature in the academic community.

Reaching Out

Here are some first-day suggestions and activities that will help you establish a level of rapport with your students. As with the previous list, feel free to select those ideas with which you are most comfortable. By the same token, consider the inclusion (and extension) of these suggestions throughout the length of the semester.

Make sure your students see you as a human being first, rather than just an authority figure. Take time early during the first day to introduce yourself. Tell students something about yourself—particularly about your life outside the classroom. This can include your youth and educational experiences, hobbies and interests, your family, places traveled, books that influenced you, and so on. Describe some of your experiences as a college student, particularly those related to the discipline you are now teaching. Tell students about your early years—where you grew up, schools attended, hobbies, interests, and places traveled. I often tell my students about growing up in Southern California in the '50s and '60s, and how I used to be a body surfer, a skateboarder, and I could play a pretty mean game of beach volleyball. This opens the door to all sorts of conversations (and revelations) critical to building good relationships.

You want your students to know that you have outside experiences and interests just like they do. In fact, I've often found it helpful to share a funny incident from my past, an embarrassing moment I had in school, or some self-deprecating humor. These humanizing touches show students that their professor is human and isn't always perfect.

From the Field

Invite a student from the previous semester to write an open letter to the students in the current class and comment on the course requirements, the professor's personality, how to be successful, study hints, and so on. I always invite the writer to comment on some of my idiosyncrasies or mannerisms (Note: Students have noted that I have a particular fondness for the word "plethora." Maybe you have, too!) Reading this letter at the first class really breaks the ice.

Divide the class into several groups. Invite each group to decide on a series of three questions (unrelated to the course) they would like to ask you. They can ask about your family life, background, education, political preferences, favorite restaurants, travel, or reading material. Invite students to record the questions on individual index cards. Collect the cards (this allows you to prescreen the questions) and respond accordingly.

Take time to share anecdotes or answer the following questions about yourself and your field of study:

◆ Why did you choose this field?

◆ What have been some of your most memorable learning experiences in this field?

◆ Did you choose the field or was it chosen for you?

◆ Who are some of the memorable people you've met in this discipline?

- What gets you excited about teaching this discipline?

- What has been the greatest lesson you've learned in this field?

- If you had to do it all over again, would you still make the same choices in this field?

Divide the class into several groups and tell them to predict your answers to some questions you have prepared for them. Here are a few possibilities:

- Where did you grow up?

- What are some of your hobbies or free-time activities?

- What kind of music do you like to listen to?

- What kind of childhood did you have?

- What do you do during the summer?

- What got you interested in this subject?

Give each group time to make their predictions, and tell them not to be afraid of bold guesses. Then have them to share their predictions with the whole class. Be sure to allow time to share the appropriate information about yourself and correct any "misconceptions"!

Prepare a set of index cards with 20 or 30 questions for students to "interview" you with. Distribute the cards and have each student take one. Provide students with the option of declining to ask a question. Here are some possible queries to record on the cards:

- What do you like so much about this particular discipline?

- Who has been the greatest influence in your life?

- Where do you like to travel?

- What was one of your most embarrassing situations?

- What kinds of books do you like to read?

- What really irritates you in life?

- When did you know you wanted to be a college teacher?

- Would you like to tell us something about your family?

◆ What is the greatest honor you've ever received?

◆ If you could have a conversation with any historical person, who would it be (and why)?

◆ What's the best advice you've ever received?

As a variation on the idea above, distribute a few blank index cards along with the cards with precomposed questions. Invite students who receive the blank cards to come up with their own question. After students have heard the prearranged questions, they will be more inclined to create their own original questions to ask you.

Take attendance the first day. Spend time learning the correct pronunciation of each student's name. Make a positive comment or ask a brief question as you go through your class list. Consider the following:

"Thanks for coming."

"I'm looking forward to working with you."

"How does the field hockey team look this year?"

"I like that outfit."

"It's good to see there's another Anthony in the class."

"How are you doing?"

"What's one adjective you would use to describe yourself?"

"I'm curious—why are you taking this course?"

"Seen any good movies lately?"

The questions you ask aren't important. What's important is making an effort to reach out to students to welcome them and learn something about them as individuals.

Start off the first class by posting a philosophical statement on the chalkboard or whiteboard. This should be a statement that is reflective of your own personal philosophy. Here are some I have used:

◆ "Imagination is more important than knowledge."—Albert Einstein

◆ "There is nothing more dangerous than a closed mind."

◆ "Education is a process, never a product."

◆ "I touch the future: I teach."—Christa McAuliffe

- "Education is not the filling of a pail, but the lighting of a fire."—William Butler Yeats

- "Humans and amoebas are both imperfect. But humans have the capacity to change."

Talk with students as to why that particular philosophical statement reflects your outlook on life or teaching. How did you arrive at that philosophy? How do you practice it? Has it ever let you down? What do you do to share that philosophy with others? Then, invite students, either individually or in groups, to design their own philosophical statements.

Just prior to the first meeting of the course, send a group e-mail to all the students and give them a brief introduction to you and the course. Welcome them to the course, provide some background information about you, talk about the exciting things you have in store for them, and invite them to reply to the e-mail with any pre-first-day questions or concerns.

"Research Says"

One impressive research study out of Harvard University concluded that for college students, "the emotional climate of the classroom is directly related to the attainment of academic excellence, however defined. Student feelings about what they will experience in class ... cannot be divorced from what and how well they will learn."

Quick and Easy Ideas

Here are a few quick and easy ideas you can use on the first day of class:

- Write an "open letter" to students that provide them with information about you—hobbies, interests, goals, childhood, teaching in general. Duplicate the letter and have a copy on each desk before students arrive for the first class.

- Meet and greet students at the door to the classroom. Shake their hands, call them by name if you know them, ask their names if you don't, and welcome them to your class. This is a critical moment that can set the tome for the rest of the year.

- Make up a "Top Ten" list (a la David Letterman) of facts about yourself. As with Letterman's list, keep the tone light and humorous. Introduce yourself, then read the list to the class.

Other First-Day Suggestions

If it's true that first impressions are lasting impressions, then what we do on the first day of class sets the tone and the expectations for the semester to follow. Here are a few more first-day tips I've gathered from colleagues around the country:

◆ This is not the time to pontificate. It's an opportunity to establish a bond between you and your students.

◆ Take time to get to know your students and give them time to get to know you.

◆ Provide study tips or note-taking tips that lead to success in the course.

◆ Make it clear that you believe the best learning takes place in a cooperative atmosphere in which everyone has an equal voice.

◆ Share your attendance policy in a positive manner.

◆ Students always want to know how grades will be determined. Make sure those procedures are clearly spelled out on the first day.

◆ Distribute index cards to students on the first day. Solicit some (or all) of the following data: Name, contact information (e-mail, cell-phone number, hours they can be reached), major, current part-time jobs, other courses taken in the discipline, other courses this semester, reasons for taking this course, personal information (about how they learn best), and a philosophical statement.

From the Field

Here's a statement I include in my syllabi: "Valuable information and ideas are presented and shared during each class session. It is to your benefit as well as the benefit of your classmates to be present for each and every class session. Your attendance, participation, and input are enthusiastically solicited and will help ensure mastery of all concepts."

The time you take on the first day or in the first week to establish positive relationships among your students and yourself will pay enormous dividends throughout the course. This is not wasted time!

The Least You Need to Know

◆ How you start the semester often determines how successful students will be during the semester.

◆ Building a community of learners is an essential component of student success.

◆ Establishing a positive rapport between yourself and your students from day one will result in positive academic achievement throughout the semester.

◆ First impressions are often lasting impressions. A great first day can lead to many other great days.

Chapter 8

Conducting a Class

In This Chapter

- ◆ Lesson design
- ◆ Opening a lesson
- ◆ Teaching the lesson
- ◆ Concluding a lesson
- ◆ A sample lesson

Somewhere along your educational journey you probably remember a class that was so intellectually stimulating and engaging that you've never forgotten it. It doesn't make any difference what the discipline was or the topic; that particular class just left a lasting impression on you and may even have contributed to your desire to become a college professor.

What do those professors do to make their classes dynamic and productive learning environments? What do other professors do that turn their course into intellectual wastelands where students feel as though their time, money, and effort are all swirling down a drain? Perhaps the best question to ask is, "How can I make sure that my class is a successful learning experience for my students?" In this chapter we'll take a look at the answers to that query.

Lesson Design

Effective public speakers always follow three essential steps of a good presentation:

1. Tell the audience what you're going to tell them.

2. Tell them.

3. Tell them what you've told them.

Those steps also hold true when designing effective college classes. In its simplest form, a good college class is separated into three critical components—the beginning, the middle, and the end. That division may seem simple, but it's a coordinated series of learning opportunities that offers students valuable information and ways of dealing with that information in productive intellectual activities. The focus is not on the information itself, but rather how that data can be processed by students and ultimately made important for them.

Let's look at each of those three stages in more detail.

Stage 1—Opening a Lesson

Good college teachers know that the first five minutes of a class often sets the tone for the rest of a lesson. These critical minutes not only provide an intellectual introduction for students, but also give you an opportunity to begin building bridges of comprehension between what they know and what you would like them to know.

You must do four things during this critical time: grab their attention, tap into their background knowledge, provide an advance organizer, and connect it with students' lives. Let's take a look at each.

Grabbing Their Attention

When I was just beginning my tenure as a college instructor, one of my colleagues used to tell me, "It's critical that you grab students' attention in the first 30 seconds of class. Remember that their minds may be somewhere out on the planet Pluto; you've got to bring them down to Earth." It's a positive stimulus to learning—it sets the tone for the day and signals students that there is something valuable ahead. Here are some tips:

◆ Start with a provocative question. ("You're a presidential candidate and have just been asked about your policy on immigration. How do you respond?")

◆ Start with a current event that relates to your topic. ("There was an article in this morning's newspaper about stem cell research. I'll read it and you can tell me what you think based on what we discussed on Tuesday.")

◆ Start with a problem that challenges their common assumptions or beliefs. ("If you had a choice between killing your father or marrying your mother, which would you choose?")

◆ Start with a "close to home" issue. ("OK, it seems like the trustees want to raise tuition again. How does this relate to our current discussion of 'competition and efficiency'?")

◆ Start with a challenge to their mental models. ("You know what I think? I think we should eliminate the welfare system. If people can't get a job, tough! Why should I have to support them with my taxes? They're bleeding us dry.")

Educators refer to this step as an *anticipatory set*. It's when students are "set up" with a question, challenge, or problem that helps build an anticipation or expectation for the learning to follow. It stimulates the mind to begin processing information, not with meaningless facts or figures, but rather with an intellectual challenge that initiates the discovery process.

def•i•ni•tion

An **anticipatory set** is an opening to a lesson that prepares students for the learning that will take place within the lesson. It introduces students to some of the lesson components at the start of class.

Tapping into Background Knowledge

Students bring a certain amount of background knowledge, prior experiences, perceptions, and misperceptions to any lesson. It's vitally important that you find out what they know (or think they know) before beginning any lesson. That background knowledge will "color" their interpretations and comprehension of the material as much as it will affect their retention of that information.

Invite students to generate two or three questions about a forthcoming topic at the beginning of each class ("After reading the chapter in your textbook about population density patterns in Canadian provinces, what are two questions that you have?").

 Red Flag

Don't make the mistake of assuming what students know. Take the time to assess their background knowledge and you'll be rewarded with more successful lessons. Bottom line: Always know what your students know!

These initial questions provide you with insights about students' thinking and how it may affect their interpretation of the material. I have also found that when students are provided opportunities to generate their own questions about a topic, then they will be motivated to seek answers to those questions.

Predictions are educated guesses about what may or may not happen. Predictions are valuable in terms of providing students with some self-initiated directions for a lesson. Predictions also give you insights about what students believe to be important or necessary ("Now that Horner has discovered the *Maiasaura* eggs, what will he do next?"). Periodically, invite students to make predictions about a topic you share with them, an upcoming reading, a future event in a chronological sequence of events, or the effectiveness of a strategy or technique.

Encourage students to brainstorm for everything they may know about a forthcoming topic. Remember that when brainstorming the emphasis is on gathering a *quantity* of ideas, never mind the quality. Brainstorming allows students to share much of their prior knowledge in a supportive arena.

Providing an Advance Organizer

Let's say you were planning a driving trip to Basalt, Colorado. What would be one of the first things you would do? For many of us, the first thing would be to get a map, find out where Basalt was on that map, and look at the highways, routes, and roads we would need to travel to get from here to there. In short, before we began we would need to know how to get there. An *advance organizer* is students' road map for a lesson.

Basically, there are four different types of advance organizers. They include …

def•i•ni•tion

An **advance organizer** provides students with an intellectual scaffold that helps them understand and retain material. It alerts students as to what is important in a lesson (from the start) and offers "anchor points" upon which students can begin collecting the necessary material in advance.

- **Exposition:** Describes the new content to which students will be exposed. It's a brief overview of the content by the instructor (time needed: 3–4 minutes).

- **Narrative:** The instructor presents information to students in a story format. It may include anecdotal information or fictionalized events (time needed: 3–4 minutes).

- **Skimming:** Students get time to quickly skim reading material in advance of reading it or in advance of discussing it in class (time needed: 5–6 minutes).

◆ **Graphic organizers:** Charts, graphs, or outlines of the essential information in a lesson provide students with a pictorial representation of the major points in a lesson and how those points are related to each other (time needed: 5–6 minutes)

The key to the success of advance organizers is that they alert students to and focus on what is important in a lesson. They give students a context at the beginning of a lesson—a framework that they can begin to fill in as you share the necessary information.

"Research Says"

Advance organizers have been studied in considerable depth in the educational literature. A synthesis of that research shows that students who were provided with advance organizers at the beginning of a lesson showed average gains (on standardized tests) of from 14 to 29 percent as opposed to students who did not experience advance organizers.

Developing a Connection with Students' Lives

Brian Furio, an associate professor of speech communication, teaches an upper division course on Communication Theory. Recently, I watched as he opened a class with a discussion of a current episode of the TV program "Grey's Anatomy" (which, through earlier assessments, he knew students watched regularly). He briefly discussed the specific episode with students and then wrote "Social Penetration Theory (Altman & Taylor)" on the chalkboard. He turned back to the class and said, "Did you know that that episode was all about 'Social Penetration Theory'—our topic for today? Let's take a look." And the lesson began.

Brian was thus able to effectively draw a relationship between students' lives and a classroom topic. It shouldn't be too surprising that he quickly had their attention and was able to begin drawing parallels between a theoretical construct and something that students could relate to.

This critical element of every lesson doesn't need a lot of time—1 to 2 minutes at most—but, it is essential to the success of that lesson. Take the time to make the connection, and you will always find it to be time well spent.

Stage 2—Teaching the Lesson

This is the heart of any lesson—you teach and students learn. Not only is it important to give some thought to what you are going to teach, it is equally important that you consider the methods of presentation as well.

I'm sure you've been in a course composed of nothing but dry, stale lectures. You undoubtedly found the course boring and wearying. The same fate awaits your students if you provide them with an overabundance of one type of teaching to the exclusion of others.

Here, in the body of your lesson, you want to focus on three critical elements:

◆ **Knowledge:** How will you present the basic information to your students?

◆ **Synthesis:** What opportunities will you give students to actually *do* something with the information they receive?

◆ **Performance:** How will you get students to use their knowledge in productive, hands-on learning tasks?

Let's take a look at each of these critical elements in a little more detail.

def•i•ni•tion

Knowledge is the basic information of a subject; the facts and data of a topic. **Synthesis** is the combination of knowledge elements that form a new whole. **Performance** refers to the ability to effectively use new information in a productive manner.

Knowledge

How do you present basic information to your students? It makes no difference whether you are teaching freshmen in an introductory English course or seniors in an advanced anthropology seminar, you must teach them some basic information. Here are the ways you can do that:

◆ **Lecture:** Share information directly with students. We discuss this form of knowledge sharing in the next chapter.

◆ **Reading information:** Assign material from the textbook for students to read independently. You may also choose to have your students read other supplemental materials in addition to the textbook.

◆ **Audio-visual presentation:** Rely on slides, movies, filmstrips, PowerPoint slides, photographs, illustrations, videos, or overhead transparencies.

◆ **Demonstration:** Students witness a real or simulated activity in which you use materials from the real world. These materials may include artifacts and objects used by individuals in a specific line of work. For example, microscopes (biologists), barometer (meteorologist), transit (surveyor), or word processing program (writer).

◆ **Observation:** Students watch an event or occurrence take place firsthand.

◆ **Field trips:** You take your students out of the classroom and into a new learning environment.

◆ **Interviewing:** Personal interviews, in which one person talks with another person, or group interviews, in which several people talk with a single individual.

Synthesis

One of the objectives of any lesson is to provide opportunities for students to pull together various bits of information to form a new whole or basic understanding of a topic. This process underscores the need for students to actually do something with the information they receive.

One synthesis strategy is small group discussions, in which the class is divided into small groups of two to four students. Each group is assigned a specific task to accomplish. The group works together and members are responsible for each other (see Chapter 11 for additional information).

Students can also participate in planned experiments, in which materials are manipulated in order to discover some scientific principle or truth.

Graphic organizers assist students in categorizing information. Most important, they help students understand the connections between their background knowledge and the knowledge they are learning in class.

One widely used graphic organizer is semantic webbing. A semantic web is a visual display of students' words, ideas, and images in concert

---

"Research Says"

Some professors think that small group discussions are nonproductive because no actual teaching takes place. Empirical research studies have shown that they are highly productive. They allow for the absorption of valuable material, a reflection on different points of view, and an informal means of assessing students' comprehension of material.

with textual words, ideas, and images. A semantic web helps students comprehend text by activating their background knowledge, organizing new concepts, and discovering the relationships between the two. Creating a semantic web follows these steps:

1. A word or phrase central to the reading material is selected and written on the chalkboard.

2. Students are encouraged to think of as many words as they can that relate to the central word. These can be recorded on separate sheets or on the chalkboard.

3. Students are asked to identify categories that encompass one or more of the recorded words.

4. Write category titles on the board. Students then share words from their individual lists or the master list appropriate for each category. Words are written under each category title.

5. Encourage students to discuss and defend their word placements. They can also make predictions about lesson content.

6. Add new words or categories to the web. Other words or categories can be changed depending upon the information gleaned from the lesson.

You can initiate problem-solving activities by giving the class, small groups, or individuals a problem or series of problems and directing them to find a solution. It is important to include problems for which you do not have a preordained answer.

Or you can have buzz sessions, temporary groups formed to discuss a specific topic. The emphasis is on either the background knowledge students bring to a learning task or a summary discussion of important points in a lesson.

Performance

Having a bunch of knowledge is one thing. Being able to pull together bits and pieces of knowledge is another thing. But the crux of a good lesson is the opportunities for students to use their knowledge in productive, hands-on learning tasks.

In independent practice, each student has an opportunity to use previously learned material on a specific academic task. For example, after learning about surrealism in an art theory class, students could create a PowerPoint presentation of a representative sampling of surrealistic paintings. In an intermediate German class, students could assemble a German/English dictionary specifically for German college students visiting the United States.

Debriefing allows students to condense and coalesce their knowledge and information as a group or whole class. Usually conducted at the conclusion of a lesson, it is an active thinking process.

In role playing, students take on the role of specific individuals (a historical or literary figure, for example) and perform the actions of that person or persons. The idea is to develop a feeling for and an appreciation of the thoughts and actions of an individual.

Simulations are activities in which students are given real-life problem situations and asked to work through those situations as though they were actually a part of them. If you have ever played the game Monopoly, then you have been part of a simulation.

Reflective inquiry is student-initiated and student-controlled. Individual students are encouraged to select a topic that they wish to investigate further. In so doing, they pose a series of questions which they wish to answer on their own. The questions are typically higher-order ones (see Chapter 12) and emphasize a variety of divergent thinking skills.

Pulling It All Together

If you'd like to make every lesson successful, you must do one thing: include a variety of teaching and learning methods in every lesson. If variety is the spice of life, then fill your lessons with lots of spice as you incorporate multiple teaching strategies.

Here's a good rule of thumb: for every lesson, try to include at least one *knowledge* method, one *synthesis* method, and one *performance* method. That way, your students are getting the necessary information, pulling that information together into a comprehensible whole, and having opportunities to use that information in a creative and engaging way.

Stage 3–Concluding a Lesson

It is essential that you incorporate some sort of closure into the lesson. This may mean a few minutes at the end when you or your students summarize some of the significant points, an activity in which students share perceptions with each other, or a time in which students recall their positive or negative perceptions of a lesson.

Be sure to summarize the important points or critical elements of a lesson for students. Discuss what was taught and what was learned. This may be the most valuable 3 to 5 minutes of any lesson.

Give students a chance to summarize the lesson as well. Inviting them to put a lesson into their own words can be helpful to you in determining how well they learned the material.

Use a question that was asked at the beginning of the class as a concluding question. If you began with a provocative question to gain students' attention, you may choose to close with that same question.

Provide feedback, and remind students what they learned and how well they were able to process the information. ("We covered a lot of ground today on the differences between good reasoning and poor reasoning. It was some tough territory, but you did well.")

Provide an anticipatory set for a follow-up lesson. ("From our discussion of the economics of the Aztec empire today, I think you're ready to begin looking at the long-term social implications—which we will do tomorrow.")

Finally, whenever possible, use a cliffhanger at the end of a lesson. This can be an unanswered question on the board, an unfinished project, or an enticing bit of information. ("Our discussion of sight and vision covered a lot of ground. But wait until tomorrow. I'm going to bring in a creature with eight eyes. You won't want to miss it!").

A Sample Lesson (Briefly)

Here's a very brief summary of a lesson Jessica Nolan, assistant professor of biology, taught one day. The lesson was part of a course on marine biology and focused on specific groups of marine invertebrates (*Porifera, Cnidaria, Ctenophora, Annelida,* and *Mollusca*).

Stage 1—Opening a Lesson

- Grabbing their attention: "Remember what we discussed yesterday? Are you ready for some critters that are even more amazing?"

- Tapping into background knowledge: "How many of you have been to the shore? How many of you have ever seen jellyfish in the water or on the beach? What did you notice about them?"

- Providing an advance organizer: At the start of class, Jessica provided students with a study guide which lists the various groups of creatures along with representative examples. The guide also included a reading list and definitions.

◆ Developing a connection with student lives: Jessica asks, "Why should we care about *Ctenophores* (comb jellies)?" She then explains that these creatures multiply very quickly and that they have taken over an entire ecological niche: the Black Sea. Discussion then centers on the implications if they were introduced into the Great Lakes or other freshwater systems.

Stage 2–Teaching the Lesson

◆ **Knowledge:** Using the study guide, Jessica reinforces the printed information with illustrations, the overhead projector, and other media. New vocabulary is always written on the chalkboard and explained.

◆ **Synthesis:** Jessica frequently brings in the knowledge students have learned in other classes to help build "connections." She then provides students with extended opportunities to view hydras and water fleas via classroom microscopes.

◆ **Performance:** Jessica engages students in a brief role-playing scene in which they pretend they are feather-duster worms. She invites them to act out the movements of these invertebrates as they slowly emerge from their shells to seek food.

Stage 3–Concluding a Lesson

◆ **Teacher summary:** Jessica provides the class with a brief overview of the important concepts they studied in the class.

◆ **Student summary:** Jessica invites selected students to provide personal insights as to why the information is important: not only in terms of marine biology, but also in terms of their own lives.

In a conversation with her afterwards, Jessica said, "I can help students succeed in two ways. First, since many students have a fear of science, I can't just throw things at them. They would all shut down. I need to take small steps and then add things as we go. Second, I have to have enthusiasm for what I teach. I put in things that I find exciting. I want students to say, 'I got excited because you were excited!' This means that I have to give them good information, but also opportunities to do something exciting with that information. It's students' interaction with me and with the material that's important!"

The Least You Need to Know

- ◆ A good lesson requires attention to three interrelated elements—beginning, middle, and end.

- ◆ The first few minutes of a lesson are often the most critical.

- ◆ Knowledge, synthesis, and performance must all be part of an effective lesson.

- ◆ Lessons must have a structured closure to be successful.

Chapter 9

Effective Lectures = Effective Learning

In This Chapter

◆ Lectures defined

◆ Four stages of good lectures

◆ A plan of action

◆ Tips and tactics

Ever since the time of the ancient Greeks, lectures have been part of almost every collegiate experience. It is the most widely used way of transferring knowledge from one individual to another and, for better or worse, what students remember most about their college days. They will remember excellent lecturers as much as they will forget those who put them to sleep.

Much has been written about lectures and lecturers. Some say they're overused, misused, or abused. Others are adamant that it is the only way to get lots of valuable information into the heads of students. Still others advocate reform in the traditional methods of lecturing to make this delivery of information meaningful, productive, and valuable. Let's take a look at the processes and procedures that will make your lectures dynamic and engaging.

The Nature of Lectures

By definition, a *lecture* is a verbal delivery of material from an expert (you, the professor) to the ears (and, hopefully, minds) of students. The basic premise is that students have a "knowledge gap" that you need to fill through the delivery of specific information.

How Lectures Are Used

College professors use lectures for several different reasons. Not all of these are pedagogically sound or research-based, but they've been part of the modus operandi of college professors since the beginning of time (or close to it). That does not, in any way, validate their use. Lecturing has simply been used for so long that the reasons for their use may be nothing more than "that's the way it's always been done."

College professors typically use lectures as their primary instructional method. Here are the reasons most often mentioned:

- A professor has a large (often overwhelming) body of knowledge to deliver in a 15-week semester.

- The discipline is so complex and the research so extensive that lecturing is the only way of presenting all that material.

- "How else can I teach 250 students crammed into a lecture hall?"

- The textbook is so complex that lecturing is necessary to explain obtuse points and convoluted theories.

- "That's the way I was taught, so that's the way I will teach."

- The professor wants to impress students (and members of the tenure and promotion committee) with his or her vast knowledge.

def•i•ni•tion

A **lecture** is the oral delivery of a body of knowledge from an expert to a novice, in college classes from a professor to a group of students.

What the Research Says

There is an enormous body of research on lectures and their value in the college classroom. Space limitations prevent me from presenting all that data in this chapter, but consider this information carefully as you plan your courses—particularly as you plan the methods and procedures of sharing information about your discipline with students.

A study of more than 80 undergraduate institutions in the late 1980s showed that lecture was the instructional method of choice in 80 to 90 percent of all courses. Another study showed that up to 15 percent of students' time in lectures was spent fantasizing.

Students' attention drifts after only 10 to 20 minutes of lecture. Several studies have indicated that when students are tested immediately after a lecture, they are only able to recall about 40 percent of the material. Most of the recalled information was delivered in the first 10 minutes of the lecture.

The human brain has "memory limits"; it can only hold or remember a selected amount of data at any one time. For college students that limit is seven "chunks" of information.

"Research Says"

One of the most important pieces of pedagogical research I ever read, and one that guides much of what I do in a classroom, is that 80 percent of what students hear is typically forgotten within 48 hours. That is to say that if I lecture students for an hour on Tuesday (without any additional or supplemental reinforcement), they will only be able to remember about 12 minutes of that lecture by Thursday's class.

One More Thought

Educational researchers tell us that genuine academic attention can be sustained at a high and constant level for only a short time. For kindergarten and first-grade students, that time limit is 5 to 7 minutes. For college students, the time limit is 10 to 14 minutes.

In the college classroom, demanding constant attention may be counterproductive. Much of what students learn cannot be processed consciously because it happens too fast. Students need time to process it. And to create new meaning, they need internal time. Meaning is always generated from within, not externally dictated. Also, after each new learning experience, students need time for the learning to "imprint."

After learning a chunk of information, the brain needs time for processing and rest. In a typical college classroom, this means a variety of supplemental methodologies. These may include rotating mini-lectures, collaborative group work, reflection, interactive discussions, individual work, and time for team projects (see Stage 2 in Chapter 8).

From the Field _____

Terry Seip, professor of history at the University of Southern California and recipient of the American Historical Association's Roelker Mentorship Award for undergraduate teaching, says that professors must "variegate every lecture. Visuals, music, sound clips, and the like are critical to a good lecture. You will lose students if you don't vary the presentation."

A Plan of Action

Good lectures don't just happen—they are the result of careful and systematic planning. The worst you can do to your students is to walk in "cold" to a lecture hall with a sheaf of yellowed notes in your hand, park yourself behind a podium or lectern, and talk *at them* for 60 minutes or more. In simple language, you've wasted their time and yours.

There are four parts to an effective lecture, whether you are teaching the evolution of European civilization, how ecosystem stability affects biodiversity, or why Pluto is no longer a planet:

◆ Preparing your notes

◆ Beginning the lecture

◆ Continuing the lecture

◆ Concluding the lecture

Preparing Your Notes

I'm going to begin this section with a loud and vociferous "don't." That is, *don't* write out your lecture notes verbatim! What often happens is that you become a "prisoner" to your own notes—and disregard the attention, interests, and questions of the students. Equally important is the fact that students process information quite differently in a verbal format than they do in a written format. Explicitly written notes satisfy your desire for detail and explanation, but often do not satisfy students' needs for participation and comprehension.

> **"Research Says"**
>
> In a 1980 study, researchers examined the lecture notes of professors at more than 75 colleges. The conclusion was that extensive lecture notes promote passivity on the part of students. When professors read from detailed notes, they lose an important component of any learning situation—eye contact. More eye contact promotes more active involvement.

Here are some "time-tested" tips that will assist you in preparing and organizing your notes for a forthcoming lecture:

Graphic Organizers

A *graphic organizer* is a visual arrangement of information, ideas, and concepts. Typical graphic organizers include semantic webs, tree diagrams, flow charts, and story maps. A graphic organizer allows you to focus on the relationships and connections that exist between ideas and information. The emphasis is not on the details, but rather on the concepts developed from those details.

def•i•ni•tion

A **graphic organizer** is any visual arrangement of words, concepts, or factual information grouped into various categories.

Color Coding

I like to write my lecture notes with colored markers. Then, as I progress through a lecture I can quickly glance at my notes and see what comes next. This frees me from an over-reliance on notes and allows me to maintain eye contact with the audience. Color coding is also a self-check that ensures that I am including essential elements of a lecture in every presentation.

Here is my coding system; feel free to develop your own:

- ◆ Red: An anecdote, story, or reading from a book
- ◆ Green: An open-ended or higher-level cognitive question
- ◆ Orange: A little bit of humor
- ◆ Black: A "connection" with students' personal lives (movie, recent sports contest, campus event, future profession)

- Purple: A problem-solving situation, small group discussion, or synthesizing activity (see Stage 2 in Chapter 8)

- Pink: A prepared visual (transparency, PowerPoint, video, etc.)

- Blue: Specific details or information

- Pencil mark: A planned stopping point or "brain break" every 11 to 13 minutes

Blocking

You may find it helpful to design a lecture in blocks. I prefer time blocks—that is, I arrange my information and all ancillary activities into individual blocks of 11 to 13 minutes each. Here are some other "blocking" strategies you may wish to consider:

- **Topic blocks:** Select the three most important topics.

- **Chronological blocks:** Arrange the information in chronological order. For example, three blocks each focusing on a single decade of time.

- **Controversial blocks:** Arrange the information in a series of blocks that moves from "pro" to "con" to "resolution."

- **Progressive blocks:** Set up your blocks so that students are introduced to the theory, research, facts, practice, and applications of a topic.

- **Hierarchical blocks:** Organize the information into a progression of blocks that move from easy to understand to more challenging information.

- **Question blocks:** This form is guided by a challenging question posed in each block. The questions may be generated by you or ultimately by your students: "Based on what we have discussed today, what questions do you need answered in Wednesday's class?"

Beginning the Lecture

The introduction may be the most important part of any presentation. It alerts students to the information to follow, taps into their background knowledge and helps them make "connections" to the new material, and provides motivation that stimulates engagement in the entire lecture. My own experience has been that the time spent on developing the introductory elements of a lecture will result in more effective lectures irrespective of the material or concepts covered.

Here are some valuable tips and ideas for your consideration:

- Begin a lecture with a story, vignette, or anecdote. This personalizes the information and places it in a memorable context.

- Start with a provocative question or interesting fact. This helps students quickly focus on the material and (hopefully) arouses their interest. For example, a mathematician might ask, "Did you know that some cultures never used the number zero?" An anatomy might ask, "Does anyone know what the largest organ of the human body is?" An oceanographer might say, "A tsunami can travel through the ocean at speeds greater than a jet airplane."

- Begin with a current event that directly relates to the material. For example, an article on declining attendance at professional baseball games would be appropriate to share in a sports-management class. An article on white collar crime would be appropriate in a business ethics class.

- Try beginning a lecture with an interesting visual. This may include a cartoon, a quote projected on the overhead, a photograph from a magazine or newspaper, or a short section of a video.

- Write or project the objectives (no more than three) for the lecture for everyone to see. This provides students with your "plan of action." Refer back to these objectives periodically throughout the lecture.

- Sometime during the first 5 minutes, relate the subject matter to students' lives. A botanist might begin a presentation on vascular plants by asking, "How many of you have ever tried to grow a plant and failed to water it sufficiently?" An economist might ask, "Has anyone ever wondered how much beer is consumed each weekend in the United States?" as a prelude to a microeconomics lecture on the interaction of supply and demand.

- Make sure students know the significance of the material. The question in the mind of every learner is, "Why do I have to know this stuff?" Make sure you answer that question right up front.

From the Field _____

Brian Furio, an associate professor of communication, suggests the use of some of the following statements: "Some of you have found this …," "Think about when you …," and "Perhaps you can remember …."

Continuing the Lecture

Now that you have their attention and they're focused on the material, it's time to concentrate on maintaining that interest. For me, a good lecture is like competitive ballroom dancing—the material must be carefully choreographed according to rhythm, flow, and pacing.

Never, *ever* cover more than three general concepts or topics in any single lecture! Most new professors make the mistake of trying to include too much in a lecture. Overloading students with material limits their ability to process and comprehend that material. Remember: Three points. Stop.

Show, demonstrate, or model how a professional in the field deals with a concept or idea. Don't just tell students about a principle or immutable fact—provide them with concrete examples of how professionals *use* that information.

Try telling students how you came to understand a particular piece of information. How did you wrestle with a concept when you were a college student? What challenges did you overcome in learning something? What kinds of questions did you have early in your career?

From the Field

Terry Seip, the USC history professor quoted earlier in this chapter, is emphatic about the need to "relate something in class to something in students' frame of reference or personal life. This lays a factual background, builds an enthusiasm for discussions, and motivates students to think more deeply."

def•i•ni•tion

A **criterion check** is a point in a lecture at which the teacher stops and checks to see if students understand the material up to that point.

Every so often, offer a mini-summary (1–2 minutes) of the material discussed. This allows students to catch up, fill in their notes, check their comprehension, and ask questions.

Whenever possible, use analogies and relate new information to what students already know. For example, a geologist might say, "Plate tectonics is like two slabs of wax sliding around on a hot plate." A political scientist might say, "Political conventions in the mid-20th century were like fraternity parties on Saturday night. There was always something happening in every room."

Insert *criterion checks* into the presentation every 12 to 15 minutes or so to see if students understand the points made up to that point. I like to drop one of the following questions periodically into my lectures:

◆ "Thumbs up, thumbs down. Did any of that make sense to you?"

- ◆ "What's one thing you still wonder about?"

- ◆ "If you had to summarize that information in just five words, what would you say?"

From the Field

Don't make the classic mistake of asking, "Does anyone have any questions?" You will *always* be faced with a sea of blank faces as a result. Instead, do something like the following: "Write down a question you have about the material up to this point. Share your question with a partner sitting by you. In a minute, I'll call on random teams to share their questions."

Consider a wide variety of visuals for any presentation. Overhead transparencies, videos, PowerPoint presentations, slides, filmstrips, and the like are all important. Remember that this generation of students is primarily visual—use that to your advantage.

Include some "compare and contrast" examples in your lecture. Present two sides of an argument and ask students to defend one. Share a controversy in the field and ask students to pose a solution. Explain a point of contention and invite students to defend or attack the point. Here are some leading questions you can ask:

- ◆ "How many of you agree with _____?"

- ◆ "Why would anyone disagree with this point?"

- ◆ "How many of you believe that _____?"

- ◆ "Who's right? Who's wrong?"

Provide students with periodic "markers" throughout a lecture. These include *signposts* to let them know what is ahead; *transitions* to let them know when you are finishing one topic and beginning another; and *summaries* to let them know what you just covered.

def•i•ni•tion

Signposts are verbal cues that inform students about material to be covered or discussed. A **transition** is when you move from one topic to another. A **summary** is when you compress a topic into a brief overview or main idea.

Vary your pacing. A good lecture is not linear, moving in a straight line from Point A to Point B. Change your tone of voice, provide information from various sources, use audiovisuals or computer technology, invite student participation, and *show*, don't just tell.

Most important, *don't read your lecture!* Your students will lose interest and so will you.

From the Field

Terry Seip stresses the need for "students to have a sense of ownership in the material. Statements like, 'What do you get from this?' and 'Why would this be useful?' give students a little bit of buy-in to any presentation."

Concluding the Lecture

A well-done lecture is a well-*finished* lecture. Don't let your presentation be ended by the bell. The conclusion must be as well-planned as every other element of the lecture. The last 5 minutes of a lecture can be just as important as anything discussed in the body of the lecture.

Here are some ideas and suggestions for your consideration:

◆ Invite students to get together in groups to summarize the lecture's main points. Invite the groups to share their conclusions.

◆ Provide a brief visual summary of the two or three main points of the lecture on the chalkboard, overhead transparency, or PowerPoint.

◆ Consider giving students a short quiz on the material covered. (Let them know you're giving one at the start of the class.)

◆ Ask each student to write a 1-minute summary of the lecture. Collect these and quickly review selected entries for the class. Use the remaining ones to assist you in planning your follow-up lecture.

◆ Invite students to take on the role of instructor. Ask each one to write down three questions they would ask if they had delivered the lecture. Encourage students to share some of their questions.

◆ End with a provocative question or setup. A physicist might say, "Now that we've studied Bernoulli's Principal, we'll see how we can use it to create the ideal paper airplane in tomorrow's class." An ethnomusicologist might ask, "Anybody wonder how the African music we studied today influenced early rock and roll? Come back on Friday and I'll show you."

◆ Invite students to compare their notes with each other for 1 to 2 minutes. Call on selected pairs to share their reviews.

◆ Provide a visual or graphic organizer to students that encapsulate the main points of the lecture on one page.

◆ Be sure to leave students with an answer to their perennial question—"Why do I have to know this stuff?"

A Plan of Action

Lectures are as varied as the people who deliver them. However, if you are looking for a format that will assist you in constructing a well-rounded lecture, you may wish to consider the plan below. Its beauty is in its simplicity and its adaptability to any discipline and any topic. You should feel free to modify this outline in line with your own preferences or specific topics. (Note: This plan is based on a class period of 1 hour.)

<u>Beginning</u>

Time: 5 minutes

Content: anecdote, question, story, vignette, graphic organizer, music

Materials: overhead projector, computer, blackboard

<u>Middle</u>

Block One

    Time: 15 minutes

    Content: Principle #1 or Idea #1 or Concept #1

    Students: Activity (e.g., 1-minute paper—What have you learned so far?

Block Two

    Time: 15 minutes

    Content: Principle #2 or Idea #2 or Concept #2

    Students: Activity (e.g., Q & A)

Block Three

    Time: 15 minutes

    Content: Principle #3 or Idea #3 or Concept #3

    Students: Activity (e.g., debate)

Demonstration, audio-visual, graphics, computer

Time: 5 minutes

End

Time: 5 minutes

Content: summarization activity, provocative question

Students: one-question quiz

Tips and Tactics

Here is a random collection of tips and suggestions collected from some of the best teachers around the country. They are designed to help you craft lectures that are educationally sound and intellectually stimulating—for your students as well as yourself:

◆ Consider using a conversational tone rather than a dictatorial one. Help students feel as though you are having a personal conversation with them.

◆ A good lecture doesn't mean nonstop talking. Pause frequently. Provide opportunities for students to process what you say.

"Research Says"

One interesting study of several college courses showed that when professors paused for 2 minutes at three separate junctures in any lecture and allowed students to discuss and/or process the material, the students retained more information than when they sat through a nonstop lecture without any "processing breaks." Another study confirmed these results and also found that both short-term and long-term memory was positively affected with the "pause procedure." This may confirm the old adage, "Less is more!"

◆ Use stories and anecdotes wherever possible. Wrap your facts around stories and students will remember the information more.

◆ Demonstrate enthusiasm for your topic. Let your excitement about a topic rub off on your students. Enthusiasm fosters comprehension.

◆ Try to make eye contact with each student at least once in every lecture (more is always advisable).

◆ Invite students to become part of the lecture. "What do you think?" "How does this relate to _____?" "What do you like about _____?" "Tell me your thoughts about _____."

◆ Vary the pace, intensity, and cadence of your lecture. A bland monotone creates a psychological distance between speaker and listener.

Red Flag _____

According to Terry Seip, "Lots of students want a 'sage on the stage.' But, interactive learning is the best—even in lectures."

◆ Use examples, models, visual cues, and demonstrations when you can. Physical objects and tangible items help students remember important concepts.

◆ Relate, relate, relate. Always relate material in your lecture to information students already know. Help students make intellectual connections between what they *do* know and what they *can* know.

◆ The best lectures end a little early (it's a psychological reward for the listeners). On the other hand, don't go past the end of the period—students won't remember (or care about) what you say.

◆ Remember: Just because you're talking doesn't mean students are listening … or learning!

The Least You Need to Know

◆ Lectures can be an effective way of delivering information to students.

◆ All lectures can be significantly improved by attending to four critical stages.

◆ Good lectures are neither spontaneous nor completely scripted, but rather well-planned learning opportunities.

◆ There are some cautions about the role of lectures in college classrooms.

Chapter 10

Effective Discussions = Effective Learning

In This Chapter

- ◆ Revisiting constructivism
- ◆ Before the discussion
- ◆ During the discussion
- ◆ After the discussion
- ◆ Troubleshooting discussions

Let's imagine it's Monday morning and there was a big game on campus the previous weekend. Students are still talking about it. Some are commenting on the results. Others have something to say about the athletes. A few may be talking about key plays or decisions. There's talk about the coach, the weather, and a dozen other factors before, during, and after the event.

What's happening here? In this discussion there is a sharing of information in a supportive environment. Students can all relate to a common experience. Sometimes there is disagreement; sometimes there is acclimation. Students are reviewing what they saw based on their experiences with previous contests or events. They're interpreting events, asking questions, airing criticisms, establishing points—and their emotions may, at times, run high.

The final score isn't what's critical to you here (unless it's a conference championship); rather it is everyone's perception, interpretation, and input that makes this an active dialogue. The same thing can be part of any class—*your* class—as well.

Revisiting Constructivism

Our earlier discussion of *constructivism* (see Chapter 2) made a distinction between a more traditional view of college teaching as a *transmission* of knowledge, and a *constructivist* view of teaching in which students use what they already know to help them incorporate and understand new material. The discussion of the big game is constructivism at its finest. Let's analyze it:

◆ Students use what they already know. Students all watched the same athletic contest.

◆ Students have prior experiences. Students have a basic knowledge of the sport being discussed (football, basketball, field hockey).

◆ Students incorporate new material. Students share their own views of the recent contest and listen to the views of others who also watched the same contest.

◆ Students understand new material. Students' positions about the contest are strengthened, realigned, modified, or thrown out when compared with other interpretations.

> **"Research Says"**
>
> Research conducted by numerous investigators over the past several decades has revealed that students pay attention and think more actively when engaged in discussion—more so than when exposed to lectures.

In the same way, students in constructivist classrooms try to assimilate new information with what they already know and understand. By incorporating discussions as a regular feature, you can promote this same process.

Discussion—Why?

Classroom discussion offers students incredible learning benefits. Here are a few:

◆ Students learn to weigh different types of evidence in reaching a conclusion.

◆ Students are able to think more deeply about a topic or subject.

- Students are able to evaluate the strength of their own position on an issue or concern.

- Students are provided with a safe environment in which to articulate their beliefs.

- Students can engage in higher-level thinking that offers multiple perspectives on an issue.

"Research Says"
A significant body of research has demonstrated the value of classroom discussion in improving student attitudes toward learning, enhancing learning and retention of material, and promoting the development of critical thinking skills.

- Students' interest and curiosity about a subject can be heightened and expanded.

- Students are engaged in active listening.

- Students have a chance to learn from others.

Good classroom discussions don't just happen—you have to plan them. You can never be sure of the ultimate destination of every discussion, but you should always have a course of action to ensure that students reap the greatest benefits. There are three stages to consider:

- Before the discussion

- During the discussion

- After the discussion

Before the Discussion

Good discussions take planning. Organizing your thoughts and helping students organize theirs will help guarantee that important concepts and necessary information are shared in a supportive arena that promotes learning through dialogue. The groundwork you lay before a discussion is directly related to the success students enjoy while participating in a classroom discussion.

Before you do anything else, establish a set of rules or behavior expectations for class discussions. It would be advantageous for students to create these rules on their own, but you may wish to at least suggest the following:

- Respect the opinions of others, even when they differ from yours.

- Give everyone the opportunity to express an opinion.

♦ A discussion is a group activity rather than an individual crusade.

♦ Personal attacks and condemnations are inappropriate.

♦ What is said here, stays here.

Schedule Discussions

As you begin planning your course—laying out the topics, arranging textbook readings, scheduling exams, and so on—you should also plan for *structured discussions*.

Here are some ideas:

def•i•ni•tion _____

A **structured discussion** is one in which the instructor takes a strong leadership role. The topic is selected beforehand, the questions are carefully planned, and the goals are very specific. In a structured discussion, there is a specific idea or conclusion you want students to reach.

♦ List structured discussion sessions (and the individual topics) in the course syllabus. Emphasize that these are as important to the coursework as lectures and reading.

♦ Along with the topic of each structured discussion, list one or two preplanned questions that will be the focus of each discussion. Again, this prepares students in advance.

♦ Make discussions a regular feature of your course. Schedule them on the syllabus (once a week, for example). Let students know in advance about these interactive experiences. As a result, they will be better prepared for them.

Classroom Design

The design and configuration of the classroom will either facilitate or hamper discussions. The worst possible configuration is the classic straight rows and straight columns. Here, students are interacting only with you, not with each other. You will see the amount and quality of your students' involvement go up when they can see, hear, and react to each other. You'll also have better luck coaxing out those who may be reluctant to participate in discussions.

Consider the following configurations (which can be set up in advance of a class or "on the fly" in the middle of a class session):

♦ The desks arranged in mini-groups of four or five with all the desks facing inward.

- All the desks or chairs in a horseshoe.

- Individual work tables with chairs all around.

- Desks or chairs arranged around the perimeter of the room—all facing inward.

From the Field

According to Angela McGlynn, a professor of psychology at Mercer County (NJ) Community College, "The classroom seating arrangement will influence both the atmosphere of the class and students' willingness to enter into discussions. Without an atmosphere of trust, safety, and connection, our attempts to lead rich classroom discussions are bound to fall short."

Start Early

Good discussions don't just happen because you've put students into small groups and given them a question to analyze. You have to give them a sense of shared responsibility and make them feel comfortable and at ease.

At the first class session, organize students into groups and invite them to introduce themselves to each other. Keep this "getting to know you" session relaxed and informal.

In the second and third class sessions, give small groups an opportunity to tackle a topic upon which they will all have an opinion or an experience. For example, "Should everyone go to college?" "What's the best thing to do on the weekend around here?" or "Why do we have to take this course?" These broad topics may not have anything specific to do with the course's content, but they help students establish important bonds that will pay dividends throughout the semester.

Early in the semester, invite students to discuss (in small groups) the value of discussions. Encourage them to establish a list of "rules" or expected behaviors that will make a discussion valuable for everyone. Invite groups to come together to establish a "master class list" or a discussion protocol.

Inform students that *how they learn* is just as important as *what they learn*. Emphasize early (and throughout the semester) the importance of discussions as a way of mastering the necessary materials.

Before Class

You can use several techniques before each class to ensure the success of any planned or unplanned discussions. Good planning ensures good discussions (and outcomes).

Whether you begin with a lecture, reading assignment, or some other class presentation, make sure students all have the same frame of reference to draw on before they begin discussions. This may include a textbook or article reading, a video, a PowerPoint presentation, a guest speaker, a demonstration, or a recording.

Determine your objectives for a lesson beforehand and develop two to four discussion questions based on those objectives. Share the discussion questions with students along with the assigned reading.

Before class, write out a series of question types as "stimulators" for classroom discussions. These can include the following:

♦ **Application:** "How could we use this information in _____?"

♦ **Interpretation:** "How do you feel about this position?"

♦ **Making connections:** "How is this like something else you're familiar with?"

♦ **Comparison:** "How is your idea similar to or different from _____'s?"

♦ **Validation:** "Why do you believe your response is correct?"

♦ **Evaluation:** "Why do you think this concept is so important?"

Prepare students in advance of any discussion. I like to give students a prediscussion sheet several days in advance of a scheduled discussion on a specific reading. This way they're able to ponder and prepare in advance. The sheet contains the following elements:

♦ **Why is this reading important?** First, I provide students with a brief explanation of the importance of the reading—as a new philosophy, a different perspective on an issue, a point of controversy, and so on. I do not provide a summary—I don't want students to rely on my summary for their interpretation.

♦ **Reading points:** I offer students two or three critical points to look for in the reading. I might pose the following: "What do you know about the author's philosophy after reading the first two paragraphs?" "Note where the author contradicts herself." "Where does the author confirm his thesis?"

♦ **Self questions:** I invite students to record three to five of their own questions as they read, or write responses to open-ended statements such as "I didn't understand when he …," "I was confused about …," "I thought that the most important point she made was …," or "I particularly liked …."

- ◆ **Discussion questions:** Here I provide students with questions we'll be addressing in class. All the questions are at higher cognitive levels (application, analysis, synthesis, evaluation). Students are encouraged to record key words or phrases from the reading, their own interpretations, or notes from another source. I also provide space for additional questions (and responses) that will inevitably arise during the actual discussion.

These discussion sheets have several advantages. Students come to class with written information as an aid to their oral discussions—their participation isn't merely off the cuff. Students sense that a discussion will not be a recitation of factual information, but will be focused on higher cognitive thinking. And, the discussions are focused and purposeful—students view them as integral elements of a course, rather than as "time wasters."

During the Discussion

Not only will you want to make discussions an integral part of any course or any topic, you will also want to make those discussions fruitful and productive for your students. Here are some time-tested strategies.

A Secret Weapon

Listen in on many classroom discussions and you'll probably hear teachers asking lots of questions. With so many questions coming at them, students have little time to think: the more questions that are asked, the less thinking occurs. Observations in classrooms reveal that instructors typically wait less than one second for students to respond to a discussion question, either growing uncomfortable with the silence or concluding that students don't know the answer or don't have anything to say.

Is this a problem? Yes! But here's an interesting solution: increase the time after asking a question—known as wait time—from the typical 1 second to 5 seconds. Believe it or not, this produces profound changes in the classroom:

- ◆ The length of student responses increases 400 to 800 percent
- ◆ The number of unsolicited but appropriate responses increases
- ◆ Student confidence increases
- ◆ Students generate more questions
- ◆ Student achievement increases significantly

Here's a tip: when you ask a question, don't preface it with a student's name, for example, "Franklin, how can humans decrease their impact on aquatic ecosystems?" As soon as you say one student's name, all the other brains in the room immediately shut down.

Instead, ask the question, wait, and then ask for a response. Interestingly, you'll discover a heightened level of involvement. Everyone has to think about a response because anyone may be called on to respond. There will be more group thinking and the responses you receive will be considerably better.

After you ask a question, let it percolate in students' heads for a while. And after a student responds, let the response percolate as well. Believe me, you'll wind up with a much better brew in your classroom.

It's only fair to tell you, however, that this sounds simpler than it is. It may be one of your greatest teaching challenges (it has always been for me) simply because teachers are uncomfortable with classroom silence. We tend to abhor it, often believing that learning can't really be going on in a quiet classroom. But with practice, you'll begin to see the incredible benefits of wait time!

Visual Organizers

I have found it very helpful to provide students with one or more visual organizers (projected on a screen, written on the blackboard or a large sheet of newsprint, or distributed as a handout) at the start of any classroom discussion:

- ◆ A web of key points, terminology, or concepts
- ◆ A taxonomy of various classes or groups of data
- ◆ A "tree" of contrasting or related features
- ◆ An outline (I, II, III, A, B, C) of important points
- ◆ A "fill-in-the-blanks" paradigm

Red Flag

Kay McAdams, an assistant professor of history at York College and a master of discussions, says that a good discussion "keeps students focused on one to two main concepts. Otherwise the discussion will dissolve into an open-ended free-for-all."

Here are two ways I like to use a visual organizer in my courses: I prepare the organizer by filling in information and details from the text in one color of ink. Then, as we discuss the reading, I record students' opinions, comments, and ideas on the organizer in another color. This helps students draw positive, visual relationships between an author's ideas and their own.

I fill in an organizer with a limited number of details. I tell students that the object of a forthcoming discussion is to complete the organizer with information they've garnered from the text or their interpretations of and opinions about the reading. Afterwards, we take time to discuss the "completeness" of the organizer.

The "Ping-Pong" Effect

One trap many professors fall into (myself included) is to make a discussion "teacher dependent." You ask all the questions and students deliver all the responses to you. It happens like this: Teacher asks … Student A answers … teacher asks … Student B answers … teacher asks … Student C answers … and so on.

I call this "verbal Ping-Pong." In reality, there is no discussion, because you are calling all the shots. But here are some alternate strategies to consider:

When a student responds, try to get other students involved. ("Sandra, how do you feel about Albert's interpretation?" "Raymond, any reaction to Sandra's opinion?") Or try establishing a rule that you will ask a follow-up question only after three different students have responded to an introductory question. (This is a good opportunity to practice wait time.)

Many students are more comfortable expressing their thoughts in small group settings. You could divide students into triads, giving one student in each group responsibility for posing a question to which the other two students must respond. Then, invite the triads to share their responses with the whole class. Or arrange students into small groups and pose a question or problem to the entire class. Each student in a group must offer a response or reaction to the question/problem before tackling another question/problem.

From the Field

Kay McAdams suggests that our primary role in any discussion is "to expose students to ideas—not to tell them what to think."

After the Discussion

You can do several things at the conclusion of a class or small-group discussion to emphasize the importance of this teaching technique to your students. Consider some of the following suggestions.

Take a few moments to summarize the major points, both orally and in writing, on the blackboard or overhead projector.

Give students opportunities to summarize the essential points in a whole class session or by asking small groups to brainstorm and record their information on the chalkboard.

You can also appoint a class scribe for each class session who is responsible for recording the essential points and conclusions. Invite the individual to take notes and copy and distribute or post them on the class website.

I often like to end a discussion with an intriguing statement, such as, "You know, we've thoroughly analyzed the elements of a good lesson plan today; however, tomorrow we're going to discuss one specific strategy that will make every single lesson successful—guaranteed!"

Be sure to celebrate *everyone's* contributions. Acknowledge their opinions even if they were different from yours or the author(s) of the reading, and congratulate them for their participation. Let students know that their engagement in course discussions is key to their comprehension and appreciation of course concepts.

Troubleshooting

It's inevitable. You've planned an exciting and stimulating discussion, but the students couldn't care less. You pose a fascinating question and all you get is a sea of blank faces. You've shared an intriguing problem or set up a conceptual conundrum and a wave of silence engulfs the room. It's bound to happen … and it will happen more than once in your professional career.

Let's take a look at some of the most common discussion problems and some ways of dealing with those challenges.

Students Are Unprepared

- In a preceding class tell students to bring a critical question to the discussion. By showing up in the next class they affirm that they are ready to discuss that question.

- Give students specific roles (within a group) ahead of any discussion. One can be the leader, another the recorder, another a questioner, and another a summarizer.

- Invite students to select a passage from the text that they would like to discuss or challenge in the next class.

Students Are Not Participating

◆ Keep the groups small. Invite students to tackle a problem or question in two-person teams or in small groups. This facilitates discussion simply because there are fewer persons "listening in."

◆ Provide multiple opportunities for students to interact and get to know each other in a variety of ways throughout the course.

◆ Invite students to write out a response to a question first. Then, encourage students to share their written responses in a larger group setting.

◆ Students respond more when they are facing each other—in a circle, for example. In this way they receive visual feedback (smile, nod, body language) that they don't get in rows and columns.

◆ Ask a plethora of open-ended questions. Instead of asking "What is the main idea of this article" (which puts a student on the spot if a wrong answer is given), ask "What do you think about this particular article?" Questions for which there are multiple answers are much more comfortable for students and they engender more participation.

The Discussion Monopolizer

◆ Divide and conquer. Assign discussion monopolizers to different groups.

◆ Invite the class to discuss the importance of equal contributions from all class members.

◆ Assign a "talker" the role of discussion recorder. Give the individual the responsibility of recording the concepts discussed and the conclusions reached.

◆ Videotape a class session and invite the monopolizer to view the recording. Often, these individuals are not aware of their actions.

◆ Pose a question and invite students to respond for a maximum of two minutes. Each speaker must briefly summarize the comments of the previous person before voicing their own opinions.

From the Field

Kay McAdams says that it is important that you "not view yourself as a sage in classroom discussions. Rather, your chief responsibility is to help students develop their own critical thinking abilities."

Controversial Topics

◆ Make sure the focus is on facts, not opinions. It's easy to get emotional when the emphasis moves from verifiable elements to personal attacks.

◆ Refer to a passage in the textbook or other written resource. Keep bringing the discussion back to proven facts that are within the student's experience—textbook readings, for example.

◆ If two or more individuals are engaged in a heated discussion, establish a rule that each person must briefly summarize the comments of the other before voicing her or his thoughts.

◆ Sometimes, you may elect to allow a "pitched battle" to continue. Oftentimes there is learning through conflict—particularly in a follow-up class.

◆ Establish a rule that the personal pronoun "you" may never be used ("you always …," "you have to be the …," "I can't believe you are …") in discussing any controversial subject.

◆ Establish time limits for any comments on controversial topics. This signals students that their remarks must be well planned, concise, and to the point.

◆ Above all, keep the emphasis on *respect!* It's alright to have a difference of opinions; however, it's not alright to use that opinion as a battering ram or personal attack weapon.

The Least You Need to Know

◆ Discussions help promote a constructivist philosophy of teaching and learning.

◆ Good discussions are the result of careful planning.

◆ There are several techniques you can establish prior to any discussions.

◆ What happens during and after a discussion can be critical to its success.

◆ There are many techniques possible to involve nonparticipating students.

Chapter 11

Collaborative and Cooperative Groups = Effective Learning

In This Chapter

◆ The nature of constructivism

◆ Collaborative and cooperative learning

◆ When students work in groups

◆ Making groups work productive

◆ Practical strategies you can use

◆ Making constructivism work in your classroom

In the traditional model of college teaching, often known as a *transmission* model, the professor talks and the students take notes, memorize those notes, and then replicate them on an exam. In this model, students are passive recipients of knowledge, rather than active processors of information.

On the other hand, in a *transactional* model (sometimes known as constructivism) students become more actively engaged in their own learning and play a greater role in the discovery process. At the heart of this model is the notion that students must actively construct their own understanding of new information and assimilate it into what they already know and understand. Let's see how you can make this work in a college classroom.

The Constructivist Classroom

In a constructivist classroom, students assume responsibility for some of the direction and depth of learning, integrating prior experiences with new information to extend or deepen their understanding. The constructivist model places students at the center of the learning process and encourages them to think about ideas, discuss them, and make them meaningful.

def•i•ni•tion

Constructivism is when students are offered opportunities to assimilate new information with what they already know and understand. It is an active involvement in learning whereby students construct new knowledge, rather than record it.

"Research Says"

A growing body of educational research suggests that providing students with less content (less transmission), but more opportunities to actively engage in the material at higher levels of cognition (see Chapter 12), results in a more productive educational experience.

So what are some of the components of a constructivist classroom?

◆ Less material covered, but more information *uncovered*

◆ Prior knowledge is incorporated into new information

◆ More emphasis on the processes of learning rather than the products

◆ Learning takes place in a social context

◆ Learning is less teacher-directed, more student-centered

◆ Higher-level thinking opportunities are emphasized over low-level cognitive skills (see Chapter 12).

◆ Student-initiated goals are valued and celebrated

◆ Students are actively involved in self-assessment

◆ Learning is integrative and active

◆ Learning is produced, not reproduced

In a constructivist classroom, you're still responsible for imparting information and materials to your students. However, you also provide opportunities for students to actively process that material, interact with the ideas, and relate the new material to concepts previously learned. This can be effectively and successfully accomplished by incorporating collaborative and cooperative learning opportunities into your courses.

Collaborative and Cooperative Learning

You can promote constructivism through cooperative and collaborative learning models. These two terms are often used interchangeably, and they share some common elements, but it's important to make a few distinctions between the two.

Collaborative Learning

Collaborative learning is a teaching technique in which the professor defines a specific learning task with more than one answer or solution and then organizes students to work it out collectively. The benefit is that students are exposed to multiple perspectives and multiple viewpoints. The completion of any task is the result of a collective judgment in which everyone has a voice.

The basic elements of collaborative learning are as follows:

- ◆ Consensus building

- ◆ Accepting divergent viewpoints

- ◆ Minimal teacher involvement

- ◆ Synthesis and evaluation

In collaborative learning, students work together to build consensus on an issue or topic. This is more than everyone simply expressing their opinion; it involves a concerted effort to reach some level of agreement. It's an intellectual "give and take" to arrive at a common response.

Divergent views and opposing arguments are recognized in an environment that celebrates differences. Students learn that they all have differing biases and perspectives that shape and influence their thinking.

def•i•ni•tion

Collaborative learning is a classroom activity in which groups of students tackle a task with multiple answers. The successful completion of the task is accomplished via an emphasis on a variety of perspectives.

The instructor's primary role is that of a manager—you set the task, arrange the groups, oversee the deliberations, and synthesize afterwards. You may need to occasionally keep the groups focused on the task, but other than that your task is to step back and let students proceed without your intervention.

When student groups have completed their tasks, reconvene the whole class and synthesize the results. Each group's spokesperson shares the results of her/his group. Afterwards, invite students to examine the similarities, differences, contradictions, and parallels among the recorded information. Guide students in reaching appropriate conclusions about the material.

Cooperative Learning

Cooperative learning is a successful teaching strategy in which small teams with students of different ability levels use a variety of activities to improve their understanding of a topic. Each member of a team is responsible not only for learning what is taught, but also for helping her or his teammates learn—thus creating an atmosphere of achievement.

Cooperative learning is beneficial for any subject or any topic. That means that it can be effectively used in an upper-division physics course, an introductory English course, an advanced algebra course, or a lower-division history course.

The success of cooperative learning is based on three interrelated factors:

◆ **Group goals:** Cooperative learning teams work to earn recognition for the improvement of each member of a group.

◆ **Individual accountability:** Each member of a team is assessed individually. Teammates work together, but the learning gains of individuals form the basis of a team score.

◆ **Equal opportunities for success:** Individual improvement over prior performance is more important than reaching a pre-established score. A student who moves from 73 percent on a test one week to 81 percent (8 percent improvement) the next week contributes just as much to a group as a student who moves from 82 percent to 90 percent.

def•i•ni•tion

Cooperative learning is the instructional practice of placing students into small groups and having them work together toward a common goal. Each group member learns new material *and* helps other group members learn important information.

However, the ultimate success of cooperative learning is based on a single and very important principle: Students must be *taught* how to participate in a group situation. Professors cannot assume that college-level students know how to behave in group settings. Here's how to do that:

Structure learning tasks so that students understand their positive interdependence—that they sink or swim together. Students need to know that each group member's efforts are required for group success and that each group member has a unique contribution to make to the joint effort.

Groups should be heterogeneous, comprised of three, four, or five members each. The membership within a group should be mixed according to academic abilities, ethnic backgrounds, race, and gender. It's also important that groups not be arranged according to friendships or cliques.

Be sure to state directions or instructions in clear, precise terms. Let students know exactly what they are to do. When appropriate, inform students what they are to generate as evidence of their mastery of the material. These directions must be shared with students before they engage in cooperative learning activities.

Give students a clear set of learning objectives, describing exactly what they are expected to learn. Let students know that cooperative learning groups are a means to an end, rather than an end in itself. Do not use ambiguous language in describing what students will learn or the knowledge they will gain.

Establish individual and group accountability by asking group members to discuss how well they are achieving their goals or how they are maintaining effective working relationships. Help students make decisions about what behaviors to continue, what to change, and what to eliminate.

Make sure there is sufficient time to learn the targeted information. Groups should stay together until the designated subject matter is learned.

What Are the Benefits?

The terms "collaborative learning" and "cooperative learning" are often used interchangeably. Although they are not one and the same, they do share several common characteristics that can have a profound and significant impact on the learning that can take place in your classroom. It's not the terminology that's important, it's the overall benefits these practices can have on students' retention and integration of course content:

◆ **A sense of community:** Both approaches place a premium on learning as a social activity. Listening and reacting to different perspectives—and valuing those perspectives—is at the very heart of group work. Students' knowledge base grows exponentially.

◆ **Respect for students:** Both approaches underscore a basic respect for students and their abilities to solve common problems and deal with "thorny" issues. Students' engagement in the learning process is valued and celebrated.

◆ **Constructive learning:** Students learn that learning is not a passive activity (listening to and recording lectures), but rather one in which they can, and should, have an active role. The process is as important as the product.

◆ **Student achievement:** The effects on student achievement are positive and long-lasting irrespective of the course or subject matter.

◆ **Information retention:** When students process information in group contexts they usually retain more of it over longer periods of time.

◆ **Improved relations:** One of the most positive benefits is that students who cooperate with each other also tend to understand and appreciate each other more. This is particularly true for members of different ethnic, cultural, social, and religious groups.

◆ **Interdependence:** When students work with, and rely on, other students, their interpersonal and social skills are maximized. They become more than observers, they become participants in the social order.

◆ **Critical-thinking skills:** More opportunities for critical-thinking skills are provided and there is a significant improvement in those thinking skills.

◆ **Oral communication improvement:** Students improve in their oral communication skills.

◆ **Improved social skills:** Students' social skills are enhanced and promoted.

◆ **Heightened self-esteem:** Students' work is valued by team members and their individual self-esteem and respect escalates dramatically.

"Research Says"

A small but growing body of research looks at cooperative and collaborative learning from students' perspective. According to student self-reports, the benefits include: higher levels of motivation to learn the material, opportunities for enhanced peer interactions, greater class interest and enjoyment, opportunities to process rather than simply record information, and an appreciation for divergent perspectives and outlooks.

Group Selection (and One Caution)

One element that has come out of the research on college-level group work deals with how students are selected for their respective groups. Several researchers point to the advantage of having teachers select the members of a group rather that having students select their own groups. When students select their own groups, they tend to engage in excessive socializing and off-task discussion.

It's better to group students heterogeneously and randomly. This ensures that each group is composed of a diversity of opinions, abilities, genders, races, and other factors.

There are any number of ways you can divide your students into collaborative or cooperative groups. Here are a few you may wish to consider:

- Whip around the classroom assigning each student a sequential number (1, 2, 3, 4). All the 1's go into one group, the 2's in another, and so on.

- Randomly distribute colored index cards to the class. All the yellow cards form one group, purple cards another, and so on.

- Assign students to groups based on their month of birth. For example, all the Februarys will work together, all the Octobers will work together.

- Remove all the face cards from a deck of cards, shuffle them, and distribute them to students. All the kings form a group, all the jacks form another group, and so on.

- Invite students to write down a randomly selected four-letter word. Those who have a word that begins with a letter between *A* and *E* form one group, those with names between *F* and *J* form another group, and so on.

- Use the last number in each student's social security number (or phone number, or student identification number). All the 9's in one group, all the 8's in another group, and so on.

- One of my favorites is to bring in several different four- or five-piece children's puzzles and mix all the pieces together in a box. Students each select a random puzzle piece then locate others with pieces that form a complete puzzle (all the puzzles are different). I sometimes create an "added value" by having an initial discussion question taped to the back of each puzzle piece.

It doesn't make any difference what method you use to determine the members of each group. It is important, however, that you use a variety of methods and that you keep the selection process entirely random.

One of the biggest issues (voiced by professors and students alike) of collaborative and cooperative learning is how to deal with "nonparticipating" students. Often there will be some students who "hitchhike" on the work of others so that the work a group does is the result of one or two highly motivated students rather than all members equally.

Unfortunately, there is no way we can completely eliminate this, but there are ways to minimize the likelihood. Develop group assignments that allow you to grade both individual and group performance. For example, each group member takes a quiz and the scores are all added up to calculate a group grade that every group member receives for the task.

Invite each member of a selected group to make an oral presentation of their discoveries and results. Let students know ahead of time that you will select one group at random (from a hat) to share their collective information. You can also ask groups members to submit a group written report to which each member must sign her or his name and to indicate the amount (percentage) of involvement of contributions they made.

In several of my courses I use a chapter log in which small groups record reactions to a textbook chapter assigned prior to class. Here's an example:

CHAPTER LOG

Name: Date:

Chapter #:   Pages:

Topic(s):

Group members:

End of chapter question: #_____

My response(s) [to be completed before class]:

Group Consensus:

A significant quote from the reading is [to be completed before class]:

Group Consensus:

Overall, my participation in today's discussion was:

_____Extensive   _____Moderate   _____Minimal

I think today's experience (chapter reading &/or group discussion) was:

_____Very stimulating   _____Interesting

_____Fairly interesting   _____Confusing

_____Boring   _____Other:

Strategies for Your Classroom

To help your students master essential material via group work, you must provide a range of classroom possibilities. You can do this by using this collection of specific cooperative and collaborative learning strategies. Of course, you're not going to use all these at the same time, nor are you going to use any one of these over and over again. (Remember, variety is the spice of life.) And keep in mind that these strategies are just part of a range of options at your disposal.

Jigsaw

Set up groups of four, five, or six students, called "home" groups. Divided the material into four, five, or six sections and assign each member one subsection. She or he works on that material and how it will be learned. Each subgroup is known as an "expert" group. After students master the material in their expert group, they return to their home groups and teach the information to the members of her or his group. Afterwards, each student can be tested independently on both group and individual activities (and learning).

Panel Discussions

Stage a panel discussion in which students are randomly assigned to several different groups, some of them "pro" and some of them "con." Each group must prepare an appropriate argument related to a specific topic (abortion, immigration, nuclear energy, intelligent design, foreign policy). Since students are randomly assigned to a group, they may have to wrestle with their own beliefs, particularly if assigned to a group that must take a conflicting viewpoint.

Trial

As a variation of the preceding strategy, invite students (in groups) to conduct a mock trial. One group of students could be the prosecuting team, another the defense team, another witnesses, another the judge, and a fifth the jury. Invite them to "try" a controversial figure or issue. For example: Osama bin Laden, creationism versus evolution, Goldilocks, the Boston Tea Party, life after death.

From the Field

One "jury trial" I often use at the start of a new course is for students to put the actual course on trial. That is, some students must defend the utility of the course, while others must argue against its place in the curriculum. Besides being fun, this activity provides me with some valuable background information about student perceptions that I can address later, in addition to letting students know that we will continue to look at many sides of various issues throughout the semester.

STAD (Student Teams–Achievement Divisions)

Students are assigned to four-person teams. Each team is mixed according to ability, gender, race, and ethnicity. After the presentation of a teacher-directed lesson, students work in teams to master the material. Buddy work, group quizzes, or focused study questions may be part of a group's efforts. A quiz is given to all group members. Improvement scores are assigned to each individual as well as the entire team as a whole.

Modified Focus Group

Provide students with a question that has different perspectives and that requires collaborative effort to solve. Invite students to each list as many responses, interpretations, or reactions to the question as possible (you may want to establish a time limit).

Divide the class into groups and appoint a recorder for each group. Each student, one at a time, shares an idea with the whole group. In round-robin fashion, students share their ideas and record them on a large sheet of newsprint. After everyone has shared all the items on their individual lists, the group works together to rank all the items from 5 (greatest importance) to 1 (least importance). Each group's final rankings are reported to the entire class. The class then engages in dialogue to synthesize and analyze the information. Different perceptions and interpretations are both solicited and encouraged.

Think-Pair-Share

This cooperative learning activity involves three steps. Students think silently about a question asked by the teacher, then pair up and share their thoughts. Finally, the pairs share their responses with other pairs, other teams, or the entire group.

Constructive Controversy

Divide your class into groups of four students each. Within each group, further divide students into two separate pairs assigned to opposing sides of a controversial issue. Each pair is responsible for gathering information to support their position, then presents its argument to the other pair. The intent is not to create a debate, but rather for students to begin appreciating the different sides of a single issue. You may wish to invite pairs to switch roles and "argue" the opposing point of view. Comprehension of the material can be assessed individually or as a group effort to master the content.

Numbered Heads

Divide the class into teams of four students each. Give each member of the team a number: 1, 2, 3, or 4. Ask questions of the entire class and have groups work together to answer the question so that all of them can verbally respond to the question. Then call out a random number ("3"); each "number 3" will give the answer.

Three-Step Interview

Have each member of a team choose another member to be a partner. During the first step, have individuals interview their partners by asking clarifying questions. During the second step, have partners reverse the roles. In the final step, have members share their partner's response with the team.

Reader's Roundtable

Divide the class into several small groups. Assign all the groups the same piece of reading (e.g., a monograph, a textbook chapter, an article). Each group is responsible for dividing the reading into several parts—one part for each member of the group. Each member reads her or his assigned section and explains it to the team. Then, each team shares an overall interpretation with the entire class. Discuss the differences in interpretation with class members.

Three-Minute Review

Occasionally during a lecture or discussion, stop and give teams 3 minutes to review what has been said and ask clarifying questions. Invite each team to arrive at a summary statement (a main idea) of what was presented, then write these on the chalkboard. Take time to discuss any differences among teams. At the end of the lesson, invite teams to review the summary statements and to arrive at the most appropriate ones for sections of the lesson or the entire lesson all together.

Case Studies

Case studies are used in medical colleges, law schools, and business courses. They provide students with opportunities to answer the question, "What would you do?" To conduct a case study, select a brief article from the newspaper, a section of text from an outdated textbook, a video clip from a national news program, or create your own case study (story) that engages students in creative decision-making (a variety of Internet sites provide a range of case studies for classroom use). Invite students, in various teams, to work out appropriate decisions or solutions using material learned in the course.

Other Options

Here are a few more options for you to consider in your various courses:

- Team interviews (of students or faculty)
- Group surveys (of community members)
- Focus group sessions (on specific issues)
- Public displays and exhibits
- Discipline-specific research projects (of professionals in the field)

As you become more familiar with cooperative and collaborative learning, you might want to create your own learning activities. Even better, challenge your students to invent and design variations of these suggestions for the classroom.

Teaching Constructively

The effective use of cooperative and collaborative learning is often built upon a four-step process. Consider the following four elements as you begin to design and implement constructivist learning into your teaching routines:

- Presentation of content
- Facilitation
- Teamwork
- You're the director, not the dictator

Cooperative and collaborative learning is *not* a self-instruction model, but rather a way for students to interact with previously presented material. In short, cooperative and collaborative learning comes *after* you have taught something to your students.

This is the time—after you've taught new material—when students are engaged in a cooperative or collaborative learning activity. The strategy is selected and explained to the entire class. Students are divided into various teams and provided sufficient time to complete their assigned duties.

Your role is primarily that of a facilitator. You are there to help groups define their goals, engage in meaningful dialogue, and work toward pre-established goals. Your primary responsibility is not to tell them what to think, but rather to provide them with the forum in which they can engage in productive and active deliberations.

Utilizing collaborative and cooperative strategies in your courses means releasing responsibility to your students. This may be uncomfortable, particularly if you've been exclusively exposed to more traditional college teaching protocols. This "loss of control" can be both frightening and exciting. But, to use a familiar educational maxim, your primary responsibility in any collaborative venture should be that of a "guide on the side, not a sage on the stage."

The Least You Need to Know

- A constructivist classroom provides opportunities for students to take an active role in the learning process.

- Collaborative and cooperative learning has many positive benefits for any course.

- Group membership should be random and arbitrary.

- There are a wide variety of constructivist strategies at your disposal.

- Four essential elements underscore constructivist teaching and learning.

Chapter 12

Thinking About Thinking

In This Chapter

- ◆ Traditional thoughts about learning
- ◆ Promoting critical thinking
- ◆ Encouraging students to think creatively
- ◆ Stimulating practical thinking
- ◆ Promoting thinking in every subject

Across the country, college faculty members overwhelmingly state that "development of effective thinking" is their primary purpose. In fact, gather any group of college professors—regardless of institution, teaching experience, or discipline—and they will universally state, in one way or another, "I want my students to know how to think."

A substantial body of evidence points to the direct relationship between students' success in a course and the opportunities they get to engage in thoughtful, productive thinking.

Thinking is not a one-semester skill to be learned and then quickly forgotten. It is a skill we can share with our students to enhance their educational experiences, our teaching effectiveness, and the impact of our courses.

What Students Think about Thinking

John Barrel, an educator in New Jersey, outlines a series of expectations that students have about the classroom. See if these sound familiar:

◆ The teacher "teaches" and the students "sit and listen" or "learn" passively.

◆ There is one right answer to any question, and it is in the textbook or the teacher's head.

◆ The answer to most questions can be given in one or two words, and the teacher won't challenge you to go much deeper.

◆ Books and teachers are always right, and we learn only from them, not any other resource in the room, such as classmates.

◆ If we wait long enough, a teacher will answer her/his own question, and we won't have to do much work. The teacher is the only one worth listening to.

◆ If we ask enough questions about a difficult assignment, we can get the teacher to make it a lot easier and less demanding.

◆ "Thinking" is not something we talk about.

◆ If I memorize enough stuff, I can get a good grade.

◆ Most tasks and tests will demand recall of isolated pieces of information, and I will not have to show how ideas are related.

Barrel calls these conditions the "hidden curriculum"—or that set of assumptions and expectations students traditionally have about education. As you look over those statements you will quickly notice that they indicate, for the most part, a passive classroom: a teacher-directed learning environment in which students have little input, little involvement, and little interest.

In Chapter 8, I discussed the various ways you have of sharing information with your students. When students become more actively engaged in the dynamics of learning, that learning becomes more personal and meaningful for them. What results is not a hidden curriculum but rather a completely new set of expectations in which student participation is active, sustained, and deliberate. Students begin to assume that their role in the learning process is to manipulate ideas, solve problems and, yes, think.

Three Types of Thinking

Robert Sternberg, a professor of psychology at Yale University, defines thinking as a triad of interlocking skills. He sees thinking as a general concept and then identifies three distinct subcategories:

♦ **Critical thinking:** the process by which students use higher-level cognitive skills (application, analysis, synthesis, evaluation) to process information.

♦ **Creative thinking:** the process by which students create something new, original, or novel.

♦ **Practical thinking:** the process by which students are able to make decisions and solve problems.

Let's take a look at each of these divisions in a little more detail.

Critical Thinking

The most effective way to stimulate and emphasize critical thinking is to ask questions. These questions provide both a model and a forum through which students become active participants. Specifically, there is convincing evidence that students tend to frame their thinking based on the questions asked by an instructor. Asking the right kinds of questions, therefore, has a significant effect on the intellectual growth of your students.

In Chapter 10, I talked about how you can use a variety of questioning strategies to promote and enhance classroom discussions. Unfortunately, most of the questioning in college classrooms is trivial, with the emphasis on memory and information giving. Seldom are students given opportunities to think about what they are reading or doing, and rarely are they invited to generate their own questions for discovery.

Questions are one of the most effective and most successful ways to engage students in the dynamics of a topic. The benefits of systematic questioning in any class are overwhelmingly positive. Unfortunately, too many professors simply plow through the material, not giving students a chance to engage in meaningful discussion or critical thinking about the subject matter.

> **"Research Says"**
>
> In one study of more than 150 class sessions in various disciplines at several different institutions, questioning of students comprised only 0.2 to 9.2 percent of class time.

The Value of Questions

There are many reasons why professors should make liberal use of questions in any type of class or laboratory experience. As we discovered in Chapter 10, the right kinds of questions get students involved in the lesson. Mental engagement can be assured whenever appropriate questions are carefully sprinkled throughout a lesson. (Example: "Now that we have discussed the policies that led to the war in Iraq, how will those policies affect our relations with other Middle Eastern countries?")

Equally important, responding to questions gives students a voice, and lets them know that their participation in the class is both valued and appreciated. As mentioned earlier (Chapter 3), student-faculty engagement is one of the most powerful motivators and most effective determinants of academic success. In other words, students place a premium on being active processors of information, rather than passive recorders of notes.

Use questions to inspire students to ask their own questions. As a model of good question asking, you can provide students with insights into the reflective and critical thinking important in any subject or class topic. As a result, students will be more inclined to come up with their own questions—and more inclined to pursue the answers. (Example: "What might be some questions you have about the implications of drilling in the Arctic National Wildlife Refuge?")

Danger! Too Much Recall

College teachers tend to overuse recall questions ("What are three causes of the Civil War?"), which inspire and produce little critical thinking.

> **"Research Says"**
>
> In one study of college professors, it was found that 89.3 percent of all the questions asked by instructors were simple recall.

It has been my experience that one all-important factor is the key to a successful college class: *Students tend to read and think based on the questions they think the instructor will ask.* So if students only get questions that require only low levels of intellectual involvement, they will tend to think accordingly. Conversely, students who get questions based on higher levels of thinking will tend to think more critically.

Knowledge

This is the lowest level of questions and simply requires students to recall information. Knowledge questions usually require students to identify information in basically the same form it was presented. Some examples of knowledge questions include …

In woody plants, what is xylem?

Who wrote War and Peace?

In what year was the Magna Carta written?

Red Flag

Observations of college classes across a range of disciplines has shown that instructors significantly overuse knowledge or recall questions. It is not unusual for instructors (both novice and experienced) to concentrate almost exclusively on knowledge-based questions.

Comprehension

Simply stated, comprehension is the way in which ideas are organized into categories. Comprehension questions ask students to take several bits of information and put them into a single category or grouping. These questions go beyond simple recall and require students to combine data. Some examples of comprehension questions include …

How would you illustrate Kreb's Cycle?

What is the main idea of this article?

If we put these three events together, what do they say about the Industrial Revolution?

Application

At this level, instructors ask students to take information they already know and apply it to a new situation. In other words, they must use their knowledge to determine a correct response. Some examples of application questions include …

How would you use your knowledge of latitude and longitude to locate East Timor?

What happens to the square footage when you increase the overall dimensions by one-third?

If you had 8 inches of water in your basement and a hose, how you would use the hose to get the water out?

Red Flag

Never end a class by asking, "Are there any questions?" This is the surest way to turn off students. Instead, say something like, "Take two minutes and write down one question you still have about the material. Share and compare your question with a partner. I'll randomly call on three people to voice their queries."

Analysis

An analysis question asks a student to break something down into its component parts. To analyze requires students to identify reasons, causes, or motives and reach conclusions or generalizations. Some examples of analysis questions include …

What are three major factors leading to oxidation?

Describe the major reasons why the United States went to war with England?

What two conclusions can you share as to why the author took this particular position?

Synthesis

Synthesis questions challenge students to engage in creative and original thinking. These questions invite students to produce original ideas and solve problems. There is always a variety of potential responses to synthesis questions. Some examples of synthesis questions include …

def•i•ni•tion

In **analysis**, you move from the whole to the parts. In **synthesis** you move from the parts to the whole.

How would you assemble these items to create a windmill?

How would your life be different if you could breathe underwater?

Construct a display that illustrates the evolutionary nature of Picasso's work over his lifetime.

Evaluation

Evaluation requires an individual to make a judgment about something. We are asked to judge the value of an idea, a candidate, a work of art, or a solution to a problem. When students are engaged in decision making and problem solving, they should be thinking at this level. Evaluation questions do not have single right answers. Some examples of evaluation questions include …

> *What do you think about your work so far?*
>
> *Why is Marx's thesis particularly appealing to you?*
>
> *What are your feelings regarding Intelligent Design?*

"Research Says"

One research study found that in only 0.3 percent to 2.5 percent of class time were students required to engage in evaluative activities or exercises.

Creative Thinking

Creative or divergent thinking promotes the idea that students can move beyond right answers and begin thinking independently. It's thinking without limits and without boundaries. Creative thinking requires an attitude or outlook that allows you to search for ideas and manipulate knowledge and experience.

However, before we launch into some strategies that will help you promote creative thinking in your courses, let's take a look at some of the factors that tend to inhibit creative thought.

Inhibitors of Creative Thinking

Students often believe that getting the right answer is more important than thinking about a diversity of possibilities. By focusing only on single right answers, they frequently inhibit their own creative thought.

College students often believe that education is a logical and practical way of looking at the world. However, when students get the chance to ask their own questions, find the answers, and consider questions that *have* no single right answer, they can stimulate their natural curiosity about the world around them.

Like all of us, many students have a fear of failure. When students are worried about getting a wrong answer, they are reluctant to venture anything. Their creativity and thinking shuts down. Students need an atmosphere that supports their efforts and encourages them to think their way through their mistakes.

> **Red Flag** _____
>
> Because they have been conditioned by rote memorization and low-level thinking skills, many college students believe they aren't and can't be creative. Students often have the mistaken impression that success in college is built on the ability to memorize bits of information and regurgitate that data on paper-and-pencil tests.

Enhancers of Creative Thinking

College instructors sometimes make the mistake of assuming that exercises and activities designed to strengthen creative thinking are intellectual fluff. Nothing could be further from the truth. In fact, creative thinking should and can be promoted in any topic or discipline.

Here are four creative thinking strategies—all of which can be incorporated into any presentation:

- Fluency
- Flexibility
- Originality
- Elaboration

Fluency is the ability to create a potpourri of ideas or lists of ideas. It involves the generation of many thoughts without regard to quality—otherwise known as brainstorming. Brainstorming is designed to produce many ideas and can be used in small or large groups of students. It should not be considered as an end in itself, but rather as a prelude to further investigation and discovery. To be effective, brainstorming should adhere to the following guidelines:

- **No negative criticism.** Defer judgment until a large number of alternatives have been produced.

- **Freewheeling is desired**. Encourage wild, off-beat, and unusual ideas.

- **Quantity is stressed.** Include the small, obvious alternatives as well as the wild, unusual, and clever ones. No value judging or evaluation of ideas is permitted during brainstorming.

Flexibility involves drawing relationships between seemingly unrelated ideas, such as, "How is a rubber band like a dictionary?" or "How is a screw similar to an inclined plane?" Locating common elements between items helps students look for many possible answers to a problem.

Originality refers to the creation of ideas that are singular and unique. It involves a willingness to take risks, be unconventional, and deviate from common patterns. The original thinker is able to analyze known information, manipulate and transform it so that new and different relationships are discovered, and, finally, recognize and decide which ideas are the most original.

Elaboration is the process individuals go through to expand an idea—to enlarge it until it is workable or feasible. It is a process of multiplication or addition that builds and "inflates" ideas into an expanded final form.

Sample Activities to Promote Creative Thinking

Here's a sampling of selected activities and questions borrowed from colleagues in various disciplines. They were all designed to help students look at a topic more creatively. The intent was *not* to have them all arrive at predetermined right answers.

Fluency:

- ◆ **Principles of Marketing:** Make a list of the marketing mix decisions that will satisfy potential customers.

- ◆ **Modern Europe:** Construct a list of the five major cultural events in Europe from the French Revolution to the present.

- ◆ **Analysis of Algorithms:** Develop a list of five fundamental algorithms.

Flexibility:

- ◆ **Tropical Ecology:** Illustrate some of the similarities between the biological diversity in a tropical ecosystem and those in a more temperate ecosystem.

- ◆ **Art Appreciation:** Make a three-dimensional model that illustrates the similarities and differences between pointillism and surrealism.

- ◆ **Physical Anthropology:** Cut out pictures of several people from old magazines. Using a combination of body types, faces, and so on, construct a character that is similar in appearance to *Homo erectus*.

Originality:

◆ **Elementary French I:** Make a cartoon strip (of at least four "boxes") in which the characters speak in French.

◆ **Modern Geometry:** Make a dictionary of descriptive words that could be used in a study of Euclidian geometry versus non-Euclidian geometry.

◆ **Nutrition:** Make a sock puppet or stick figure and present basic nutrition facts to elementary school students through a 5-minute play.

Elaboration:

◆ **English Literature:** If you were the author of the story, in what further episodes, events, or discoveries would you have the characters participate?

◆ **Engineering Physics:** Write a letter to the author of the textbook regarding his emphasis on the use of vectors.

◆ **State and Local Government:** Develop a PBS radio show interview that addresses the unique problems of contemporary urban politics.

Practical Thinking

Practical thinking is sometimes defined as problem solving. When we say to students, "Here is a problem. How would you solve it?" we are asking them to engage in practical thinking. Practical thinking has direct applications to real-life situations or events.

Problem solving is a process—an ongoing activity in which we take what we know to discover what we don't know. It involves overcoming obstacles by generating hypotheses, testing those predictions and arriving at satisfactory solutions.

Problem solving involves three basic functions:

◆ Seeking information

◆ Generating new knowledge

◆ Making decisions

def•i•ni•tion

Problem solving is the ability to identify and solve problems by applying appropriate skills systematically.

Problem solving is, and should be, a very real part of any course. It presupposes that students can take on some of the responsibility for their own learning and can take personal action to solve problems, resolve conflicts, discuss alternatives, and focus on thinking as a vital element of a course. It provides students with opportunities to use their newly acquired knowledge in meaningful, real-life activities and assists them in working at higher levels of thinking.

Here is a five-stage model that students can put into action and which has direct applications for any course.

1. Understand the problem.

It's important for students to understand the nature of a problem and its related goals. In short, students need to frame a problem in their own words.

2. Describe any barriers.

Students need to be aware of any barriers or constraints that may be preventing them from achieving their goal. In short, what is creating the problem? Encouraging students to verbalize these impediments is always an important step.

3. Identify various solutions.

After the nature and parameters of a problem are understood, students will need to select one or more appropriate strategies that will help resolve the problem. Students need to understand that there are many strategies available to them and that no single strategy will work for all problems. Here are some problem-solving possibilities.

- **Create visual images:** Many problem solvers find it useful to create "mind pictures" of a problem and its potential solutions prior to working on the problem. Mental imaging allows the problem solvers to map out many dimensions of a problem and "see" it clearly.

- **"Guesstimate":** Students should be given opportunities to engage in some trial-and-error approaches to problem solving. It should be understood, however, that this is not a singular approach to problem solving but rather an attempt by the problem solver to gather some preliminary data.

- **Creating a table:** A table is defined as an orderly arrangement of data. When students have opportunities to design and create tables of information they begin to understand that most data relative to a problem can be grouped and organized.

- **Using manipulatives:** By moving objects around on a table or desk, students can develop patterns and organize elements of a problem into recognizable and visually satisfying components.

- **Work backwards:** It is frequently helpful for students to take the data presented at the end of a problem and use a series of computations to arrive at the data presented at the beginning of the problem.

- **Look for a pattern:** Looking for patterns is an important problem-solving strategy since many problems are similar and fall into predictable patterns. A pattern, by definition, is a regular, systematic repetition and may be numerical, visual, or behavioral.

- **Create a systematic list:** Recording information in list form is a process used quite frequently to map out a "plan of attack" for defining and solving problems. Students should be encouraged to record their ideas in lists to determine regularities, patterns, or similarities between problem elements.

4. Try out a solution.

When working through a strategy or combination of strategies it will be important for students to engage in the following:

- Keep accurate and up-to-date records of their thoughts, proceedings, and procedures. Recording the data collected, the predictions made, and the strategies used is an important part of the problem-solving process.

- Try to work through a selected strategy or combination of strategies until it becomes evident either that they are not working, they need to be modified, or they are yielding inappropriate data. As students become more proficient problem solvers, they should feel comfortable rejecting potential strategies at any time during their quest for solutions.

- Carefully monitor the steps undertaken as part of a solution. While it may be natural for students to rush through a strategy in hopes of getting a quick answer, it is incumbent upon you to encourage students to carefully assess and monitor their progress.

- Feel comfortable putting a problem aside for a period of time and tackling it at a later time. For example, scientists rarely come up with a solution the first time they approach a problem. Students, too, should also feel comfortable in letting a problem "rest" for a while and returning to it later.

5. Evaluate the results.

It's vitally important that students have multiple opportunities to assess their own problem-solving skills and the solutions generated from using those skills. Students frequently depend too much upon teachers to evaluate their performance.

The process of self-assessment is not easy. It involves risk-taking, self-assurance, and a certain level of independence. But, you can effectively promote by asking students questions such as "How do you feel about your progress so far?", "Are you satisfied with the results you obtained?", and "Why do you believe this is an appropriate response to the problem?"

From the Field

Here are some techniques that will help students understand the nature of a problem and the conditions that surround it:

- ◆ List all related relevant facts.
- ◆ Make a list of all the given information.
- ◆ Restate the problem in their own words.
- ◆ List the conditions that surround a problem.
- ◆ Describe related known problems.

Bloom's Taxonomy

In 1956, Benjamin Bloom of the University of Chicago developed a classification system we now refer to as *Bloom's Taxonomy* to assist educators in recognizing their various levels of question asking (among other things). The system contains six levels of thinking arranged in hierarchical form, moving from the lowest level of cognition (thinking) to the highest, or from the least complex to the most complex:

- ◆ Knowledge
- ◆ Comprehension
- ◆ Application
- ◆ Analysis
- ◆ Synthesis
- ◆ Evaluation

def•i•ni•tion

Taxonomy is an orderly classification of items according to a systematic relationship (e.g., low to high, small to big, simple to complex).

What does all this mean? Several things, actually! First, it means that there are several different kinds of questions you can ask your students. If you only focus on one type of question, then your students may not be exposed to the diverse and complex levels of thinking necessary to a complete understanding of a topic. If, for example, you only ask students knowledge-based questions, then your students may think that learning is nothing more than the ability to memorize a select number of facts.

Second, although Bloom's Taxonomy is primarily focused on the types of questions we ask students, it provides you with a way to craft meaningful and significant classroom experiences (see Chapter 10). Students become more engaged in the dynamics of a topic when that topic is approached via multiple viewpoints and perspectives.

Third, it offers several intriguing out-of-class learning opportunities. Projects, written papers, library research, and other assignments can be built around a variety of critical thinking opportunities. For example, a sociology class may wish to *analyze* recent public policy statements regarding child care. Students in a biology class might *synthesize* recent research on global warming to present to the entire class. Music majors could *evaluate* the public's preferences for various types of music (classical versus hip-hop).

Fourth, you can use this taxonomy to help craft a wide range of in-class and out-of-class learning experiences—from low-level thinking (knowledge) to high-level thinking (evaluation). If variety is the spice of life, you should sprinkle a variety of critical thinking opportunities throughout every lesson, irrespective of the discipline or topic.

Fifth, and most important, students tend to think based on the levels of thinking modeled and promoted by the instructor. If they only get knowledge-based questions, they'll only engage in knowledge-based thinking. Students will tend to approach a topic at higher levels of critical thinking if they are presented with an abundance of higher-level thinking activities.

"Research Says"

One study of college classes discovered that the level of thinking promoted by a professor was directly related to class size. For example, the median cognitive level in classes of 15 or less students was *analysis*. The median level of thinking in classes of 16 to 45 students was *comprehension*. In classes with more than 45 students, the median level of critical thinking was simple *knowledge*.

Thinking About Thinking—Revisited

Ken Bain, director of the Center for Teaching Excellence at New York University, posits that five essential ingredients promote thinking in a college course or classroom. They are also emblematic of what the best college professors do, irrespective of their discipline. They are: providing meaningful information, raising questions, providing authentic tasks, making decisions, and engaging in intellectual inquiry.

You can promote and emphasize thinking by including the following factors in every lesson or presentation:

◆ **Pose an intriguing problem.** This is a problem or situation grounded in relevant course concepts or real-life situations.

◆ **Ask high-level cognitive questions.** Students learn to think by listening to and emulating the questions you ask them in class. Raising questions is more important than providing answers.

◆ **Engage students in higher-order intellectual activities.** This may mean wrestling with problems that have no clear-cut answers, tackling situations that have a host of viewpoints, or integrating other disciplines into a single topic (for example, using poetry, art, and math to describe the design of a polyhedron).

◆ **Invite students to pose their own questions.** The best kinds of questions are those that students ask of themselves. And, the best answers are those that students seek and develop on their own, too.

◆ **Encourage self-discovery.** One of the best ways to conclude a class is to provide students with an opportunity to draw their own conclusions. Instead of providing them with your preconceived conclusions, allow them to develop their own conclusions.

The Least You Need to Know

◆ Students often have preconceived notions and expectations about learning.

◆ Critical thinking can best be promoted through the types of questions we model for our students.

◆ Creative-thinking opportunities allow students to "think outside the box" and move beyond right answers.

- Practical thinking activities offer students opportunities to apply course content to real-world situations.

- Thinking should be an inherent and necessary part of every course and every subject.

Part 4

Connecting with Students

Successful college teaching is much more than delivering what you have in your head to the heads of your students. College teaching is like an exotic tropical drink—it's one part this, two parts that, a dash of something else, and a sprinkle of another thing—all shaken up in a blender (the classroom) to create a delicious taste sensation (learning) with an umbrella on top (an A grade!). It's fair to say that one of the most important ingredients in this concoction is the students themselves.

In Part 4, I'll share what college students really expect from a course. You'll learn how to efficiently manage large classes, how to effectively get your lessons across to the diverse group of students in each class—and how to deal with the problem students you're likely to encounter. The bonds you establish with students will be the ultimate determinant of your instructional success—much more than the "stuff" of your discipline or field. Let's take a look.

"Question up there. You're jbd235, right?"

Chapter 13

What College Students Want

In This Chapter

- Student wants
- How students learn
- Building relationships
- A supportive classroom environment
- The human factor

When you go to see a new movie you probably go with several expectations. You want to be entertained, maybe even intellectually stimulated. You want believable characters and a storyline that is interesting or provocative. If the movie satisfies your expectations, then you'll probably conclude that it was an enjoyable film. If it doesn't, then you may feel that your money (and your evening) was wasted.

College students also come to class with a set of expectations. They want some bang for their (tuition) buck; after all, they will be spending the next 15 weeks or so of their lives in your course, and they want to know that it will be time well spent. Let's take a look at some of those student expectations and how they might shape the design and delivery of your courses.

Give Them What They Want *and* What They Need

Each year I visit the classroom of selected colleagues at my institution. I select different classes, various disciplines, and a variety of levels (freshmen, seniors). My goal is to solicit information on how students learn and how I can meet their learning needs in my own classes.

In each class I distribute a blank index card to each student and ask her or him to respond anonymously to two or three specific questions. I select the questions from the following list:

♦ At the beginning of a new course, what do you expect of a professor?

♦ What should professors do to help you learn?

♦ What is the most positive learning experience you've ever had (in school or out)?

♦ What factors inhibit your ability to learn a new subject or topic?

♦ If you could give one piece of advice to every college professor, what would it be?

This little survey only takes about 5 to 6 minutes, but it has yielded some incredibly valuable information that has helped me design courses with student needs in mind. That's not to say that every one of my courses or every element of my classes is in response to what students want, but it helps me plan effective teaching methods, so I can offer "well-developed characters and an engaging story line" throughout the semester. It may not seem like it, but the production of an effective college course is quite similar to the production (and directing) of a memorable movie.

What Students Say

Based on information I've gathered over several semesters, here are the most frequent responses students give to the first question, "At the beginning of a new course, what do you expect of a professor?"

♦ Everyone is treated fairly and respectfully.

♦ The instructor has clear expectations and is organized.

♦ The instructor is knowledgeable about his or her subject matter.

♦ The instructor is approachable and willing to help.

♦ The instructor is enthusiastic about teaching the subject.

- The instructor is human; he or she has good rapport with students.

- There is a connection between the material and real life.

- The instructor creates a safe and comfortable learning environment.

- The instructor is flexible; he or she is willing to adjust or adapt as necessary.

- The instructor has a sense of humor.

From the Field _____

Dominic Delli Carpini, an associate professor of English at York College of Pennsylvania, says, "We need to be able to bridge the gap between our passion and students' needs. Second, students need to know us as people, not just as professors. There is a deep emotional bond that facilitates learning and the bottom line is that teaching is all about real relationships with real humans."

Whether or not student expectations match our goals will have a significant impact on students' success. If we want to help students learn, we have to pay attention and respond to their immediate and long-range needs. This is not coddling students, it's showing respect for their needs ... and responding to those needs. Let's examine some ways we can do that.

Red Flag _____

In a study of 700 undergraduate students, respondents were asked to list complaints about teaching behaviors they observed in all the college courses they took. Two of the most frequently mentioned complaints were: "being unhelpful and unapproachable" and "intellectual arrogance—talking down to or showing a lack of respect for students."

The Big Five

Numerous studies around the country over the past decade have identified several factors that have a significant and permanent impact on how well undergraduate students learn. This research has focused on identifying the needs or expectations students bring to class, and the ways professors can respond to those needs while staying focused on the necessary course content. I like to call these "The Big Five":

- Real-life experiences

- Comprehensible presentations

- A supportive and engaging classroom environment

- Approachability and respect

- Enthusiasm for teaching

Real-Life Experiences

It's probably safe to say that it's a small number of students in your freshman History of Western Philosophy course that really cares about "the development of epistemology, metaphysics, and ethics within several historically important systems of philosophy." The same holds true for all the nonmajors in your Principles of Economics (Micro) course, not to mention their affection for "price and output determination as explained by the interaction of supply and demand."

Nevertheless, the impact of any lecture, presentation, or class discussion is often determined by how well students "see" its relationship to their own lives. Students need to understand the connection(s) between a specific topic and their lives and/or experiences outside the classroom. Without that connection their level of comprehension diminishes significantly. Consider the following:

- Ask questions that focus on connections between a topic and students' lives. ("How might the disturbance at the game last Saturday be comparable to the current debate in the U.S. Senate?")

- Design and develop assignments that help students use course information in practical real-life situations in the outside world.

- Provide relevant anecdotes, especially those from your own (or your colleagues') experiences in the field.

- Whenever practical, discuss the movies, books, or websites that students read or view. Draw parallels between those media and specific course concepts.

- Periodically construct and use classroom *simulations* to illustrate important ideas.

- Incorporate role-playing activities into your course as appropriate.

def•i•ni•tion

A **simulation** is an abstraction of a real-life event. The board games *Monopoly* and *Life*, and computer software such as *Oregon Trail* and *Sim City* are simulations of events, circumstances, and conditions that exist in the outside world.

Comprehensible Presentations

As professors and practitioners, we are passionate about our subjects. We have spent considerable time and tuition learning as much as possible about our respective fields. The depth of our knowledge and the enthusiasm we have for that knowledge is extensive. We are steeped in the concepts, philosophies, and terminology of our respective professions. Students, however, are not!

This does not mean that you should talk down to students, but you do need to be supportive as well as instructive. True, that's often challenging, given some of the complex theories and concepts we need to present.

Today's students are visual learners. Whenever possible, supplement a presentation or lecture with some sort of visual aid. These may include charts, graphs, maps, PowerPoint presentations, flowcharts, videos, DVDs, and illustrations.

Always provide opportunities for students to share and discuss course concepts in small group sessions. Learning occurs best when students have opportunities to talk about the implications of course content as well as their understanding of those concepts. Focused in-class assignments and projects are critical to their understanding.

Students often stumble over new vocabulary. Plan to provide alternate definitions and explanations apart from those in the textbook. Invite students to participate in small group discussions about difficult terminology. Ask students to maintain vocabulary notebooks as they read which can be shared and discussed in class. One suggestion from Lana Becker and Kent Schneider at East Tennessee State University is "to create a 'living' glossary on [your] website where new terminology is added, explained, and illustrated throughout the course."

When possible, provide students with opportunities to have a say in selecting what will be studied and how it will be approached. Offer students options on reading assignments, test design (essay, multiple choice), or written assignments.

Make the course progressive. Begin the course with easy-to-comprehend concepts and principles. Offer multiple opportunities for students to succeed at this level with exams and out-of-class assignments. As their confidence grows, gradually increase the difficulty level of the information as the course progresses.

Don't assume that students will tell you when they don't understand something. Always say, "This seems to be a challenging or difficult piece of information. How can I help you understand it?" One of the best motivational devices at your disposal is to anticipate their intellectual discomfort and be proactive in responding to it.

A Supportive and Engaging Classroom Environment

One of the most valuable ways we can promote a supportive classroom environment is through the feedback or responses we provide them both in and out of class. Feedback, to be effective, must be prompt, frequent, and efficient. Students want to see a direct connection between any effort or completed task (such as reading a text-book chapter or midterm exam) and a response from you. Here are some suggestions for providing successful feedback:

◆ Make feedback immediate. ("I'm returning the test you took in the last class.")

◆ Always frame your feedback in positive language. ("Wow, it looks like we're really on a roll today with quantum theory!")

◆ Allow students to revise their incorrect responses. ("I'm not sure that's a sufficient response. Is there another way we could explain this?")

◆ Use verbal as well as written feedback. ("You must be feeling pretty good about the progress you're making on this project.")

◆ Always make eye-to-eye contact in asking a question as well as when giving feedback. Let each student know that she or he has your complete and total attention. ("Sandy, I see that you're a little unsure about some of the philosophical influences on the American system of education. What can I do to clarify?")

◆ Allow students to control some feedback. ("How do you feel about your effort on the titration experiment?")

◆ Make comments specific, and suggest corrections. ("You provided a good overview of current thinking about the neural/hormonal regulation of sexual behavior, but you might want to address the topic from a historical perspective, too.")

◆ Offer feedback in terms of a student's progress, not her or his comparison with others. ("Look how you improved from 78 percent on the first terminology quiz to 91 percent on the second one.")

◆ Always comment on students' answers and always use part of a student's answer in your response. ("Let me see if I can rephrase that. What you're saying is that the League of Nations was doomed from the very beginning—right?") (Note: This tip is so important that it should get five stars—★★★★★!)

Dominic Delli Carpini (whom you met earlier in this chapter) is a master of classroom discussions. In any verbal engagement with students, he doesn't just accept a student's response to a question. Rather, he prompts their thinking through one or more of the following:

◆ Always provide a reaction to a student's verbal contribution ("I like your interpretation of [the author's] main thesis.").

◆ Always relate a student's comment back to the text. ("Your summary of this article seems to concentrate on the author's last two points.")

◆ Always use a student's words in framing a response. ("You said that you thought that the author was 'less than honest, less than candid' in his summary. Would you care to elaborate?")

◆ Always turn a student's response into one or more higher-level questions. ("Given your position on this issue, how could we use that information to interpret [another author] thesis?")

Another way college professors promote the concept of an engaging classroom is through the use of humor. Humor, when appropriately used, helps create a more relaxed, informal, and comfortable learning environment. It also has the advantage of revealing you as someone other than "just" a college professor. In short, it humanizes both teaching and learning.

"Research Says"

A research study in 1996 found that college students rated the use of humor as very effective to extremely effective in reducing their anxiety, increasing their ability to learn, and improving their chance of performing their best on problems and exams. Another 1999 study that reviewed several decades of research on the uses of classroom humor discovered a strong positive correlation among teacher uses of humor in the classroom, student evaluations of teaching, and student reports of learning.

This doesn't mean that you need to be a comedian in order to be an effective professor. It does mean that humor is a vehicle that can "lighten" a subject or specific subject while creating positive bonds of communication.

You can open each class with a humorous quote posted on the chalkboard. ("There comes a time in the affairs of men when we must grab the bull by the tail and face the situation."—W.C. Fields)

Include a cartoon or two on your course syllabus, exams, or other written documents, or post a humorous cartoon or saying on your personal website or office door. Be sure to replace these at regular intervals.

If you're comfortable with it, use self-deprecating humor. At the start of a new course, I often make fun of my increasing loss of cranial hair by asking, "You know how people figure out that I've been teaching for more than three decades?" I wait a few moments, bend over, and point to the top of my head saying, "This is the result!"

Often the best humor is spontaneous or situational humor—the kind that arises unexpectedly during a class discussion, an event outside the classroom window, a glitch with some form of technology, or a thousands other situations.

Once, in the middle of an intense, whole-class discussion of educational theory, one of my students dropped her purse, scattering the contents to the four corners of the classroom. Without thinking, she blurted out, "Oh, s**t!" She realized what she had said, put her hand over her mouth, and she (and everyone else in the class) waited for my response. I said, "That's OK, I probably would have said the same thing. It's just that the dean docks my pay whenever I do."

Everyone smiled, the situation was defused, and we moved on in our discussion. (Note: After class, the student and I had a brief, pleasant conversation about appropriate classroom language.)

From the Field

Professor Richard Leblanc of York University in Ontario, Canada, winner of the Seymous Schulich Award for Teaching Excellence, says, "Good teaching is about humor. It's about being self-deprecating and not taking yourself too seriously. It's often about making innocuous jokes, mostly at your own expense, so that the ice breaks and students learn in a more relaxed atmosphere where you, like them, are human with your own share of faults and shortcomings."

Approachability and Respect

Repeatedly, in study after study, college students report that the "availability," "openness," and "mutual respect" of the instructor was a critical factor in how well they learned a subject and retained that information long after the course was over. Students want to be treated fairly and respectfully. Their self-esteem and learning potential are significantly diminished whenever they are treated like "second-class citizens" without a voice or an identity.

Get to know each student by name. This may be challenging, particularly if you teach large lecture courses, but the dividends are worth it. Conversations with students reveal that they feel more comfortable with and positive about a class when the professor takes time to learn (and use) students' names.

Demonstrate that you care about students' enrollment, attendance, and participation in the class. This can be as simple as a friendly greeting to an entire class as you enter the classroom or asking to see random students after class to thank them for their contributions or progress on an assignment. Also, take roll in every class. This not only encourages attendance, but provides an opportunity to share (and learn) each student's name.

Red Flag

Experienced professors know that college students learn best in humanistic (as opposed to dictatorial) classrooms. There is convincing evidence that they want teachers who are *real* people, who recognize them as human beings— teachers who care about them.

Remove yourself from the "teacher role" every so often. Allow students to see you as something other than just a college professor. I do this by sharing *relevant* anecdotes or stories about myself or my family periodically throughout the semester. I also share some of my foibles, mistakes, or learning challenges to let students know that I am certainly less than perfect.

Always demonstrate respect for your students. Never put them down; never be disrespectful of their culture, religion, gender, beliefs, or opinions; and never make a joke at their expense. Use sarcasm sparingly, if at all.

Open each class by posing a question for students. Invite each student to respond. You can begin the semester by asking general questions. ("Who is your favorite actor? "What type of ethnic food do you enjoy?) As the semester progresses, ask more specific questions. ("What is the most important lesson you've ever learned?" "Where would you like to be in 25 years?") You can also add some content-specific questions to your repertoire, too. ("What is one unanswered question about organic chemistry that you have?" "If you could tell the author of this poem one thing, what would it be?")

Make it a point to frequently react to the ideas or comments of students. Acknowledge and validate each student's contributions to the class. You can do this through verbal responses ("thanks for sharing that with us"), body language (smiling, nodding), or via an after-class e-mail ("I liked the question you raised today about the prospects for democracy in post-war Iraq").

Enthusiasm for Teaching; Enthusiasm for the Subject

Use a variety of teaching strategies and techniques (see Chapter 8). Vary your presentations each day, each week. Don't turn the semester into a nonstop series of lectures—not only will students be "turned off," so will you. For each class consider an assembly of teaching options such as small group discussions, case studies, demonstrations, audiovisual presentations, guest speakers, debates, role playing, brainstorming, and simulations. Not only will student interest be maintained with this variety, so will yours.

Frequently tell students about some of the exciting research you're doing, presentations you're making, or articles/books you are writing. Occasionally inject some of your passion and enthusiasm into the course. Let students know what excites you about the discipline or field.

"Research Says"

A significant body of research has demonstrated that an instructor's enthusiasm is a crucial factor in college students' motivation and eventual success—irrespective of the discipline or difficulty of material. According to Barbara Gross Davis of the University of California, Berkeley, "an instructor's enthusiasm comes from confidence, excitement about the content, and genuine pleasure in teaching."

Periodically share some of your teaching philosophy with students. Why did you become a college professor? What have you learned in your years in the classroom? What has been your most interesting teaching experience?

The former mayor of New York, Ed Koch, used to stop people on the street and ask them, "How am I doing?" You can do the same thing with your students. Halfway through a presentation ask them to fill in a simple two-minute evaluation form. (What do you find interesting so far? What is less than interesting?) Periodically, invite students to engage in a short debriefing session about their level of enthusiasm for a topic relative to your level of enthusiasm. Invite a colleague to visit your class and assess your enthusiasm for a challenging or difficult topic.

Whenever practical, use community resources. These may include local government officials, businesspeople, scientists, researchers, technicians, environmentalists, museum directors, and the like. "Outside" people provide you with opportunities to see your discipline through new eyes.

Form a student panel and invite them to challenge your philosophy or viewpoints. Reverse roles and vigorously oppose your beliefs (students will defend your position).

Provide opportunities for students to assume the role of a professional in your discipline (teacher, biologist, chemist, economist, mechanical engineer, respiratory therapist, paleontologist, psychologist, etc.).

Take students with you when guest speakers, visiting performers, or other visitors come to campus. Plan time afterwards to discuss the work or information in terms of basic course concepts.

Dominic Delli Carpini exercises his enthusiasm within a class and throughout a course with a three-pronged approach. This includes:

◆ Enthusiasm for the text ("Now, here's a really interesting statement for you!").

◆ Enthusiasm for student responses ("Congratulations. You really nailed it with that response!").

◆ Enthusiasm for what he is saying ("I think this is one of the most exciting ideas we've studied so far! Let me tell you why.").

The Least You Need to Know

◆ Students have perceived ideas and expectations about a course that need to be addressed.

◆ It's important to demonstrate the connection between course content and the real world.

◆ Creating a supportive classroom environment is critical to academic success.

◆ Humor is an essential ingredient in any academic endeavor.

◆ Students want to be respected. Respect engenders academic growth.

Diverse Students, Diverse Populations

In This Chapter

- ◆ A diversity of students

- ◆ Knowing yourself

- ◆ Knowing your students

- ◆ Knowing your course

- ◆ Knowing your institution

It was a lesson well learned. For the first several weeks of the semester I shared my ideas, presented the latest research, and engaged students in an array of interactive activities. But one student never made eye contact with me. Try as I might, I couldn't make a visual connection with her. So, I asked if she could see me during my office hours. During the course of our conversation, I mentioned the fact that she never seemed to look at me in class. She politely informed me that in Japan (her native country) it is considered rude to stare at a person of higher rank, such as a college professor.

The demographics of college enrollment over the past several decades have shown a significant increase in the ethnic, gender, and cultural diversity of students enrolling in colleges both large and small. Ensuring that everyone has equal access to an educational atmosphere of respect, trust, and appreciation is sometimes a challenge—particularly for white, European American professors. This chapter offers some considerations and practices that may be appropriate for your classroom.

A Little Background

Since the Civil Rights movement in the 1950s, we have seen a significant increase in the diversity of students in college classrooms. Typically under-represented groups of people were enrolling in college classes all across the country in significant numbers. The educational opportunities for Asian Americans, Latin Americans, African Americans, Native Americans, gays, lesbians, women, and various socioeconomic groups were increasing dramatically. At the same time this diverse population was occasionally at odds with the backgrounds of the teachers they faced in the college classroom.

Although the educational opportunities were increasing, even at the most progressive and desegregated institutions, many students were subjected to subtle forms of *discrimination* and *stereotyping*.

def•i•ni•tion

Discrimination is the differential treatment of an individual due to minority status. The minority status may be either actual or perceived; e.g., "Of course she's failing English 101, she's an immigrant."

Stereotyping is generalizing about a person while ignoring the presence of individual differences; e.g., "He's like that because he's from California. Everyone from California is crazy!"

"Research Says"

According to the Institute for the Study of Social Change, discrimination often takes the form of facial expressions, in not being acknowledged, in how white students "take over a class" and speak past students of color, or in small everyday slights in which minorities perceive that their value and perspective are not appreciated or respected. These behaviors have an understandable effect on students' personal, academic, and professional development.

This chapter is designed to help you work with the wide diversity of students in your classes. However, according to Professor Richard Suinn of Colorado State University, it is imperative that college teachers avoid what he calls the *deficit model*, the view that inadequate performance from an ethnic person automatically means the student is academically deficient, unmotivated, uninterested, or poorly prepared.

def•i•ni•tion

The **deficit model** postulates that poor academic performance on the part of students from various ethnic, gender, and cultural groups is the result of academic deficiencies, lack of motivation, disinterest, or inadequate preparation.

Know Thyself

Our behavior, speech, and attitudes are reflections of our beliefs. What we say in class may be subtle indicators of internally held stereotypes, biases, or patterns of discrimination. Your background, your upbringing, and your life experiences color your perceptions and treatment of other individuals. Here are some factors you need to be aware of.

Stereotypes

Be aware of any "grouping" practices that you use. For example, do you assume that males are the only ones who are qualified for scientific careers? Do you assume that all African Americans are in an ethnic studies program? Do you assume that people with foreign accents are unable to write comprehensive and coherent papers?

By the same token, be aware that, even within groups, people are different and often like to celebrate their differences and individuality. For example, just because you have several Asian American students in your class, don't assume that they all socialize together. Just because you have several African Americans in the class, don't assume that they all belong to the black student union. And, just because there are several Latinos in your course, don't assume that they all celebrate Cinco de Mayo. It's important to look past the cultural or ethnic label and recognize each and every individual.

Language

The language we use is often an indicator of our biases, prejudices, and preferences. Here are a few questions you may wish to ask yourself:

- Do you use the pronouns "she" and "he" equally in your lectures, written comments on papers, and in casual conversations?

- Do you refer to homosexuals as gays and lesbians, or as "queers" and "homos"?

- Do you refer to African Americans as blacks or Negroes?

- Do you refer to all Asian Americans as Orientals rather than South Asian, Japanese Americans, or Chinese Americans (among others)?

- Do you use socioeconomic terms such as "poor white trash" or "trailer trash?"

- Do you refer to all people with a non-English accent as immigrants?

Nonverbal Behaviors

The nonverbal behaviors you exhibit both in and out of class will have an impact on students from various ethnic and cultural groups. Cultural norms and expectations vary among different groups and your awareness and respect of those norms may affect their learning potential. Consider the following:

- As mentioned previously, eye contact between a professor and a student may be deemed disrespectful in some cultures.

- The preferred personal space between two people often varies according to culture or tradition. In some cultures closeness is valued; others prefer a comfortable distance.

- How you use your arms (body language) sends different signals. In some cultures folding your arms while talking is disrespectful; in others it denotes arrogance.

- Hand gestures are viewed differently throughout the world. For example, the "OK sign" (thumb and forefinger formed into a circle) is considered an insult in some parts of the world.

> **"Research Says"**
>
> According to several studies, African Americans and Hispanics tend to stand closer to someone they are conversing with than do white Americans. On the other hand, Asians tend to prefer a greater distance.

Self-Fulfilling Prophecies

An old maxim says that students tend to perform as we expect them to perform. (This is sometimes referred to as the "Pygmalion Theory," after George Bernard Shaw's play of the same name.) That is, when we expect more from our students, they will learn more. Conversely, when we have lower expectations, students will learn at lower levels. Thus, if we believe that African Americans, second-language learners, or overweight people won't be able to learn a subject as well as "mainstream" students, our expectations will be fulfilled in their lowered achievement rates.

"Research Says"
The research on this issue is clear and definitive! An instructor's expectations often become self-fulfilling prophecies. That is, students who sense that more is expected of them tend to outperform students who believe that less is expected of them—regardless of the student's actual abilities.

Know Your Students

One of the themes promoted throughout this book is the value of knowing each and every one of your students. Knowing students' names, background, and experiences that will help or hinder their success are critical to their scholastic progress. This is equally (if not more) true with students from various ethnic and cultural groups. Here are a few ideas for your consideration:

Learn the Culture

Make an effort to learn as much as you can about the history and culture of groups other than your own.

- ◆ Read books and articles written by people of a specific ethnic group or culture.

- ◆ Talk with students informally after class and ask them to share some of their cultural beliefs and traditions.

- ◆ Speak with colleagues from other departments—particularly those from different cultural groups.

- ◆ Check out websites to learn about the history, traditions, beliefs, and culture of a specific group.

- Contact cultural centers and religious organizations in your town. Ask for printed information or opportunities to chat with members.

- Attend cultural celebrations in your area. Take time to talk with people, enjoy the food, and listen in on conversations.

- Attend campuswide activities that celebrate diversity or ethnic heritage.

Don't Generalize

It may be tempting to ask a Japanese American student to discuss her feelings about the internment of all Japanese Americans during World War II, but be careful that you do not single out one member of a cultural or ethnic group as a "representative" of that group. It would be a mistake to assume that one member of a minority group is an authority or expert on a culturally related topic. Just as there is a variety of opinions and viewpoints among white Anglo-Saxon males, so too is there an equal variety of viewpoints and opinions among the members of any other ethnic or cultural group.

Respect Differences

Some students are not active participants in debates, confrontations, or arguments. That may be more the result of cultural expectations and behaviors than any lazy or willful nonparticipation. Some students, depending on their cultural norms, may not ask questions or become verbally challenging because to do so would feel rude and disrespectful to them. Know that students (of any culture) learn in different ways—not necessarily those practiced by white European Americans.

def•i•ni•tion

ESL is an acronym for English as a Second Language. ELL is the acronym for English Language Learner.

Respect Language

Students from other countries may not be as fluent in English as native speakers. They may need assistance in both oral and written language via *ESL* or *ELL* courses offered on campus. You may wish to check with the instructors in these on-campus courses for advice on grading papers, exams, and other assignments.

Meeting with Students

Plan to meet with students informally after (or before) class. Invite students to meet with you for a cup of coffee at the student union, ask them to stop by your office during your scheduled hours, or talk with them informally as you cross the campus or stroll over to the faculty lunchroom. Regular and constant contact with students outside of class does much to ensure good teacher-student relationships and mutual understanding. These times may be group endeavors or private one-on-one sessions.

> **"Research Says"**
>
> One 1989 study provided evidence that frequent and rewarding informal contact with faculty members is the strongest predictor of whether or not a student will voluntarily withdraw from a college.

Challenge Inappropriate Comments

Some students may make comments about certain ethnic, cultural, or racial groups out of habit or ignorance. Don't allow these comments to pass unnoticed. Make sure students know that discriminatory comments are inappropriate and unacceptable. Immediately give the student an "I message." An I message is composed of three parts:

1. Include a description of the student's behavior. ("When you use that racial slur ...")

2. Relate the effect this behavior has on you and other students. ("... I and the other students become very upset ...")

3. Let the student know the feeling it generates in you. ("... because we know it is both inappropriate and unacceptable.")

Take Advantage of the Diversity

Knowing the culture, ethnicity, and origins of the students in your course can help you shape your assignments and requirements to address the under-representation or discriminatory practices in several academic endeavors. For example:

◆ In a history course, invite students to examine the roles of both males and females in a specific historical event.

◆ In a sociology course, invite students to look at racial discrimination from the perspective of nonwhites.

◆ In an anatomy and physiology course, invite students to look at the contributions of African-Americans (the tragically ironic story of Charles Drew comes immediately to mind).

◆ In a mathematics course, invite students to examine the contributions of Middle Eastern civilizations.

Know Your Course

At this point you may be wondering if you need to design a course that will be "all things to all people." That would probably be an overwhelming challenge and might lead to more frustration for you and less satisfaction for your students.

What's more important is to design your course to be respectful of each individual and celebrate the mix of students.

Select Appropriate Texts

In reviewing possible textbooks (see Chapter 5), check for any cultural, gender, or ethnic biases. Make sure the language is not gender specific (a preponderance of "he's"), that all ethnic groups are fairly and equitably represented, and that no single culture is held as an example of all minority groups (for example, "Native Americans, just like every other minority group in this country, once …"). Be aware of any stereotypes—those that are overt as well as those that are more subtle (for example, "It is well-known that all Latinos …").

Partner with Students

Many cultures value modesty and humility much more than drawing attention or showing off one's knowledge. Many cultures also have an ingrained respect for people in power or authority, such as teachers. Being aware of the cultural values held by students in your class can be helpful in designing in-class activities, particularly discussion. For example, instead of asking a student, "Tell us everything you know about the Portuguese empire in the New World," which would place a student on the spot, you may want to recast the request as follows:

◆ "Work with a partner on an appropriate response and then share that in a small group."

- "Can you help me with some of the details about this topic? At my age I sometimes forget a few."

- "Can you write four critical facts on the board, after which I'll write three critical facts?"

Guest Speakers

Consider bringing a variety of guest speakers into your course. Speakers may include colleagues from your department or other departments on campus. Consider individuals from the local community as well as various social agencies.

Establish Trust

One of the most important things you can do in any course is to establish an atmosphere of trust. That is, students need to feel comfortable in sharing their thoughts and opinions without recrimination or negative comments from the teacher or other students. One way to do this is by choosing your questions carefully. Questions should be framed in such a way that students do not feel threatened or challenged, but rather that their eventual responses will be valued and respected. Here are a few examples:

- Establish a partnership: "So that I can remember where we left off in the last class, can someone remind me what we said about remote sensing?"

- Celebrate a student's response: "I like your interpretation of the differentiated roles of men and women in World War II. How did those roles affect post-war America?"

- Use his/her words in the response and follow-up question: "You said that the American secondary school today is rooted more in tradition than in innovation. Does that hold true for other educational institutions?"

Red Flag

Ed Ransford states that "a balanced approach to any topic engenders trust. Students tend to lose trust if things are presented one-sided. Students need to hear all sides, as well as opposing views, of an issue."

Gender Sensitivity

A growing body of research has conclusively demonstrated that college instructors respond differently to male and female students—irrespective of the instructor's gender. Both male and female professors tend to call on male students more, tend to acknowledge male students more than female students, and tend to provide more positive responses to the contributions of male students than those of females.

Red Flag

Your gender bias often shows up in the pronouns you use in class. Relying exclusively on masculine pronouns (he, his, him) is not only inappropriate, but demeaning for your female students. Strive for a balance between feminine and masculine pronouns in your lectures, presentations, discussions, and written documents such as course syllabi.

Assess the Climate

As part of the evaluation process, invite students to comment on the climate in the classroom. Invite them to share anything that makes them or other members of the class uncomfortable or uneasy. Are there things that you do (or don't do) that may be construed as culturally insensitive or inappropriate? You may wish to include one or more of the following questions on an end-of-the-semester course evaluation form:

- Is the instructor fair and equitable in her/his treatment of all students?

- Does the instructor show preference to any single student or group of students?

- Does the instructor demonstrate biases (for or against) any race, culture, or ethnic or gender group?

- How comfortable are you with the instructor? With other students?

- What does the instructor do to make you feel comfortable in class?

- Is the instructor respectful of each individual?

From the Field

Do you demonstrate any biases in the classroom? Do you provide differential treatment of various cultural or ethnic groups? Do you give preference to one group of students over another? If you're not sure of the responses to these questions, ask a colleague to videotape one of your class sessions. Afterwards, sit down with the colleague and examine your habits, language, directions, comments, questions, and in-class attitudes. What do you notice? Are any changes necessary? Is there room for improvement?

Know Your Institution

One of the best ways to respond to the diversity of students in your classes is to learn as much as possible about your institution—its history, its traditions, and the social and cultural environment in which it operates. In a way, you are a reflection of the institution you work for—know your territory and you can also know your students.

Check Out the Catalog

Read the college catalog—particularly its mission statement—and get to know its philosophy and its goals. What does the college (the administration and the board of trustees) believe? What are their operational guidelines? What is their philosophy about the education of all students? Having that information in hand will help you craft a course that is sensitive to and respectful of all students, irrespective of their culture, gender, or ethnic group.

College Services and Resources

Find out everything you can about your campus's various support services for students. Is there a tutoring service or academic support center? What services does the academic advising office provide students? What types of cultural or ethnic student groups, organizations, or clubs are there? Does the college have a minority affairs officer or a minority recruitment officer? Is there a women's study program or major?

In Your Department

How does your department respond to or address diversity issues? You may wish to suggest that selected topics be included in departmental meetings. For example, are course requirements equitable for all students? Are course prerequisites fair and just? What type of orientation program is provided for new students, new majors, and transfer students? What are the graduation rates and job placement data for majors? What types of extracurricular activities and support services are available for students? How does your department interface with the English as a Second Language program?

In the Community

While learning about the college it would also be valuable to learn as much as you can about the community in which the college exists. What has been the historical relationship between the college and the local community? What is the current atmosphere between the community and the college? It would also be valuable to seek out and investigate any ethnic, cultural, or racial support groups, clubs, or organizations in the local community.

A Final Thought

As we've discussed, the more opportunities students and teachers have to get together (in class and outside of class), the more every student will invest in learning. Showing a preference for one group of students to the exclusion of another negates the educational benefits of this principal.

Exhibiting disrespect or inappropriate verbal responses to students of minority backgrounds creates an environment of power rather than one of pedagogy. In short, teaching college is not about how much you know, but rather it's about how well you interact with students—all students!

The Least You Need to Know

- ◆ The diversity of students in college classrooms provides unique learning opportunities.

- ◆ It's important that everyone be treated fairly and equitably.

- ◆ Good relationships with students are built on trust and understanding.

- ◆ Working toward a balanced course should be a priority.

- ◆ Most institutions have a variety of resources to offer minority students.

Chapter 15

Teaching Large Classes

In This Chapter

- ◆ Organization is the key
- ◆ Getting students actively involved
- ◆ Written assignments
- ◆ Outside reading assignments
- ◆ The anonymity factor

You've just walked into your first college course: an 8:00 Introduction to Psychology class. It's a cavernous lecture hall with endless rows of theater seats. Filling those seats are 250 undergraduates—those in the front rows are awake, those in the back are quietly dozing. Elsewhere there is an atmosphere of controlled chaos—some students are shaking off the effects of last night's fraternity party, several are having intense cell phone conversations, others are doodling, many are consuming a semi-nutritious breakfast of a latte and a donut, and a good number would probably prefer to be somewhere else. There's also a wandering dog or two for added effect.

How do you teach all these students? How do you make your presentation engaging and meaningful? How do you *keep them awake* for the next 50 or 75 minutes? Each year, these questions strike fear into the hearts of new professors. Let's take a look at how you can address (and teach) large groups of students for maximum effect and maximum learning.

Same Old, Same Old

You may remember your days as an undergraduate in a large lecture hall. You were once one of scores (or perhaps hundreds) of other students (typically freshmen and sophomores) taking a required liberal arts course. The professor may have seemed distant (physically and psychologically) and you may have felt distinctly disconnected from the instructor, the material, and the whole class. You may have felt like nothing but a number—a small cog in a very large machine.

Now, it's your turn to teach one or more of these enormous courses. How can you do it successfully while still maintaining your sanity? Let's take a look at some suggestions.

Organization Is Crucial

Large classes take lots of extra planning. It is virtually impossible to give a lecture to a large group of students off the cuff. Don't walk into a large lecture hall without a complete and detailed set of notes about what you are going to teach. If you've got nothing but a few "war stories" from your days as an undergraduate student or a practitioner in the field, you will be setting yourself up for failure. I can't stress enough the need for planning (indeed, overplanning) to ensure that students' time (and yours) is well spent. For the most part, students don't like these large, impersonal formats; don't add to their "uncomfortableness" by being less than prepared.

Mike Messner, a professor of sociology at the University of Southern California, says that he designs large lecture courses in four steps: "Prior to class, I want students to do lots of reading. Then, in class, I give them lots of examples of my own past, including personal anecdotes and things that have happened to me. These stories help students grasp the concepts in a lesson. Third, I provide a PowerPoint presentation with important concepts. Finally, I finish the lecture with information on how the key concepts impact them."

Here are a few tips: first, review the chapter on effective lecturing (Chapter 9). What applies in small classes also holds true for large sections, too. Let students know that you are organized and prepared for them. Remember to model the same kinds of behaviors that you expect of them. Spend the first 3 minutes of class briefly outlining the information, activities, objectives, and procedures for the class. If you're comfortable with it, use the same style as the 1-minute "promos" delivered by your local news station ("This afternoon a noted celebrity donated $100,000 to a local cause. Tune in at 11:00 for all the details.").

If you use PowerPoint, project your notes on the screen for everyone. I prefer to use an overhead projector that projects the three or four objectives of the lesson. As I discuss each one, I use a transparency pen to check it off. This provides students with visual proof of what was "covered" and what's to come.

If possible, provide students with a set of lecture notes as they enter the room. This can be a detailed outline of the topics and concepts to be shared in class, or I prefer to provide a set of questions I'll answer in the day's presentation. In front of each question is a small box that can be checked off when the question has been addressed. I've also found these useful at the end of class when I invite students to ask any unanswered questions on their lists.

Red Flag

The minimum font size for any overhead transparency (or PowerPoint presentation) is 24 points—no less! If you don't know whether a transparency is 24-point or not, lay the transparency on the floor and stand over it. If you can't read it without bending over, the font is too small.

Post a study guide for each lecture on your class website. You may elect to have this guide posted before class or immediately after. There are advantages to both. If you post it in advance, students can see the primary points to be covered and bring questions. If done after class, the guide can help students fill in any blanks left in class.

Red Flag

Jessica Nolan, an assistant professor of biology, posits an interesting notion that guides her courses. She says, "Concepts lead to class discussions, while facts lead to more lecture."

The downside of this approach is that students may feel that they don't need to attend class, and instead just look at the notes each week. You can address this concern by posting an abbreviated form of the material.

Active Student Involvement

Nothing does more to disinterest students in a topic or a course than knowing that every one of their large class sessions will be done in the same format or style. If students expect that every class will be a long-winded lecture, they will be considerably less involved in the dynamics of the course and considerably less motivated to learn the material.

As shared in previous chapter, variety is the spice of life. This is equally true in large classes as it is in smaller seminar-type classes. Here are some techniques you can use in your large sections:

Start the class with a question ("Someone once said that 'Art defines a culture.' What does that mean? Turn to the person sitting next to you and create a response. You have 2 minutes."). By letting students know that they will be intellectually engaged right at the beginning of class, they will be more prone to staying engaged throughout the class.

If possible, bring a small group of students to the front of the room or on stage. Divide this group into two camps, pro and con. Give the two groups a concept or principle to debate. This will be unscripted, but if you provide students with guide sheets or hand-outs describing how a debate "works" this can be a valuable teaching tool—particularly if used several times throughout the semester. Students will tend to pay (more) attention when their fellow students are on stage.

Invite colleagues or outside experts into the class to debate an issue or concern with you. Each individual can take an opposing position and defend his or her thoughts. Invite selected students to comment afterwards.

Consider using a "fishbowl" in selected classes. Randomly select six to eight students and invite them to discuss some of the concepts, principles, or ideas shared during the class. Have the remaining students observe the discussion and record the information shared. Afterwards, have them write a brief summary of the events. They may also wish to pose any unanswered questions—questions that you can respond to in a follow-up session.

From the Field

Brian Furio, an associate professor of communication, makes it a point to insert some key phrases at the end of each "block." Here are some he especially likes: "The real key component is ...," "This is important because ...," "Here's the critical part/element ...," and "The one thing you want to remember is ...."

If you have teaching assistants, invite them to place themselves throughout the lecture hall. Provide time during the presentation for students to direct their questions to the teaching assistants. Schedule one or two in-class Q&A sessions in which a group of students interacts with a teaching assistant. Afterwards, ask the teaching assistants to share some of the information discussed in the various groups.

Make sure you divide any presentation into "blocks." You may wish to review the information in Chapter 8— it's relevant for small classes and large lectures, too. Consider using two or three teaching methods in every large presentation, just as you would for a smaller class.

The conventions for many professional organizations schedule "poster sessions." These are informal opportunities for one or two persons to discuss their latest research or observations about a specific topic. There is usually a board or wall on which charts, graphs, or other display items can be posted. The presenter may give a brief talk and then be available for questions. This technique would also be appropriate for large class sessions, too. Students will need some instructions and directions in order for it to be successful. A few poster sessions can be scheduled throughout the semester.

Red Flag

Richard Fliegel, assistant dean of Academic Programs at the University of Southern California, says that it is important to remember that "classes are different from each other. No single class is the same. If something doesn't work with one class, that doesn't mean it won't work with another."

Write On

If you've got 250 students, you've also got the task of grading any work they submit as part of your course assignments. You probably don't want to assign five or six writing assignments to a large section since the time necessary to grade all that work would be simply unimaginable.

Since grading written work becomes almost prohibitive in a large section of students, you may wish to consider some of the following alternatives.

I've often used the "one-minute paper" as a writing tool in large sections. At an appropriate point in the presentation, invite students to each take out a sheet of paper and respond to a question, issue, concern, or piece of information in 60 seconds or less. When the time's up, invite students to submit their papers to you for review, or have students exchange their papers with each other for written or verbal comments or review.

Consider the "one-page-only paper." Invite students to respond to a question raised in class. They may use only one side (single or double-space) of a single sheet of paper for their response. These become very easy to read because the length of each response is limited to 250 to 500 words.

The "30 percent rule" is another way of addressing a large number of written assignments in a large class section. Provide a brief writing assignment to the class, but announce that you will randomly select 30 percent (or any other percentage of your choice) of the papers to review and grade.

By reading just a limited number of papers, you will get a generic idea of how all the students think about a topic or how they interpret a principle or concern. You will also reduce your reading time. You can then share and discuss the common factors with the class as a whole. This strategy releases students from the burden of having every paper graded and also provides you with important information on how they are thinking about a topic.

Invite students to exchange, read, and review each other's papers. Provide students with a standardized rubric (see Chapter 17) each of them can use to "grade" their classmate's work. Students may wish to share their reviews in a scheduled follow-up session or submit them to you for evaluation.

If you have teaching assistants for the course, invite them to thoroughly review a selection of assigned papers using a standard rubric (be sure you provide them with adequate training on the use of the rubric). Afterwards, you can quickly review the papers and record a brief comment or message on each one.

The trick is to have a balance between the number of papers you want to assign, the number of students in a class, and the number of hours you will have available to evaluate that written work. There is no magic formula. However, as the examples above prove, you can deal with written work in a variety of ways without sacrificing your course goals or the learning opportunities for students.

To Test, To Test

Evaluating student performance in a large class can be both problematic as well as demanding. Imagine trying to read, review, and grade five or six essay questions for a midterm exam given to a class of 300 students. It would be a physical, psychological, and mental impossibility. However, with some modifications and a little creativity, you can create an evaluation system that respects your time limitations and effectively evaluates students' performance.

I heartily recommend that you *not* use "pop quizzes," in large or small classes. Pop quizzes may seem easy to construct, administer, and grade, but the negatives far outweigh the positives.

These random assessments do nothing to create good relationships between professors and their students. Second, they're often viewed as punitive measures by students—something done to test content rather that teach concepts. Third, any quiz or exam given to a large section must be carefully planned out and designed. The questions must be carefully executed, time must be allocated for the preparation and duplication process, and a sufficient amount of grading time must be allocated. Pop quizzes are often viewed as a "gotcha," something that is done *to* students at their expense, rather than as a teaching or learning tool carefully woven into the course design.

Take the time to carefully plan and construct any objective questions for a test. Just as you would with a smaller section, include a selection of question types from different levels of cognition (see Chapter 12). The use of a multiple-choice exam provides you with the opportunity to grade it using scan sheets and appropriate software.

Provide students with an essay exam composed of several different questions. Invite them to each select one question to which they will respond, or randomly assign the questions according to last name, seat, birthday, or some other device. The advantage is that students will prepare by studying all the necessary information, but won't know in advance the question they will need to answer. You have the advantage of grading only one question per student, while still observing how your students are absorbing the concepts learned up to that point in the course.

Provide students with an objective test (multiple choice questions, for example). Include one essay question at the end. Tell students that they have the option of answering the essay question if their grade is on the borderline between two grades. Or, tell all students to answer the essay question, but that you will only grade it if it will significantly raise their test or course grade.

Several weeks before the end of the semester, provide students with a take-home final exam. Tell students that they may elect to complete the take-home exam only if they would like to have it factored into their final grade for the course. Students who are comfortable with their grade for a course need not take the final if they so choose.

You may find it advantageous for students to take exams in a group format. Divide the class into several different groups. Give the exam to each group and have them work together. Be clear that all group members will share in the final grade! Besides significantly reducing your workload, this technique provides meaningful discussions between students (which alerts you to any misperceptions or inappropriate conclusions) and fosters cooperative learning techniques.

Outside Reading Assignments

One of the other factors you must consider when teaching a class of many students is the utilization of outside reading resources—those resources in addition to the course textbook. One of the challenges is the simple availability of sufficient copies of those resources for every student in the course. Three hundred copies of a monograph by a leading researcher in your field would be problematic for the college library to obtain or provide. As a result, the need for outside reading assignments must be carefully considered in the planning for any large course.

Here are a few considerations you may wish to think about relative to outside readings. Choose your textbook carefully. Does it provide students with a balanced approach to your subject, or does it need to be supplemented with outside readings? Those readings may include additional materials purchased by students or materials that can be made available through the resources of the college library. If in doubt, always take time to talk with the college librarians about the practicality of assigned library readings versus purchased materials.

Consider providing students with a list of specific websites or electronic articles in lieu of printed materials. Many college libraries also have an electronic reserve system which posts copies of specific reading materials on the library's computer. Students can access the material in the library or other locations on or off campus.

Consider the use of course packets. There are several commercial firms who will gather together articles and other publications (along with the necessary copyrights) and duplicate them in a packet for students to purchase along with the textbook. As a professor, you can specify which articles, monographs, handouts, conference proceedings, or other items you want in these packets. Many research institutions have their own procedures for producing these packets in-house. Check with your department chairperson or appropriate dean to determine the procedures in place at your specific institution.

Consider setting up a class website on which you can post selected articles (or the Internet links to those articles). This allows large numbers of students the option of accessing that information at their convenience.

The Anonymity Factor

Large classes are often the rule at large institutions. They are the administrative method of choice for teaching required courses to large masses of students. But they come with a price—many students become anonymous, disengaged, and often disconnected in these classes.

It is easy for some students to "hide" in a large class than in a small seminar. Admittedly, some students prefer this sense of disconnectiveness, yet we know that anonymity tends to create lower levels of motivation, less involvement in the subject matter, and more opportunities for uncivil behavior (see Chapter 16). Students' feelings of anonymity determine, in large measure, their engagement (and ultimate success) in a course.

"Research Says"

Social psychologists have drawn parallels between the size of a group and the degree of anonymity experienced by any single individual within that group. In short, the larger the group, the more disconnected a person feels. In college classes there is a direct correlation between group size and students' sense of self (larger classes = more anonymity).

With large classes it will be a challenge to establish and maintain connections with your students. Yet, the efforts can be well worth it—particularly in terms of student engagement, participation, and identity.

If you are in a large lecture hall, see if you can get a wireless microphone. Walk up and down the aisles looking at students, asking specific questions, and listening carefully to their responses. Moving away from the podium or stage and down into the audience has long been used by performers to significantly shorten the distance between themselves and their audience.

Come to class a few minutes early and walk among students. Greet them by name, welcome them to the day's class, and spend a few moments talking about the big game last weekend, a cultural event on campus, or some bit of national or regional news. Don't begin a class by walking in and immediately perching yourself and your notes behind a podium or lectern.

Create a seating chart that has student names (and photos, when available). When you pose questions to the class, make sure you ask specific students, by name, and spread your attention around the room.

Provide an opportunity in each class for student pairs or triads to work together. Ask a question and invite students to turn to one or two neighbors to discuss a possible response. You may wish to invite these small groups to define some terminology, create a question that they would like answered, or to recapitulate a portion of the class for others. Randomly call on selected groups to share their response with the whole class.

Offer opportunities for students to engage in buzz sessions or small discussion groups.

From the Field

According to professor of sociology Mike Messner, "A good lecturer is clearly organized. He or she tells stories in order to connect with the audience in personal ways. Then, the lecturer connects the stories to concepts. The stories are the hook; the concepts are the meat of the course."

Pose a problem and invite students to tackle it in groups. Circulate among the groups (if possible) and listen in on their conversations.

Ask students to create "snowball" groups. Ask a question at a specific level of cognition (see Chapter 12). Invite two students to discuss a possible response then join with another two students to arrive at a mutually satisfactory response. Then, ask one four-person team to join with another four-person team to create an answer acceptable to all eight individuals. Randomly call on two or three eight-person teams to share and defend their responses.

Invite students to participate in informal discussion groups after class. Provide some coffee and donuts. Encourage students to set the agenda (which may or may not be class-related).

Once a week, set up an informal buzz session in your office or commons area. Send out invitations to students randomly selected from your class list (Note: Send out at least twice as many invitations as the number of students you expect).

As students arrive, randomly pass out 5 to 10 simple class evaluation sheets such as the one below. Meet with the students after class to discuss their observations. If time is a factor, you may wish to respond to their comments via a group e-mail. Consider incorporating their views and opinions into a subsequent class.

Class Reaction Form

Name: _____ E-mail: _____

Course: _____ Date: _____

Please complete this form by the conclusion of today's class. You may hand it to me or drop it in the box in the back of the hall. Please be honest in your assessment. I may wish to contact you for further details or information. Thank you in advance.

1. One point or piece of information that was particularly clear:

2. One question that I still have about the topic:

3. Something else I'd like to know:

Most large classes are supplemented with regularly scheduled seminars or discussion groups. These are often led by teaching assistants. Plan to stop by these sessions occasionally to chat with students or listen in on their conversations.

Assist students in setting up study groups outside of class. Use your institution's technology to establish chat rooms, a calendar of available meeting rooms and times, instant messaging groups, or videoconferencing sessions across campus.

As practical, provide opportunities for breakout groups to work on a problem or a specific task. Divide the class into groups of 15 to 20 students each. Invite them to use corners of the room, a hallway, a nearby empty classroom, or some other space to meet. Each group then reports on their deliberations (to the whole class) after a specified period of time. The trick to making these sessions work is to keep the time frame limited and tight (15 minutes maximum). Plan to circulate among the groups during their deliberations.

From the Field _____

Richard Fliegel of the University of Southern California says that the bottom line is "students want a live faculty member who is engaging and cares about them."

Four Keys to Success

Here are four essential points that you should keep in mind as you begin designing a course for a large number of students:

◆ Don't turn the course into an endless series of impersonal lectures.

◆ Provide students with multiple opportunities to become actively engaged in the dynamics of the course. Use a variety of teaching methodologies.

◆ Connect with students as often as you can. Meet with them before and after class in both planned and unplanned sessions.

◆ Use technology to your advantage. Consider technology as a way to present information to large numbers of students as well as a way for large numbers of students to access information relative to your course.

The Least You Need to Know

◆ Large classes require extra planning and organization.

◆ Students can become actively engaged in large classes with the proper activities.

◆ Written assignments and exams need to be structured differently.

◆ Outside reading assignments should be adjusted and modified.

◆ In large classes there is a tendency for students to lose their identity.

Chapter 16

Problem Students (and the Solution)

In This Chapter

- ◆ Unprepared students
- ◆ Inattentive students
- ◆ Aggressive students
- ◆ Discouraged students
- ◆ Attention-seeking students
- ◆ Teacher behaviors

Imagine the following classroom scenarios: you walk into the room and a student approaches you and tells you to "take a hike" (or other words which can't be printed here) after getting a less-than-memorable paper back. A small group of students talks during your entire presentation. A third student has his hand raised for every question you ask in class. Another student is busy drawing doodles in the margins of his textbook. A fifth student comes up to you after class and says how much she "loves your course" (it's the eighth time this semester she's said it). A sixth student tells you that her grandmother is sick back home and she must miss the next 2 weeks of class—can she take the midterm exam when she returns?

Such class situations may be out of the ordinary, but one or more of the students profiled above will find their way into your courses. How do you deal with these "problem students"?

A Community of Learners (Revisited)

Earlier in this book I talked about the value of establishing a "community of learners" in your courses. When students feel a connection with other students and the professor, their likelihood of academic achievement blossoms accordingly. Conversely, when students feel disenfranchised or disconnected from the class, their academic performance suffers, as does their self-concept.

The key to any successful academic venture is to create a community that values all participants and their contributions. Will that eliminate all the problems students bring to class? No, but it will provide you with a foundation from which you can approach and deal with the most common problems in a supportive and encouraging environment.

In short, students are not the enemy. True, they bring their own unique characteristics and personality dynamics to a classroom (just as we bring ours). It's not a matter of isolating those behaviors from the mainstream, but rather of working to involve those students into the culture of the classroom.

Let's take a look at some of those challenges.

Unprepared Students

It is quite common to have unprepared students in your classes. They may neglect to read the assigned chapters in the textbook, fail to turn in papers on time, be unprepared for discussions or group work, or seem disconnected from the other students in the course.

In my own work with students and in conversations with other professors, I've discovered some practical and universal ideas that will help you deal with unprepared students. Here are some suggested approaches.

Make sure that the assigned readings, scheduled exams, and other course requirements are clearly and sufficiently detailed in the course syllabus. Unprepared students often don't know the precise expectations of the course. If necessary, list each day of the semester and the readings, quizzes, exams, and papers due for each particular date. My own preference is to list each week of the semester in a spreadsheet and the specific assignments and responsibilities scheduled for that time frame.

Sometimes, at the beginning of the semester, I will tell students that each day they come to class I will provide them with a one-question quiz on the assigned reading for that class. When students arrive, there is a slip of paper with a single question on each desk—a question that can only be answered after having read the assigned pages in the text. They have 3 to 4 minutes to answer the question. These are collected and factored into each student's final grade. Later in the semester, instead of having these every day, I may reduce this to a weekly event. The message, however, is very clear. The assigned material must be read in order to respond to the one-question quiz each class. Students cannot be unprepared.

Start each class with focus groups. Let students know that when they arrive to class they will be working with other students on a specific topic or problem-solving experience. Each student must be prepared in order to contribute to the group. Walk around the room and monitor each group's activities. Consider some of the cooperative learning strategies in Chapter 11.

Another technique I've used with considerable success is to purchase a set of wooden craft sticks from a local hobby store. Each student is given a stick and asked to write her or his name on it. I collect all the sticks and store them in a small box. Each day I bring the box to class and ask someone to randomly select one or two of the sticks. I then call on the students whose names appear on those sticks to respond to a question about a reading assignment or to provide a brief summary of the assignment. Each day no one knows whose names are going to be chosen, so everyone must be prepared to respond just in case. This activity, which only takes about 5 minutes, sends a clear message that preparation before class is both necessary and important.

Inattentive Students

Typically, inattentiveness in students arises as a result of one of two factors. If the material is too complex or confusing, many students tend to zone out and disconnect from the class. They often engage in conversations, catnaps, doodling, or other inappropriate behaviors. It's also possible that they're just not aware of or practiced in appropriate social graces or expectations.

Here are some suggestions for you to consider. Be clear about your expectations for classroom behavior on the first day of class. State those expectations verbally and be sure to back them up in writing throughout the syllabus.

Always have a physical presence throughout a classroom. If you're always parked behind a podium for the duration of every class, students—particularly those in the back of the room—will have more of a tendency to disconnect from the class. Move around the room, call on students from every quadrant of the class, speak from the front, sides, and back of the room. Your physical presence throughout the classroom is a major deterrent to inattentiveness.

Examine the material you are sharing with students. Is it too complex? Is it confusing? Is there too much theory and not enough practical applications? If inattentiveness is a persistent problem in your courses, it may a result of the material rather than a fault of the students.

Once again, I strongly suggest that you provide at least one activity in each class in which students work in small groups. I like to randomize the groups each time so that the same students are not always working together. I'll assign random numbers to individuals ("All the 3's will form a group"), or assign students to groups based on birthdays, the color of their shoes, or some type of random sorting. If there are several inattentive individuals in a class, this ensures that they would be equitably distributed throughout the groups. These students then become responsible to the members of a group and their successful completion of a specific task. I always make it a point to "travel" around the room to monitor each group's progress as well as the contributions of each member.

Use low-profile intervention. When you spot an inattentive student, use the student's name in part of your presentation. For example, "As an example, let's imagine that Darren is John Scopes. How does he rationalize the teaching of evolution during this time period?" Darren, who has been whispering to a fellow student, hears his name and is drawn back into the lesson. Sprinkling these interventions periodically through-out a course helps keep everyone on their toes.

Aggressive Students

It's not unusual for some students to want to challenge their professors. They may have some previous knowledge about a topic and want to assert their beliefs or opinions. Or, they may simply be confrontational individuals who relish the thought of engaging in verbal battle. Doing so—particularly with a person in authority—often gives them a sense of power and control.

If you have an aggressive or challenging student in your class, there are two things you must never do. One, do not ignore the behavior. Doing so only adds fuel to the fire and raises the intensity of the individual's argument and frustration. Second, never verbally attack the student—particularly in front of other students. You will immediately lose any credibility and will come off as dictatorial, unsympathetic, and dogmatic.

Rather, here are some suggested tips for dealing with aggressive students. Take the time to listen carefully to the student's argument. Provide the student with an opportunity to get her or his position out in the open, where it can be addressed and/or discussed.

Acknowledge the student's anger. ("You seem to be quite upset by this.") This alone will diffuse some of the anger, let the student know that you are listening to her or him, and begin to build a common ground on which an ensuing discussion can begin.

From the Field

Robert Rotenberg, a professor of anthropology at DePaul University, says, "Anger is often a mask for fear. If you respond to the fear instead of the anger, you can diffuse it. Always allow [the student] a way to gracefully retreat from the confrontation."

As appropriate, bring other students into the situation. For example, "Marcia is quite upset about my position on this issue. Does anyone else feel this way?" Invite others to express their feelings or perceptions. True, Marcia may gain additional allies, but even more important, she no longer feels cornered and alone, and her anger is dissipated among members of her peer group. This also gives you additional time to ponder an appropriate response. In many cases you can turn the experience into an interesting class discussion by posing a series of leading questions ("Are there other feelings we're not expressing here?" "Would others look at this in the same way?" "How could we organize these thoughts on the chalkboard?")

Whenever a student becomes angry and/or verbally adamant about a certain point, I usually invite her or him to come up to the front of the room. (The physical act of walking to the front of the room tends to dissipate some of the anger and allows the student a little time to rethink or reconsider the initial argument.) While the student is coming forward I locate two chairs, place them side by side in the front of the room, and invite the student to sit down. (It's much harder to be aggressive when sitting down than when standing up.)

I'll invite the student to restate her or his case (another way to defuse the anger) and then ask if I could restate my position. Then I'll invite other students to enter in on either side of the "debate." Irrespective of the position they choose (mine or the angry student), a conversation has been started which can lead to new observations or new insights. I've found this to be an important way of modeling critical thinking—that is, informed people must be able to look at all the evidence—both pro and con—in reaching a decision. Listening to and considering divergent views on a topic is academic growth at its finest. In addition, the act of sitting side by side not only reduces the physical distance between individuals, it also reduces the emotional distance.

If it seems that a student's anger is directed at you rather than at your ideas (for example, the student believes that your course requirements are excessive, or you assigned a grade on a paper that was unfair, or even that you are incompetent), invite the student to meet with you personally to discuss the situation. Here are some specific tips:

- Listen carefully and respectfully.

- Don't prejudge. Encourage the student to state her or his case or rationale completely *before* making any comments or decisions.

- Never put down the student or her or his opinion.

- Don't assume an authoritarian or defensive position. Let the student know that it may be possible to reach a mutually agreeable decision.

- By the same token, let the student know that you have a responsibility to be fair and equitable to everyone. Your final decision may not be the one the student wants to hear, but it will be based on an assessment of all the evidence.

- If applicable, let the student know that you would be willing to revisit the concern at any time. Promote an open-door policy.

- Thank the student for the meeting and for taking time out of her or his busy schedule to discuss the issue.

The key to dealing with angry or aggressive students is to become an "active listener." In active listening you respond to a student by using some of the student's remarks, thoughts, or ideas in any feedback. Here are some examples:

Student: "You know, I think this whole thing about birth control is way off base. What gives those religious zealots the right to determine how I should live my life?"

You: "So, Sarah, you think that religion is dictating how you should live your life. Is that right?"

Student: "You know, your grading policy really sucks! Nobody's ever going to get an A in this class."

You: "Karl, you seem upset by the fact that my grading procedures appear harsh and unfair. Would you care to elaborate?"

Discouraged Students

Frequently, students begin the semester with a great deal of enthusiasm and energy. However, as the assignments begin to pile up, the requirements become more demanding, and the pressures escalate, some students experience a sense of discouragement. They may miss classes, submit papers after the dues date, or maintain a lethargic attitude in class.

While this is not an unusual condition, there are some surprisingly effective measures you can implement to deal with this "condition."

In previous chapters we've discussed the value of an open letter to a class from a previous student or students. These letters have many advantages, particularly as a way to address the needs of students who are easily discouraged. The effect is amazing—students quickly realize that their contemporaries were able to successfully "survive" the course with a little extra effort, time with the instructor, new resources, or other strategies and devices. Among other things, these letters really help to get a new course off on a very positive note.

From the Field

Here is part of a letter a previous student addressed to the new students in a course I teach every semester:

"Dear Fellow Students:

Welcome back to a new semester! By now, I am certain that you have been given the class syllabus and are feeling slightly confused and/or overwhelmed. Hopefully, when you have finished listening to this letter, you will feel more confident in your ability to complete the assignments given to you. I would like to present you with an overview of what to expect from this course and [the professor], as well as what to expect of yourself. I will also provide you with advice that should be useful in accomplishing the tasks outlined in your syllabus."

Here's a modification of the previous suggestion. If there is a particularly challenging assignment that you give students each semester, invite a student from a previous class to write an open letter specifically on how she or he was able to tackle that specific assignment, what was learned, the personal benefits, and perhaps one or two study techniques. Read this letter to students in the current class immediately after you make the assignment or midway through the period of time students would be working on that assignment. You will probably notice an immediate and significant improvement in students' overall attitude toward the assignment. When students hear that their contemporaries have successfully "made the grade," they are inspired to do the same.

Wilbert McKeachie of the University of Michigan suggests that you may want to consider bringing in a student from the previous semester and inviting that person to describe their experiences of frustration and self-doubt and how they surmounted them and survived. This pep talk alerts students to the fact that the situation is temporary and can be successfully addressed.

If you notice that a student is persistently discouraged and down, invite that individual to meet with you in your office. Take time to find out the root cause of the discouragement. It may have nothing to do with you or the course, but may involve family issues, personal crises, or work-related problems. Be sure to have contact information readily available about the campus counseling center, tutoring bureau, mental heath center, campus ministry, or learning disabilities office. Make the appropriate referrals as appropriate and follow-up with the student within a week to see if the necessary contacts have been made.

Attention-Seeking Students

You've probably seen them. They're the ones who always have something to say, the ones who always have their hand in the air when a question is asked, and the ones who are always hogging the instructor's time both before and after class. Not surprisingly, you can expect them to show up in your courses, too.

Here are a few ideas for your consideration. I sometimes tell students that, in order to be fair and equitable to everyone, whenever I ask a question, I won't ask for hands. I'll merely direct the question to a specific individual in the class. In this way I can rotate the questions around the room and ensure that everyone has an opportunity to contribute during a single class. Also, since students don't know who will be called on and don't have the luxury of deciding if they do or do not want to respond to a question, they must all pay attention.

"Divide and conquer" is another effective technique in handling attention seekers. Since they want attention from the largest audience possible, reduce the size of the audience. Every other class or so, I make sure to have at least one activity in which students must work in pairs (or perhaps triads). I'll often put each attention seeker in a position of authority—she or he is the recorder for the group's activities, deliberations, or decisions.

Red Flag

Interestingly, some students have "marked" new professors for extra attention because they think that the novices won't have the "thick skin" of more experienced faculty members and that they'll be easier to influence. Be forewarned!

After about the third week of the semester, present students with a mini-lecture on importance of having everyone contribute to the class. Solicit suggestions and ideas from students on how to facilitate that process for the remainder of the course. Students will often come up with practical and useful ideas that will dissipate the influence of attention seekers. I sometimes convert their ideas into an overhead transparency or chart which can be reviewed on an as-needed basis throughout the semester.

As a last resort, invite a colleague to videotape one or two class sessions. Invite the attention seekers to view the videotape and comment on their "performance." Ask them to discuss how their actions may be influencing the opportunities for all students to participate in the dynamics of the class.

"The Fault, Dear Brutus ..."

Many interesting observations have been made about student's behavior in college classes, and what we see is that the instructor often inadvertently fosters and creates problems through certain types of management procedures.

How many of the following teacher behaviors have you experienced or seen (in elementary school, high school, or college):

◆ **Extreme negativity:** The instructor's comments to the class are frequently couched in negative and/or highly authoritarian terms. ("It's obvious that nobody knows anything about Kreb's Cycle. It looks like many of you will fail the midterm on Thursday.")

◆ **Excessive authoritarian climate:** These instructors desire to be the absolute and complete authority figure in a course. All decisions are theirs. ("It's my way or the highway!")

◆ **Overreacting:** This instructor creates mountains out of molehills by escalating minor infractions into major ones. ("I'm tired of your inattentiveness. From now on if anyone is caught not paying attention in class you will be asked to leave the room.")

◆ **Mass punishment:** These instructors hope peer pressure will result in a change or behavior for a few select students. ("It's obvious that the two of you just can't stop talking, so I'm going to have to make up the time by eliminating the video I had planned for today.")

◆ **Lack of instructional goals:** Often instructors will attempt to engage students without a clearly defined or clearly understood (by students) goals for the lesson. ("OK, is there anything anyone wants to talk about before we begin?")

◆ **Repeating or reviewing already understood material:** In an effort to make sure students are exposed to important material, professors might constantly repeat material over and over again in the same way. There is no challenge. ("All right, I want you to look up the definitions for these 20 words, write them in your notebooks, and then record them again on this wall chart.")

◆ **Fixating on a single student:** This teacher often disrupts her or his own instructional rhythm by spending an inordinate amount of time on one student. ("I can't believe that, once again, you are late for class, Jennifer. I've talked to you over and over about your tardiness." [Five minutes of lecture ensue.])

A combination of these teacher behaviors can create and promote significant student problems in any classroom. Avoiding these behaviors will go a long way toward creating a climate of trust and caring that will significantly reduce any potential misbehavior.

Tips for Achieving Discipline

Discipline is not about getting students to do what you want. That's what dictators do, and you're not a dictator—you're an educator. Discipline is providing an environment in which positive teaching and positive learning can occur simultaneously. Discipline is not control from the outside; it's order from within.

In conversations with colleagues, I've discovered some practical and universal ideas that will help you achieve discipline in your courses. Tap into the experience of these pros and turn your classroom into a place where students learn and enjoy the process.

Interact with your students on a personal level every day. Greet them by name, interject a positive comment or observation, and welcome them into the classroom. I make it a practice to come to each class at least 5 or 6 minutes early. I can chat with students about vacation plans, a recent athletic competition, a musical group on campus, even the weather. These small conversations help establish the classroom as a positive and supportive environment. They also personalize the professor/student relationship and make discipline problems less likely.

Get students focused and be sure you have their attention before you begin. Don't try to talk over students; you'll be initiating a competition to see who can speak louder, and also let them know it's OK to talk while you're talking.

Use positive presence. Don't park yourself in the front of the room for an entire class period. Move around the room continuously, and get in and around your students. Make frequent eye contact, and smile with students. Monitor students with your physical presence.

 Red Flag

> Teachers often make the mistake of using "stop" messages rather than a "start" message. For example, "Stop talking in the back. We need to get started." A better message is "Please turn to page 11 of Thompson's monograph on commercial banking systems." The effect is tremendous. It establishes a productive, businesslike tone for the lesson. The focus is not on the (negative) behavior, but the importance of the lesson.

Verbal reprimands should be private, brief, and as immediate as possible. The more private a reprimand, the less likely you will be challenged. The more immediate the reprimand, the less likely the students will feel you condone her or his behavior. And keep reprimands brief. The more you talk, the more you distract from the lesson and the more you "reward" a student for inappropriate behavior

Be consistent! Although this is easier said than done, the key to an effective discipline policy in your classes is consistency. Make these principles part of your daily action plan:

- ◆ If you have a rule, enforce that rule.

- ◆ Don't hand out lots of warnings without following through on consequences. Lots of warnings tell students that you won't enforce a rule.

"Research Says"

The research is overwhelmingly clear: model the behavior you want students to produce. If you exhibit respectfulness, trust, enthusiasm, interest, and courtesy in your everyday dealings with students, they will return the favor in kind.

◆ Be fair and impartial. The rules are there for everyone, and that includes blondes as well as redheads, athletes as well as nonathletes, 18-year-olds as well as 40-year-olds, and happy people as well as grumpy people.

The Least You Need to Know

◆ There are several strategies that will engage unprepared and inattentive students.

◆ Dealing with aggressive students requires a special set of skills.

◆ It's important to address the immediate needs of discouraged students.

◆ Attention-seeking students should be dealt with quickly and compassionately.

◆ Some of the problems in a classroom may be exacerbated by teachers.

Part 5

Challenges and Possibilities

Teaching college is much more than standing in front of a group of students and talking about your vast knowledge of a subject. All sorts of challenges await you around every corner and throughout every semester.

In Part 5, I'll offer you some interesting insights into what some may call "administrivia." Specifically, I'll share with you how you can effectively and efficiently evaluate the progress of your students. I'll also introduce you to the conditions of good internships and productive long-distance education courses. We'll also spend some time looking at some of the causes and cures of the stuff they never tell you about in the interview—attendance, tardiness, cheating, and late assignments. It's a jam-packed section, so hang on!

"What I have here is an honor code that you signed at the start of this semester."

Chapter 17

Evaluation of Students

In This Chapter

- ◆ The nature of evaluation
- ◆ Performance-based evaluation
- ◆ Learning-centered evaluation
- ◆ Student self-evaluation
- ◆ Some final thoughts

If truth be told, there's a gremlin lurking in every college course. Evaluation—how we determine whether our students have accomplished the goals of the course—is a gremlin that hovers over the class, provides anxiety for teachers and students alike, and is often the ultimate perception of the difficulty (or utility) of a course in the life of a college student.

Too often, evaluation is viewed as something that does not celebrate effective teaching or honor good learning. Frequently, it sends a chilling message that the product is more important than the process. It is often viewed as an ingrained system of reward and punishment that may have little connection to the primary goals of helping us become more effective teachers and helping students become better learners.

The Nature of the Beast

Evaluation is not a new concept for you; however, in most previous situations you were probably the one being tested. As you move into college teaching, you will assume the responsibilities of an evaluator. You will be required to determine how well your students are learning, gauge their performance, and measure the appropriateness of the content and the effectiveness of the methods and techniques utilized in your classroom.

Effective evaluation is a continuous process, not just something you do at the end of a unit or semester. Much more than determining the products of learning, it is rather a way of gauging learning over time. Learning and evaluation are never completed; they are always evolving and developing. You should integrate effective evaluation into all aspects of a course, providing both students and yourself with relevant and useful data to gauge the class's progress and determine the effectiveness of the materials and procedures you're using.

A variety of evaluative tools are necessary to provide the most accurate evaluation of students' learning and progress. Your dependence on one type of tool to the exclusion of others deprives students of valuable learning opportunities and robs you of measures that help both students and the courses you teach grow.

Evaluation must be a collaborative activity between you and your students. Students must be able to assume an active role in evaluation so that they can begin to develop individual responsibilities for development and self-monitoring.

Evaluation also needs to be authentic. What does this mean? It means it must be based on the natural activities and processes students do in the classroom and in their everyday lives. If you rely solely on formalized testing procedures, you may send a signal to students that learning is simply a search for "right answers."

Evaluation is much more than writing a test, giving it, scoring it, and handing it back with a grade. Indeed, it involves a combination of procedures and designs that not only gauge students' work but help them grow in the process.

Evaluation: Two Views

For traditional college teachers, evaluation has meant little more than giving two midterms and a final exam. Instructors lament the time necessary to create and grade these instruments of torture, and students moan and groan about "cramming" information into their heads and regurgitating it on a pencil-and-paper test—which they'll scarcely recall a day or two later. The "traditional means" of evaluation seems to be a burden for all parties involved.

Part of the reason it has persisted is that evaluation has been viewed very narrowly by many teachers. The belief is that student success in a course is equated with an accumulation of points; the more points accumulated, the higher the grade. The accumulation of knowledge is prized more than the comprehension and application of that knowledge. It's also easier to measure.

From the Field _____

In interview after interview, I discovered that the two basic questions that every outstanding college teacher asked (relative to student evaluation) were, "Will this help my students become better learners and thinkers?" and "Will it tell me how well I have helped my students learn?"

Yet, in reviewing the literature on evaluation, and in talking with outstanding professors around the country, a predominant theme appears over and over: *Evaluation should be used to help students learn, not to sort them into categories.* The overall consensus is that well-crafted evaluative measures are a means to an end, not the end itself.

Performance-Based Evaluation

You are probably most familiar with this type of evaluation, also known as *product evaluation.* Typically, it involves some sort of pencil-and-paper test or quiz on how much of the course content has been committed to memory and can be reproduced on a written exam. The number of correct responses is tallied and a grade given. The more one memorizes, the higher the grade.

Here are some of the typical indicators of *performance-based evaluation:*

Red Flag _____

One of the inherent dangers of performance-based evaluation is that it often takes place at the conclusion of a unit or course. This tends to underscore learning as simply an accumulation of facts and figures to be memorized and regurgitated on terminal instruments.

- An over-reliance on product-oriented tests (multiple-choice, true/false, short-answer completion, matching)
- Points off for late papers
- Giving "extra credit" assignments for students with marginal grades
- Ability testing

◆ An accumulation of points

◆ Class participation rewarded with points

From the Field _____

L. Dee Fink, a professor of geography at the University of Oklahoma, says, "This approach to … evaluation is typically based on backward-looking evaluation, with exams that look back on what was covered during the last several weeks and aim *simply at determining whether the students got it or not.*" (Emphasis added.)

Learning-Centered Evaluation

Learning-centered evaluation is markedly different from performance-based evaluation, both procedurally and philosophically. Basically, it means that learning is viewed developmentally rather than as the simple acquisition of knowledge, that learning is a process and a reflection of intellectual growth and development over time. What is important isn't the facts learned, but rather what students are able to do with the content (in intellectual increments) over time.

In short, learning-centered evaluation is centered on two fundamental principles:

◆ Evaluation is used to help students learn—to progress from unknown to application.

◆ Intellectual development is highlighted over information accumulation.

def•i•ni•tion _____

Performance-based evaluation is product-oriented. The ultimate objective (for students) is the overall accumulation of knowledge. That accumulation is translated into points or grades. **Learning-centered evaluation** is developmentally oriented. It's when students are provided opportunities to demonstrate their understanding of important concepts through the manipulation of those concepts.

This form of evaluation concentrates not so much on what students have learned but on how they learn or pursue learning. Learning-centered evaluation may include the development of teacher or student-initiated projects in which students pursue a particular area of interest—for example, constructing a timeline of historical events leading up to World War II. It may also include measures in which the teacher provides materials and procedures for using those materials and then observes how students perform on the specified tasks. The objective in this form of evaluation is not on whether students have learned a series of right answers, but on how they go about learning.

Here are some practices found in courses that embrace learning-centered evaluation:

- Base-line information is collected on students at the start of the semester.

- Students can submit multiple drafts of a written assignment.

- Students are involved in self-evaluation activities.

- Due dates for outside work are flexible.

- The accumulation of points is de-emphasized.

- Students use knowledge in productive exercises both in and out of class.

A learning-centered approach to evaluation can provide both you and your students with valuable information to gauge progress and assess the effectiveness of the instruction. You can help your students assume an active role in the evaluation process and make your courses more of a collaborative effort, instead of one in which you assume all the responsibilities for teaching and evaluating.

There are many forms of learning-centered evaluation, but I will concentrate on just a few. I don't mean to imply that these are the only forms and formats, only that they have been proven over time to yield important data for teachers and students alike. Consider these (or modifications thereof) for your own courses, but be willing to try other evaluative measures in keeping with your philosophy of teaching and your students' developing abilities and attitudes.

Knowing Your Students

Effective evaluation is not based on the traditional model of "I know what is best for my students." Rather, it is founded on the principle of knowing where students are starting from and taking them to where you would like them to be. That means, quite simply, that you need to know your students' backgrounds. It means that you need to take the time early in the semester to discover as much as possible about your students. In doing so, you are creating a course that is responsive to their needs, rather than one managed by the dictates of content.

Good college teachers use a variety of techniques and strategies to assess their students at the start of a course. Here are a few you may wish to consider:

- Survey students on what they believe are their strengths and weaknesses relative to the objectives of the course. ("How comfortable are you in using algorithms?" "What is your level of expertise in staining slides?")

◆ Provide students with a list of the 8 to 10 major objectives of the course. Invite students to indicate their level of interest in each of those objectives.

◆ Offer students the opportunity to write a brief essay on what they hope to gain from the course. Divide the class into groups and ask each group to arrive at a consensus opinion.

◆ Talk with students informally outside of class (student union, off campus) about their goals and expectations for the course.

◆ Give students a pretest on important vocabulary, significant concepts, or relevant data (the information you would like them to know at the conclusion of the course).

◆ After several weeks in the course, invite students to form groups and answer the following questions: What have you learned so far in this course? How has the instructor helped you to learn that material? What modifications in the course design or delivery would you like to suggest?

Knowing your students (and checking in with them throughout the course) is an essential prerequisite of effective teaching and evaluation. Evaluation is focused on how students change (intellectually, socially, individually). To know if students have changed, you also need to know where they started.

Standards and Criteria

One of the most important elements of good evaluation is to have clear *standards* and appropriate *criteria* for those standards. That is to say, what students should know at the end of the course, and how you (and they) will know how well they learned it.

def•i•ni•tion

A **standard** is a description of what students should know and be able to do. Here's an appropriate standard for an English Composition course: Students will write a persuasive piece that includes a clearly stated position or opinion. A **criterion** is a level of performance that determines how well the standard has been mastered. For example: Very Well, Good, Adequate, Poor, Unacceptable.

The use of standards and criteria for those standards would seem to be a rather obvious element for any course. Yet, surveys of professors around the country indicate that this essential course component is barely addressed or nonexistent. This may stem from the traditional model of college teaching as lecturing, recording, and testing.

Evaluation is not something done to students, but rather a means to help them grow and develop. When students are measured against each other, then evaluation is often haphazard, arbitrary, and punitive. Grades should not be used to rank students, but rather they should represent clearly stated levels of achievement. In short, students must meet certain standards of excellence that are well defined and explained in advance. If an assignment is returned to students and they ask, "How did I get this grade?" or "Where did this grade come from?" then the standards and criteria of the course were either poorly explained or nonexistent.

> **"Research Says"**
>
> In one study of 140 college teachers, only 8 percent were able to identify the key criteria and standards by which they evaluated the quality of student learning.

How can you do a better job of clarifying the criteria and standards for your courses? Here's a plan:

1. Divide your course content into logical segments, topics, or concepts.

2. For each one write one to three standards (what you want students to know or be able to do).

3. For each standard, construct a rating scale that includes descriptive statements of good to poor versions of students' performance. (How well do you want students to know or meet the standards?)

4. Provide students with your established standards and the criteria by which they will be assessed.

Authentic Evaluations

By definition, authentic evaluation is grounded in the same tasks, duties, and procedures that practitioners of the course's study in the "real" world do. Authentic evaluation provides students with a context for learning and a model that they may well encounter in the future. Paper-and-pencil tests are often divorced from learning; they are isolated from the practical applications of that knowledge. The bottom line is that students have opportunities to use their knowledge, rather than merely demonstrate their knowledge.

As an example, I teach a course entitled Teaching Elementary Science and Health, a junior-level course required for elementary education majors. We study the levels of questions (Bloom's Taxonomy) that teachers can ask students and how those questions shape student's perceptions of science. I present the levels, examples of questions from each level, and the verbs that are used to construct each question type.

To evaluate students' knowledge of question types, I could give them a multiple-choice, true/false, or fill-in-the-blank test. Unfortunately, this type of testing would only tell me what students knew about the topic (surface knowledge), not whether they would be able to use the topic in a productive way (deep structure knowledge).

Instead, I provide them with the following exercise:

> *Imagine you are a third-grade teacher and have just completed a lesson on the Amazon rainforest. You want to know how well your students have mastered the material as well as how well they can use that information in their everyday lives. Using each of the six levels of cognition, design a "hands-on" activity in which students must develop a campaign that alerts the public to the amount of rainforest deforestation taking place throughout the Amazon basin.*

Each time I use this activity I am impressed by the level of inquiry and the quality of the overall engagement of students. Typically, this is a group activity, and the dialogue (which I carefully monitor) is reasoned and purposeful.

Is this an activity that future third-grade teachers would use in their science curriculum? You bet! Thus, it becomes a way of authentically assessing my college students on their knowledge of question types, *and* their ability to use that knowledge in real-life or occupational situations.

Here are a few more content-specific suggestions for authentic evaluation:

◆ Ecology—Using your knowledge of species interactions (competition, predation) construct a monitoring project that gauges the long-term implications of an outside species introduction (for example, wolves being introduced back into Yellowstone National Park).

◆ Probability and Statistics—Design a project that will identify most of the discrete and random variables that would affect the outcome of the local mayor's race.

◆ Industrial and Organizational Psychology—As the manager of a cardboard-box manufacturing company with 200 employees, design an annual performance evaluation system focused on productivity.

◆ The Presidency—Construct a convincing set of newspaper articles or letters to the editor advocating the elimination of the electoral college.

In order to create effective authentic evaluations, you need to be able to answer this question, "As a result of having studied and learned about ABC, is the student ready to do (perform) XYZ?" Authentic evaluation focuses on *use* of information, not on the information itself.

Rubrics

A rubric is simply a one-page document that describes varying levels of performance (from high to low) for a specific assignment. Rubrics have the advantage of letting students know the expectations for an assignment before they begin work on that assignment. In fact, they clearly define what a student must include in an assignment in order to demonstrate competency. As such, they may be general in nature (all the homework assignments in math) or specific (an assignment that focuses on the use of details in an expository writing paper).

Here is an example of a rubric that I often use (and present to students at the beginning of the semester) for written assignments:

Standards
❑ Project adhered to all requisites of assignment
❑ Project adhered to most requisites of assignment
❑ Project adhered to some requisites of assignment
❑ Project adhered to few requisites of assignment

Opinions
❑ Opinions are well formed and clearly supported
❑ Opinions are evident and moderately supported
❑ Opinions are minimal and barely supported
❑ Opinions are nonexistent and/or unsupported

Accuracy
❑ Factual data is accurate
❑ Most data is accurate
❑ Some information is accurate
❑ Little accurate information

Organization
❑ Material is presented logically
❑ Material is reasonably logical
❑ Material is minimally organized
❑ Little or no organization is evident

Creativity
- ❏ High level of creativity and originality
- ❏ Moderate level of creativity and originality
- ❏ Some creativity and originality
- ❏ Little or no creativity and originality

Focus
- ❏ Project is focused and detailed
- ❏ Project is moderately focused and detailed
- ❏ Project is minimally focused or partially developed
- ❏ Project shows little focus; unclear ideas

Interest
- ❏ Project is very interesting to read
- ❏ Project is interesting to read
- ❏ Project is minimally interesting
- ❏ Project is not interesting

Here's another type of rubric you may wish to consider, listing criteria, their possible levels of success (high to low), and the group or student's score.

1. The author adhered to all of the requisites of the assignment.
   3–1/_____

2. Factual data is covered in detail and supported with citations.
   5–1/_____

3. The author's position is strong and substantiated.
   4–1/_____

4. The author has integrated appropriate course concepts in the work.
   5–1/_____

5. The material is presented logically.
   5–1/_____

6. The author has employed proper mechanics (grammar, spelling, etc.)
   3–1/_____

7. The author has crafted an interesting and compelling paper.
   5–1/_____

   Total: 30–7/_____

You can use rubrics in a variety of educational tasks. Their advantage is that you and your students can develop them together, so that everyone knows exactly what criteria will be used to evaluate an assignment or group of assignments as they are being developed or completed.

Here is a brief outline of steps you can use to develop rubrics:

1. With your students, look at a series of completed assignments that represent various levels of success (good to poor).

2. Develop a list of criteria for assessing the assignment.

3. Reduce the list to a manageable number.

4. Develop approximately four levels of performance for each criterion. These can be 4, 3, 2, 1 or A, B, C, D.

5. Use the rubric on a sample assignment to see if it "works." Revise as necessary. Share the results with students.

Additional Evaluation Strategies

Here are a few more evaluation strategies you can consider for the courses you teach:

Provide students with a series of graduated exams or quizzes (based on levels of cognition) throughout the course. This places an emphasis on learning as an evolutionary process. As an example, design a quiz for the third week of the course that emphasizes *knowledge*. For the fifth week, develop a cumulative quiz that focuses on *comprehension* of that material. For the seventh week, produce a cumulative quiz that emphasizes *application* of the information. Keep the quizzes "moving up" the cognitive scale.

Knowledge is cumulative, never stagnant. You can emphasize this when you provide students with evaluative measures that are comprehensive and cumulative (they include everything from the beginning of the course up to the current date). Exams that focus on "packages" of isolated information send the message that learning is episodic, rather than ongoing.

You can also provide time periodically for students to craft a two minute response or reaction to new material. How well did they understand it? In what ways will they be able to use it?

You may recall that in Chapter 12, I shared a basic fact of all college courses: *Students tend to think based on the questions they think they'll get from an instructor.* Make sure your evaluation measures emphasize higher cognitive abilities. In short, de-emphasize simple recall (multiple choice, true/false, fill-in-the-blank) and emphasize analysis, synthesis, and evaluation (essays, project designs, and authentic tasks).

Consider providing students with ungraded quizzes periodically throughout the course. Afterwards, take time to discuss the material tested, why it is critical to the course, and students' individual or collective comprehension of that material.

Student Self-Evaluation

There is convincing evidence that students develop an internal sense of responsibility (or locus of control) over their learning in courses in which they take an active role in the evaluation process. When college students evaluate their own progress, they begin to see learning as much more than the accumulation of points or grades. They become more focused and invested in the processes of education instead of the products.

Students who come from traditional educational backgrounds believe that evaluation is the responsibility of the professor. However, self-evaluation is firmly ingrained in the real world—in business, science, mathematics, and almost every other field of endeavor. Learning how to assess the quality of one's own work can be a valuable byproduct of any college course.

Self-evaluation can take many forms. Simplest of all would be in the context of student/teacher discussions, which allow you to pose several types of questions to get students to "look inward" and gauge their learning.

Another format for self-evaluation is a self-report form. Provide students with a questionnaire about their activities in the course so far. Ask them to be honest—their comments will be helpful in shaping upcoming elements of the course. Have them address the following questions:

1. What are some of the concepts/ideas you have learned so far?

2. What are some of the areas that have given you trouble or have challenged you?

3. Do you believe you have improved in this course? Why?

4. What are some of the concepts/ideas you'd like to learn more about?

5. How would you rate your performance (or contributions)?

Here are some additional ideas you can use to help students self-evaluate:

◆ **"Muddy" response:** Invite students to periodically draft an anonymous response to the following query: "What was least clear to you (this session, up to this point in the course)?" or "What information was 'muddy'; that is, didn't make sense?" These reports allow you to stay abreast of how well students comprehend course content or your methods of presentation.

◆ **"Clear" response:** Ask students to compose a brief reaction to the following: "What was most meaningful about today's or this week's class session?" or "What made the most sense to you?" Spend time at the start of the next class discussing the students' responses.

◆ **Student-designed criteria:** Invite students to brainstorm for a set of relevant and appropriate criteria for a forthcoming assignment.

◆ **Student-designed questions:** Ask students to design a set number of questions and/or activities for a forthcoming exam. Invite them to focus on higher-level thinking skills (application, analysis, synthesis, evaluation).

◆ **Peer evaluations:** Invite students to read and evaluate a paper of their classmates using a previously designed rubric.

◆ **Introspective evaluation:** Ask students to evaluate their own work using a class-designed rubric.

◆ **"The Last Word" evaluation:** Invite students to include a self-analysis paragraph at the end of each written assignment, perhaps in response to the following query: "To what extent did this assignment further your understanding and/or appreciation of the course content?"

When students get the chance to assess themselves, they are more deeply involved in the dynamics of learning. Not only does this provide them with valuable insights into their own learning, it can also provide you with important data on students' intellectual growth and development throughout the course.

Some Final Thoughts

I don't recommend that you grade on a curve. Studies of outstanding college teachers have shown that the majority graded on pre-established standards, rather than on a curve. These exceptional teachers believed that grading on a curve made their classrooms more competitive, rather than cooperative. It also sent a signal to students that the accumulation of points was much more important than the accumulation and use of knowledge. Cumulative evaluation measures place a premium on deep learning, rather than the superficial (and quixotic) learning promoted via competitive or curved grading.

Keep in mind that evaluation is a process, and the best kind of evaluation offers opportunities for growth—teacher growth, student growth, and program growth. It's one thing to assess and evaluate student performance, it is quite another to do something with that information. If all you do is administer an endless battery of tests, quizzes, and written assignments and do little with the results, then your evaluation is close to worthless. Use the data you gather from all forms of evaluation productively, to help students develop the skills, processes, and attitudes that make learning an important part of their lives.

Evaluation is an integral part of the learning process that must be sensitive to the needs, attitudes, and abilities of individual students as well as the class as a whole. Be careful not to over-rely on one or two forms of evaluation just because they are easy or convenient for you. Be aware that evaluation involves some part of a student's self-esteem and that affective factors are an important ingredient in evaluation. In other words, *what* you evaluate is just as important as *how* you evaluate.

Learning to become an effective evaluator takes time. It is not easily learned, nor easily practiced. It is, however, an essential element of the effective and successful college classroom.

The Least You Need to Know

- Evaluation is a continuous process throughout a course, not just at the end.

- Performance-based evaluation (least effective) focuses on the products of learning.

- Learning-based evaluation (most effective) focuses on learning as a developmental process.

- Authentic evaluation tests students' ability to use knowledge in a real-world context.

- Students' self-evaluation has a positive effect on their perceptions and appreciation of course content.

Chapter 18

Expectations, Issues, and Concerns

In This Chapter

- ◆ Student expectations
- ◆ Attendance and tardiness
- ◆ Academic integrity
- ◆ Late papers and assignments

I wish I could tell you that being a college professor was as simple as sharing your love and passion for a subject with an eager and enthusiastic group of undergraduates patiently absorbing your words of wisdom with affection and sincerity.

I wish I could tell you that—but you probably know better. College students come with various expectations, experiences, and goals. They also come to your courses with their own ideas about how the teaching/learning paradigm works. After all, they are the products of 12 or more years of education—they have some ideas about how the "system" should operate. Unfortunately, there is sometimes a conflict between their beliefs and yours. Let's take a look at some of the more common ones and how you can effectively address them.

Expectations vs. Reality

Many college students come to class with a set of expectations shaped by their family, their experiences in high school, their peer group, or the media. Sometimes those expectations are in agreement with yours; at other times they are in disagreement.

From the Field _____

Richard Fliegel, assistant dean of Academic Programs at the University of Southern California, says that "it's important to remember that freshmen do not have a lot of life experiences." He cited the observation of a colleague who noted that "incoming freshmen are only six years out of sixth grade."

When students are engaged, when a class runs smoothly, and when students rise to the demands of the course, we can say that student expectations are in agreement with teacher expectations. When there is discord between student and teacher expectations, then some sort of conflict may ensue.

Steven Richardson, vice president for academic affairs at Winona State University in Minnesota, makes the case that traditional-age college students are still "apprentice" adults, and therefore not fully mature. It becomes necessary for us, as college professors, to model appropriate behavior and make our expectations for class conduct and course requirements well defined and clear.

Classroom Decorum

Richardson proposes a set of guidelines through which college teachers can establish appropriate models of behavior and classroom decorum. I've presented these below with some additional annotations:

◆ Make behavioral expectations clear in your syllabus. Be sure to use positive, constructive language, not threats of reprisal. Students respond best to clear, concise language that leaves little or no room for doubt—or interpretation.

◆ It is most valuable to talk about yourself and let students know what you value. "Apprentice adults" need models to emulate. You can offer a positive model simply by sharing your beliefs and values in a comfortable arena.

◆ Learn as much as you can about your students. Find out about their hopes and dreams. In doing so, you show that you are interested in them as human beings, rather than simply as students.

◆ Earn trust by being trustworthy. Be consistent in applying your expectations to students. In other words, say what you'll do and do what you say.

◆ Establish a classroom environment in which learning is promoted as a process, rather than as a product. When students' investment in a course is celebrated and valued, they will have a stake in the success of that course—for themselves and for others.

From the Field

Richardson says that the traditional lecture format—a one-way transmission of knowledge—may be counterproductive to appropriate classroom behavior. Interactive instruction styles (cooperative learning, constructivism, active discussions) are more likely to engage students and significantly reduce inappropriate behaviors.

◆ Cooperative projects and group discussions provide opportunities for students to establish personal expectations. Additionally, when students engage with each other in productive exercises, learning blossoms and behavior is aligned with group goals.

◆ It is vitally important that college professors model the behaviors we expect of our students. Students take their cues from the adults in front of them. If you're enthused, they will be enthused. If you are honest with them, they will want to be honest with you.

◆ Do not ignore minor events in the classroom. A combination of minor events can add up to a major situation or crisis. As Barney Fife (on the old *Andy Griffith Show*) would say, "Nip it in the bud!"

◆ Be willing to adjust your own behavior. Don't set yourself up as a "perfect" example; show students your human side, too. Provide students with opportunities to learn from your example.

◆ Talk with colleagues in your department or other departments. What expectations do they have for students? How do they articulate those expectations? What do they do when there is a mismatch between their expectations and those of their students?

From the Field

Ed Ransford, a professor of sociology at the University of Southern California, says, "Let a little of your personal self out. Don't get gushy, but there's no need to be totally objective all the time."

Brian Furio, an associate professor of communication at York College of Pennsylvania, seconds that when he says, "I find that self-disclosure is a way of bonding with the audience. It's a way of connecting with students while personalizing instruction."

Stating Your Expectations

Typically, you will want to put your expectations for the course in your syllabus. You may choose the option of developing a separate document which focuses specifically on your expectations. Many institutions have a set of expectations which are provided to faculty members as required elements of any course syllabus.

In stating your expectations for the course, it's important that you include the following:

- ◆ **Clear and concise language.** This is not the time to pontificate.

- ◆ **A positive tone.** Students will quickly read between the lines to determine if you have their best interests in mind.

- ◆ **A democratic atmosphere.** Let students know that their involvement and participation are valued.

- ◆ **An in-charge attitude.** You will need to strike a delicate balance and let students know that you are in charge, but without sounding authoritarian.

Now, let's take a look at some common course expectations and how you can effectively communicate them to students.

Attendance

In my experience there are two "camps" with respect to attendance. One group of professors says that students pay their tuition and they can, therefore, make the decision about whether or not they wish to be in class. They should be prepared to suffer any consequences (i.e., bad grades) with respect to their nonattendance or nonparticipation in the scheduled events of the course. In short, it is not the duty of the professor to "force" students to attend.

The other camp says that students need guidelines and expectations that are clearly stated and clearly enumerated. Without those guidelines, students may get a feeling that attendance is not important and that their engagement in the course is not valued. The opinion of many professors is that an attendance policy places a value on students' participation in every aspect of a course.

My personal philosophy is that students are more inclined to attend class when attendance is valued (and recorded) and when there are some consequences tied to attendance "lapses." An attendance policy establishes a model of behavior and expectations that contributes to academic success.

One Example

Listed below is the attendance policy I include in every course syllabus. Feel free to use or modify this example in your own syllabi:

> *Class attendance is both mandatory and necessary. Valuable information and ideas are presented and shared during each class session, and it is to your benefit as well as the benefit of your classmates to be present for each and every class. In fact, it is your primary academic responsibility to attend all classes. Roll will be taken periodically throughout the semester. Your final grade for the course may be affected as follows:*
>
> *3 unexcused absences = deduction of 1 full grade*
>
> *4 unexcused absences = deduction of 2 full grades*
>
> *5 unexcused absences = deduction of 3 full grades*
>
> *Excused absences (for health or family emergencies) must be verified with a physician's note or a memo from the Student Affairs Office.*
>
> *Materials, assigned work, and information missed due to absence are your responsibility and will need to be made up on your own time. Each student is responsible for making sure all course requirements are completed and on time. The instructor is not responsible for reminding students of missing work.*

This incorporates several elements that you should consider in your own attendance policy. There is a rationale for this policy. I let students know that their attendance is tied to their success in the course. Use of the word "may" (in the fifth sentence) allows me to keep my options open. If there are some unique or special circumstances (death in the family, severe illness), then I've given myself some leeway.

The responsibility for making up missed work is the student's, not mine. Specific consequences for missing class are clearly stated. Students are aware, from the first day of class, what may happen as a result of nonattendance.

While students may say that an attendance policy is unnecessary or demeaning at the college level, the experiences of several colleagues has shown that there is a positive correlation between a clearly stated policy and student success. On end-of-the-semester evaluations, students will often state that the attendance policy stated in the syllabus was a motivation to come to class regularly.

Tardiness

There is often a direct correlation between the time a class is offered and the rate of tardiness. Tardiness is higher in early-morning classes (sleeping in until the last minute) and late-afternoon classes (part-time or full-time work schedules). It tends to be lower in classes held between 10 A.M. and 2 P.M.

You may wish to consider including a statement about tardiness in your course syllabus. Doing so will send a message that all the time in the class is important and that all students are expected for the entire duration of each class.

Here is the tardiness statement I include in my syllabi. As with the attendance policy above, consider this (or a modification thereof) for your own use as well.

> *LATE POLICY: It is the practice and tradition of the instructor to begin class at the scheduled start time. All students are expected to be seated and ready for instruction at the start of each class. Any student who arrives late (during or after the opening activity) should see the instructor after class to change the absence (as indicated on the periodic attendance sheet) to a lateness. Two latenesses equal one absence.*

Academic Integrity

It is a sad fact of academia that students cheat. In fact, many new professors might be quite surprised at the level of cheating that takes place in higher education. Here are a few eye-opening statistics to consider:

- Numerous studies have found that from 40 to 90 percent of all students cheat on classroom tests.

- Several studies have shown that between 75 and 98 percent of college students surveyed each year report having cheated in high school.

- In one survey of 6,000 students at 31 institutions, 67 percent of students reported having engaged in one or more questionable academic behaviors.

- In another study, 78 percent of all college students reported that they had engaged in at least one type of cheating.

- In 1993, 84 percent of the college students surveyed in one study admitted to cheating on a written assignment.

- In one national survey of over 2,000 undergraduates, more than 50 percent admitted to cheating, and half of those individuals admitted to cheating more than once.

Why Students Cheat

Obviously, the reason college students cheat is to get a better grade, but there are several reasons why they actually go through with it. For many students a combination of factors is at play. Here is what the research indicates as the primary factors that influence student cheating:

◆ Peer pressure or peer influence (in many studies this is reported as the number-one reason)

◆ Low self-esteem or self-confidence

◆ An overwhelming belief that they won't get caught

◆ A feeling that the professor doesn't care or doesn't place a high enough value on academic honesty

◆ Unclear or ineffective policies (by the institution or individual professors)

◆ The rewards outweigh the potential consequences

◆ It's easy

How Students Cheat

There are probably as many different ways to cheat as there are college students. The methods and procedures are becoming more and more sophisticated via technological advances and innovations. Here is a list (definitely not a complete one) of some of the ways in which undergraduate students cheat:

◆ Downloading Internet articles and submitting them as their own (through "cut and paste")

◆ Paying someone to take an exam

◆ Paying someone to write a required paper

◆ Downloading test answers on a PDA, cell phone, or other device

◆ Facts and formulas written on various articles of clothing (prior to an exam)

◆ Looking at someone else's paper during an exam

◆ Copying material from another source (including other students) and submitting it as their own

- Providing answers to someone during an exam

- Stealing an exam

- Presenting another person's work as one's own

- Falsifying bibliographic entries or data

- Making false statements

Preventing Cheating

The prevalence of cheating on college campuses makes it seem like a virulent disease—one impossible to totally eradicate. Yet, we can implement practices and measures in our courses that will significantly reduce the "need" to cheat by students and establish an atmosphere that values honesty and academic integrity. I have found that the incidence of cheating is directly related to the classroom culture that is established and promoted throughout the semester. In its simplest terms, this is a culture of unity, a culture of "we" rather than "teacher versus students."

Here are some suggestions and ideas on preventing cheating culled from a number of sources, colleagues, and colleges. I've also included my own practices over the years. What is most interesting is that these recommendations have remained fairly consistent over the years and between investigators of this phenomenon.

Establish a clear policy on cheating and make that policy known to students on your syllabus and in discussions with the class during the first week of a course. Many colleges have an institutional policy which is required on all syllabi.

Here is the policy used at my institution and required on every course syllabi:

> *Academic dishonesty will not be tolerated at [this college]. Academic dishonesty refers to actions such as, but not limited to, cheating, plagiarism, fabricating research, falsifying academic documents, etc., and includes all situations where students make use of the work of others and claim such work as their own. Thus, it is expected that all assigned work for this course will be entirely original. In cases of academic dishonesty, the student involved may receive a grade of "0" for the course and the matter will be reported to the Department Chairman and the Dean of Academic Affairs.*

The greater the psychological distance between the instructor and the student, the greater the inclination for cheating. That is, if the professor is seen as simply a mechanical dispenser of information, or if students feel that they are nothing more than a number on a seating chart, then the likelihood of cheating will mushroom accordingly. The more of a community you can create in your classroom and the more personal interaction you share with your students, the less likely they will want to cheat.

For example, I make it a point to identify and briefly talk with one new student after each class. In one class, I complimented a young lady on her ever-present smile. In another class, I thanked a young man who contributed a thoughtful response to a question during class. In still another class, I talked with a soccer player about an upcoming contest with a conference rival. Maybe you can't talk to every student personally, but each of these individuals will share her or his conversation with other classmates and peers, thus spreading the interpersonal bonds I hope to promote.

Provide multiple opportunities for students to demonstrate their mastery of course materials. The traditional "two quizzes and a final" places undue pressure on students to make the grade in a very limited number of assessments. Although each course and each discipline will be different, work to have a balance of quizzes, tests, papers, projects, and other assignments so that students can demonstrate their knowledge in an array of evaluative measures.

Consider the length of your exams or assigned papers. A test with 150 multiple-choice questions or a paper requiring a minimum of 25 references or 50 pages will seem excessive to students. They will view these assignments as excessive and even punitive, and may retaliate with some form of academic dishonesty. Also, examine your grading policies to ensure that they are consistent and fair. Whenever possible, de-emphasize grades and provide students with opportunities for self-evaluation.

Foster the principle of academic integrity regularly. It's important to discuss academic honesty at the beginning of the course, and also appropriate to bring it up periodically throughout the semester. You may elect to have a brief statement included on an exam or quiz. Invite students to talk about academic honesty prior to a final exam. Re-emphasize your standards about a third of the way through the course and invite student comments. Frequently refer to the academic integrity statements on your course syllabus.

From the Field

Art Crawley, director of the Center for Faculty Development at Louisiana State University, says, "Professors need to create an atmosphere of trust in the classroom. That can be accomplished when we make our standards clear and then adhere to those standards fairly. This environment of trust tends to mitigate student desires to cheat."

Think about methods that significantly reduce any tendencies to cheat. Depending on your specific circumstances (size of room, number of students, and so on), you may wish to consider using multiple forms of an exam, reassign seats for a final examination, stagger the seating pattern throughout the classroom or lecture hall for midterm exams, create exams with scrambled questions, rotate the assignments for a course from semester to semester, physically move around the room during an exam, or invite monitors to help you proctor an exam.

Red Flag

I have discovered that cheating tends to escalate when the emphasis on written assignments or exams is on low-level thinking. This includes memorizing facts, simple recall of information, or knowledge-based responses (see Chapter 12). When the emphasis on papers and tests shifts to higher levels of cognition (application, analysis, synthesis, and evaluation), then the potential for cheating tends to diminish.

Try to identify and reach out to students who are struggling early in the semester. Take the time to discover the reasons for their academic problems and counsel them as necessary. If necessary, refer them to the academic assistance center or tutoring center on campus.

Meet with small groups of students regularly. Set up discussion groups and talk with them periodically. For larger classes where teaching assistants meet with students, drop in every so often to chat with students. Small group encounters allow you to meet with students on a more personal basis and address any concerns or issues they may have.

Consider the use of technology as a deterrent to cheating. There are a number of web-based antiplagiarism services available such as www.turnitin.com. These programs automatically compare student papers with text on the Internet and in published work. Many colleges use cheat-proof software to prevent cheating on computer-based tests by blocking students from using other applications, such as e-mail and web browsers. Other colleges use thumbprint scanners and digital cameras to thwart test-taker impersonations.

Finally, promote and adhere to your institution's policies on academic integrity. Regularly talk with students about those policies, disseminate them on printed materials (including tests and syllabi), and clarify your expectations for student behavior throughout the semester.

It is an unfortunate fact of life that cheating is common on college campuses, and students will sometimes resort to extreme measures. Several years ago on our campus, one student broke into a professor's office to steal a forthcoming exam. Frustrated by his inability to locate the exam, he eventually resorted to setting the office on fire. He left a trail of clues, was quickly discovered, arrested by the local police, and expelled from school.

Late Papers; Late Assignments

As long as there are college students, there will always be papers turned in late or assignments that need "just a little more time." The challenge for professors is how to deal with the "lateness factor," and the excuses that seem to be attached to almost every assignment.

Reducing the Problem

Unfortunately, there is no magic formula for eliminating late assignments. They are as persistent as mosquitoes at a lakeside resort. However, here are a few suggestions on how you can reduce the incidence of lateness in your courses.

Invite students to submit written assignments in stages. That is, ask that they turn in an outline of a paper first. This submission is checked off in your grade book. Then, a few days or weeks later, they can submit a draft of the paper for your comments and suggestions. Finally, they can turn in the final paper for a grade.

You may wish to consider including a hierarchical series of penalties for late work. These deductions should be clearly stated on the course syllabus. For example, 1 or 2 days late equals one grade deduction, 3 or 4 days late equals a two-grade deduction, and so on. Or, deduct 10 points for every day a paper is late.

One strategy I've used with considerable success is to eliminate due dates for all written assignments. I tell students that it is their responsibility to determine the actual due dates of specific assignments. This requires them to balance the assignments in my course with those in other courses. It also eliminates the lateness factor, because they now have latitude to determine the amount of work necessary for each assignment.

> **"Research Says"**
>
> In one study, researchers found that about 67 percent of students surveyed admitted to making at least one fraudulent excuse while in college. Most of the excuses were made to gain extra time in order to complete an assignment.

I realize that this technique won't work for every course or every instructor; but it has, over the years, promoted a sense of individual responsibility and self-initiative in students.

Some instructors offer a bonus for papers turned in prior to the due date, with extra points added to a paper's score if it arrives 1, 2, or 3 days in advance of the due date. Besides the incentive to turn in work early, this also has the advantage of potentially allowing you to spread out the reading of those papers over a longer period of time.

Inform students that if all their assignments are turned in on time, they will have the option of dropping their lowest grade on any single assignment. Not only will this option spur students to complete all assignments in a timely manner, but it also offers them an incentive or bonus. Conversely, students who are tardy in their submissions are "penalized" by having every grade count. For this option to work, it would be necessary to have a range of writing assignments for students to tackle.

The Least You Need to Know

- The expectations of students and those of professors may differ.

- Students need a clear attendance policy.

- Academic integrity is a persistent challenge on college campuses.

- Cheating can be significantly curbed by attending to some specific details early and throughout the entire semester.

- There are several strategies you can use to reduce the number of late papers. These may include submitting papers in stages or inviting students to select their own "due dates" for written assignments.

Part 6

Life as a College Teacher

Let's be honest—life as a college teacher is not what Hollywood would have us believe. It's much more than talking with perky co-eds in your office or casual conversations with beefy athletes on the practice field. Life as a college professor is like a sprint through a busy airport terminal to catch a connecting flight. It's a mad rush, there are people to dodge, you're lugging two bags, you've forgotten something on the previous flight, and when you get to the gate—there's a 2-hour delay.

In Part 6, I'll share several survival strategies that will ease your journey. We'll examine the roles and responsibilities of adjunct professors and teaching assistants, look at the challenges of teaching adult education courses, and see how course evaluations can help make you a better teacher. We'll also examine the most important part of the educational equation—you! I'll give you practical ideas on how you can maintain a standard of excellence and be a lifelong learner.

Chapter 19

Adjunct Professors: Making the Grade

In This Chapter

- ◆ Who are they?
- ◆ Positives and negatives
- ◆ Different types of adjuncts
- ◆ Keys to success
- ◆ From adjunct to full time

The Ancillary Army. Freeway Flyers. Roads Scholars. Turnpike Teachers. These are some of the nicknames given to part-time college teachers. They may teach one or two courses at a single institution, or, in some cases, they may teach multiple courses at multiple institutions. Often, their "office" consists of the front seat of their car, and their "desk" is a cardboard box. Their lunch is whatever they can grab at McDonald's while zipping through traffic to their next scheduled class.

The life of an adjunct professor isn't easy. For some, the thought of teaching one or two courses part time is appealing—a nice way to supplement their income—but for others the life of an adjunct professor is hell on wheels—literally and figuratively. This chapter provides you with an overview of adjunct life and ways to survive it.

Who Are They?

By definition, an *adjunct professor* is a part-time professor often hired on a contractual basis to teach one, two, or three courses a semester—a teaching load that is below the minimum necessary to earn benefits such as health and dental care, retirement, and life insurance. The positions are not permanent and may be canceled any time due to low enrollments or changing course requirements.

def•i•ni•tion

Adjunct professors are individuals who teach college courses on a part-time basis. Their positions are not permanent and they are not eligible for typical faculty benefits. Their teaching load at a single institution may consist of one, two, or three courses each semester.

Positives for the Institution

The employment of adjunct professors has several positives for a college or university:

◆ The institution does not have to pay any benefits.

◆ The institution can eliminate a teaching position at the last minute.

◆ The institution can tap into the local talent pool without spending a lot of money.

◆ The institution can reduce personnel costs (the largest chunk of a college's budget) significantly.

◆ General education courses (which tenured faculty often avoid) can be covered.

Positives for the Individual

There are several benefits for individuals wishing to work as adjunct professors:

◆ Adjunct instruction allows you to share your expertise in a specific field.

◆ Adjunct instruction can supplement the paycheck of your regular job.

◆ The duties of an adjunct instructor do not include administrative assignments such as committee work or research responsibilities.

- At many institutions the hours are flexible.

- You may decline a course at any time.

- If you have a family or cannot work full time, adjunct instruction can be a way to keep current in a selected field.

- For retired individuals, adjunct instruction offers a way to provide students with real-world experiences and practical information.

From the Field _____

Molly Roll, an adjunct professor of nursing at Sinclair Community College in Dayton, Ohio, says that one of the biggest benefits of her position is that she has considerable time to work on her course design. "Not having to sit on committees or get involved in the politics of the campus gives me lots of time to work on my presentation material," she says.

Negatives for the Individual

However, there are several negatives you should consider before accepting or continuing an adjunct teaching position. Here are a few:

- The pay can vary depending on the institution's policy, your degree, funding variables (state funds versus institutional funds), gender, and tradition.

- There is no job security. At most institutions the position of adjunct professor is on a semester-by-semester basis, and is highly dependent on student enrollment, instructor evaluations, and the teaching preferences of full-time faculty members.

- There are no benefits. Life insurance, retirement contributions, and health care are not part of the contract with the institution. Costs for these benefits must come out of the instructor's own pocket.

- There will probably be no office space available to meet with students. If office space is available, it will be shared with several other adjunct professors in a common "bullpen."

- There will probably be no telephone, photocopying, secretarial services, or technological support available. These benefits will often be the responsibility of each individual instructor.

- Your teaching schedule can be unpredictable from one semester to the next. Courses taught on a regular basis may disappear, and new courses offered at the last minute may suddenly appear without advance notice.

According to recent surveys by the American Association of University Professors, the average salaries of part-time instructors (per course) in select disciplines were as follows:

	English	History	Philosophy
Up to $1,500	24%	17%	16%
$1,501–$2,500	43%	55%	51%
$2,501 and up	34%	28%	32%

Community colleges tended to have the lowest adjunct salaries (as little as $800 per course), while private research universities had the highest (up to $5,000 per course).

A Growing Trend

The employment of adjunct professors at most colleges and universities is on the rise. In the early 1970s, the percentage of adjunct professors was approximately 22 percent of higher education teaching staffs. By the end of the 20th century, that number had grown significantly—fully 43 percent of the professors on college campuses nationally were adjunct. At my institution, for example, part-time instructors outnumber full-time instructors two to one.

Teaching Multiple Courses at Multiple Colleges

Adjunct instructors cobble together a dizzying array of courses (anywhere from three to seven from multiple institutions) each semester from an equally dizzying array of colleges in a broad geographical region. It is not unusual for these individuals to teach one course, jump in their car and speed to another course at another university, grab some indistinguishable fast food for lunch, and get back on the road for another course at another institution—all while maintaining not only their sanity but, hopefully, their teaching expertise and enthusiasm.

> **"Research Says"**
>
> According to figures issued by the United States Department of Education, between 1995 and 1997 more than two thirds of all new professors were hired as adjuncts. Currently, nearly 65 percent of all college and university teachers are adjuncts.

Red Flag

According to Kim West, an associate professor of clinical education at the University of Southern California, and an employer of many adjunct professors, "There is a potential for a conflict of interest with 'Freeway Fliers'—particularly if you are in the same program at three different institutions. There may be competition between the institutions, you may be a 'cheerleader' for one institution over the others, and you are a potential recruiter for every single institution."

Teaching Multiple Courses at the Same College

Adjunct professors who have the "luxury" of teaching one or more courses at the same institution have their own set of challenges. They may teach one course at 8 in the morning, teach another at 3 in the afternoon, and a third at 8 in the evening. That leaves lots of "free time" in between. However, without an office or work space they may decide to leave campus, go home, and do the commute all over again.

Or, quite possibly, they may have two or three courses back to back with no break or preparation time in between. They may have to teach all evening courses, or weekend courses, or any courses scheduled for times that the full-time instructors shun. They are also often at the mercy of administrative decisions into which they have little, if any, input.

Teaching One Course a Semester

If they are one of the lucky ones (e.g., they still have a "day job"), these adjunct professors may just teach a single evening course once a week. These individuals are typically not reliant on adjunct work for their livelihood or have some free time after retirement to teach a course each semester.

Often, these individuals come in just to teach a course and then disappear for an entire week. Without an office, a telephone, or even an e-mail address on campus, it may be difficult for students to get hold of these individuals for counseling or assistance with course requirements.

Surviving and Succeeding

Suffice it to say, life as an adjunct professor can be a challenge, but there are several things you can do to enhance your teaching effectiveness as well as your presence on campus.

Learn the Culture

Your success in the classroom may be determined by how much you know about the institution(s) at which you teach. Learn the culture of the institution—every college has its own unique set of traditions, customs, and practices.

Your success as a college instructor may depend on how "connected" you are to the institution. At the very least, you should be aware of the mission of the institution, its long-range plans, and the core values that shape its daily life. Here are some specific ideas:

Read the college catalog from cover to cover. If you don't understand something, be sure to ask. Read the faculty handbook, advising manual, student handbook, and other documents prepared by the institution. Can you discern the institution's philosophy from these publications? Also watch the local newspaper for articles and information about the college. How is the institution viewed in the local community?

Find out if there is an orientation program for new faculty members. Plan to attend all the sessions scheduled for just such a program and read all the materials distributed. This can be one of the most beneficial ways to learn about the college and its expectations for instructors both full time and part time. Talk to colleagues in your department whenever possible. When time allows, have a cup of coffee or lunch with members of the department. What do they talk about? What do they think about the administration or the student body?

From the Field

Kim West states that the first three things you need to do as an adjunct is to "complete all paperwork regarding pay, get a copy of a course syllabus that's been used before, and grab an orientation handbook."

Talk to students informally about some of the traditions of the college. Who's the big rival? What do students do on the weekends? Is it a party school? If practical, attend athletic contests, visiting speakers, guest lecturers, concerts, and other extracurricular activities.

The key is to know as much about the institution as you can. The more you know, the better you will be able to fit into the culture of this particular college.

Focus on Teaching

Your primary responsibility as an adjunct professor is to teach students. Perhaps you have been in the business world all your life and have no teaching background whatsoever. Perhaps you just received a graduate degree and haven't had the opportunity to pick up important and necessary teaching methods and strategies. Or, maybe this is your first time in front of students at any level—you have lots of information or experiences to share, but aren't sure of what will work. Here are a few suggestions:

Contact a member of the education department on campus. Ask for recommendations of books and periodicals about teaching. What are some excellent resources that can provide you with the strategies and techniques that will make you an effective teacher?

Visit the campus library. Access the books and magazines in their collection on teaching. Inquire at the information desk for print and nonprint resources that may provide you with specific teaching information.

Watch for conferences or seminars in your local community. Read the local newspaper regularly, and make a point to peruse the campus newspaper frequently. Stay in touch with individuals in the College of Education at your institution. Find out about teaching conferences and attend them whenever you can.

Talk with outstanding teachers (both elementary and secondary) in your local school district. What kinds of tips and techniques can they offer you on motivation, lesson plan design, teaching methods, technology, homework, and special needs students?

From the Field

Molly Roll says, "My chair was very helpful and sent me to a weeklong seminar for new nursing educators. It was really helpful. I was able to network with new educators from all over the country as well as some 'seasoned educators.' "

Red Flag

This book has been specifically designed for college teachers of any discipline, any topic, and any status. Whether you are full time or part time, the strategies, methods, tips, and procedures detailed in each chapter are designed to help you become a more effective instructor. All of these chapters represent the best that your colleagues throughout the country have to offer. This information is just as important for adjunct professors as it is for full-time professors.

Get on the Internet. There are many wonderful websites that offer college teachers an array of lesson plans, teaching strategies, and motivational techniques that can significantly enhance your classroom performance. Here are a few to get you started:

- The Chronicle of Higher Education (http://chronicle.com)

- American Association of University Professors (http://www.aaup.org)

- Gateway to Educational Materials (www.thegateway.org)

If practical, ask if you can enroll in an undergraduate or graduate education course offered by your institution. This would be particularly appropriate if you have never taught before and would like a good introduction into the world of education. You may also want to consider adult or continuing education courses offered in your local community.

Connect with Your Department

In your role as an adjunct professor, it is quite easy to feel out of touch with the institution as well as with the members of your department. Working to establish and maintain good relationships with department members can go a long way toward ensuring success—both in the classroom and outside.

Whenever possible, talk with members of the department (full time and part time) in a variety of informal conversations. Talk about the weather, a recent political situation, or the status of students.

Ask if you can attend department meetings (if your schedule allows). Listen to the various topics and challenges under discussion. If allowed, volunteer your views and perspectives.

If practical, volunteer your services to the department. Can you put together a newsletter or informational brochure for the department? Can you offer some type of technological support? Because of your expertise, can you help design a new course? Do you have contacts out in the community that could be tapped by department members?

Stay in touch with your department chair. Keep that individual informed about your availability for future courses as well as your progress in teaching your current course(s). Stop by the department office every once in a while to say hi.

def•i•ni•tion

A **mentor** is someone who acts as a guide, counselor, tutor, or coach to one or more individuals. He or she provides expert advice, counsel, and instruction in a specific field or endeavor.

Get a Mentor

One of the most effective ways you can help yourself both as a teacher and as a colleague is to find someone who is willing to act as your *mentor.* Not only can a mentor keep you up-to-date on classroom procedures and institutional policies, that individual can also help you feel more comfortable in the academic community.

Find out if your institution has a mentoring program for new faculty members. Contact the individual (typically, another faculty member) in charge of the program and ask to be assigned a mentor.

Talk with your department chair about being assigned a mentor from the department. Would someone be willing to take you under their wing for your first semester or academic year?

Talk with other full-time department members. Is there someone who would be willing to work with you on teaching methodologies, course design, or syllabus construction?

Consider having a mentor from another department. Not only will you obtain varied perspectives and viewpoints from an outsider, you will also gain a fresh outlook on ways to effectively teach undergraduates.

> **From the Field**
>
> Molly Roll says that one of the most beneficial experiences she has had was when she "spent a quarter with the team leader for our course. She lectured and I listened. The next quarter I spent with another seasoned faculty member and we split the lecture material. She sat in on my lectures and we debriefed afterwards. It was extremely helpful."

Look into any faculty development opportunities on your campus. Many institutions have a faculty development office or a special faculty committee devoted to faculty enhancement. Investigate the possibilities of working with one or more individuals associated with those endeavors.

For the Long Term

Your success as an adjunct professor can be ensured when you consider and plan long-term goals. Whether you are teaching one course at a single college or multiple courses at several institutions, you need to devote some time to career-planning strategies that will enhance your teaching effectiveness as well as your personal growth and development as a college instructor.

Based on conversations with adjunct instructors at several institutions as well as faculty development plans in place at select colleges and universities, here is a Personal Development Profile for your consideration.

- ◆ Short-term goals. What do you hope to accomplish in the next one to two years?

- ◆ Long-term goals. What do you hope to accomplish in the next three to five years?

- What college/university services will help you accomplish those goals?

- What off-campus services will help you accomplish your goals?

- What funding requirements will help you accomplish your goals?

- What professional conferences or meetings do you plan to attend? What workshops or seminars are you planning to attend? In the next year? In the next two years? In the next five years?

- In what departmental activities do you plan to participate (retreats, departmental meetings, workshops)?

- What grants or other funding resources will you apply for?

- What additional education or training will you need?

- What community resources, contacts, or materials will you need?

- What travel will be necessary to maintain or upgrade your skills?

- What special writing or research opportunities will you pursue?

- What members of the department will you consult?

- How will you monitor your progress?

Creating a personal development plan can be a critical step in your journey as an adjunct professor. Besides providing specific personal and professional goals, it underscores the resources necessary for your current and continuing success. Having a plan of action can make you a more effective teacher and your students more successful learners.

A Persistent Myth

Many individuals teach college courses on a part-time basis in the hope that it will lead to a full-time or permanent position. Unfortunately, the reality is that that seldom occurs. I hate to tell you, but the odds are stacked against you if you are planning to use your part-time status as a stepping stone to a tenured faculty position. Here are the sad facts:

It is considerably more cost efficient for an institution to hire a part-timer to teach six courses an academic year at an average salary of $25,000 (with no benefits) than it is to hire a full-time tenure-track faculty member to teach those same six courses at an average salary of $80,000 (plus benefits). With a rise in operating costs, a slashing of budgets, and a need to keep tuition down, institutions are looking to reduce their largest expenditure—salaries.

Adjunct professors provide a college or an academic department with fluidity. That is, if students lose interest in a discipline or enrollment goes down, adjunct instructors can be let go. By the same token, if a new area of concentration or interest emerges, adjunct professors can be hired to fill the demand until the discipline "proves itself."

Many universities and colleges require that their full-time professors hold terminal degrees (Ph.D. or Ed.D.) in their field. Without the terminal degree, full-time employment is not possible. Some fields (for example, the humanities, education, and history) continue to generate an overabundance of Ph.D.s. This oversupply means that these folks are often in a constant and continual scramble to snap up all the full-time positions available.

One of the most discouraging facts of life is that search committees, who must go through scores of applications in order to fill a single full-time position, may question the qualifications of someone who's only taught on a part-time basis for several years.

I don't mean to discourage you if your ultimate goal is to obtain full-time employment as a result of dipping your pedagogical toes into the part-time waters. Every year people do it (two of the recent full-time hires in our own department were folks who had done an outstanding job teaching part time for a number of years). Be realistic, however—adjunct work is not an automatic ticket to a tenure-track position. Although national statistics are hard to come by, my conversations with people on several campuses seem to indicate that less than 10 percent of adjunct professors will eventually move into full-time teaching positions.

At some institutions, having an adjunct position is a distinct disadvantage. ("If they're good teaching on a part-time basis, let's keep them there. We'll save lots of money on benefits and won't have to hire one of those expensive full-time profs.") At other institutions it is a way for them to "screen" potential full-time hires; however, the 10 percent figure used above was fairly consistent over the two dozen colleges I surveyed.

Adjunct professors are frequently the lifeblood of a department or college. Not only do they bring in experiences from the real world, so, too, do they bring in their own unique brand of excitement and enthusiasm. In a nutshell, they do it because they love to teach and they love to share their expertise with a new generation of learners. The benefits are not necessarily in a paycheck, but rather in the mutual energy they share with students.

The Least You Need to Know

◆ There are positive aspects of an adjunct professor's job. These include a flexible schedule, limited institutional responsibilities, and a way to stay current in your respective field.

◆ Adjuncts provide colleges with an enormous bank of instructional resources.

◆ Life on the road can be challenging and difficult.

◆ Seeking a mentor or establishing a support system is often the key to success for adjunct professors.

◆ Very few adjunct professors move into full-time teaching positions.

Chapter 20

Teaching Assistants: Into the Void

In This Chapter

- ◆ Your specific duties
- ◆ Establishing good lines of communication
- ◆ How to be flexible (bending over backwards)
- ◆ The keys to effective planning
- ◆ How to get students engaged and involved

Congratulations! You've been appointed as a graduate teaching assistant. You're now able to put into practice all that you've learned about your field, develop teaching skills that will last a lifetime, and provide yourself with financial assistance that will cover your living expenses and tuition. You're on your way toward an advanced degree as well as a host of dynamic learning opportunities.

It has often been said that the best way to learn about a subject is to teach it. In preparing materials for others, in organizing research and current thinking, and in discovering ways to make material comprehensible and relevant for other learners, you, too, will discover more about a discipline than you ever thought possible. You'll also discover more about yourself, too. Let's take a look at your dynamic new position.

Roles and Responsibilities

The duties, assignments, and responsibilities of your position as a *teaching assistant* will vary according to the institution at which you work, your major professor(s), and the demands of your respective department.

def•i•ni•tion

According to the University of California at San Diego (UCSD), a **teaching assistant** is defined as someone who "assists in the instruction of an upper or lower division course … under the supervision of a faculty member. The TA primarily assists the faculty member … by conducting discussion or laboratory sections that supplement faculty lectures and by grading assignments and examinations."

Suffice it to say, your responsibilities are primarily determined by your major professor or the traditions of the department. Typically, those responsibilities will be one of two types:

If you're given full teaching responsibility, you and you alone will be responsible for teaching an entire course from the first day of classes all the way to the assignment of final grades for the semester.

If you have partial teaching responsibility, your major professor (or some other tenured faculty member) will teach a course. Your duties may entail a variety of administrative tasks, including the grading of exams for that course, reading papers, conducting discussion sessions, setting up laboratory equipment, or advising students.

It is vitally important that you communicate early with your major professor about your duties and assignments so that you can begin any necessary preparation prior to the first day of classes for the semester. That individual will assist you in designing a course, obtaining necessary materials, outlining expectations and goals for students, and communicating other details of the course for your benefit.

What to Expect

Although every department, discipline, and campus is different, the following list outlines some of the major duties of teaching assistants at most universities. You may be responsible for just one of these tasks or a combination, as stipulated by a faculty member. Make sure you are clear about your specific responsibilities before the start of the semester or quarter:

- Conduct and monitor classroom discussions
- Conduct laboratory (science or language) sessions
- Read and grade assigned papers
- Read and grade quizzes, tests, and final examinations
- Teach an entire course
- Teach a portion of a course
- Attend lectures, conferences, and seminars
- Advise undergraduate students
- Hold office hours
- Clean, organize, and inventory laboratory equipment
- Set up audio-visual equipment for a presentation
- Meet with your major professor on a regular basis
- Maintain records
- Take attendance
- Lead field trips
- And, of course, the always dreaded "other duties as assigned"

Communication Is Essential

Your success as a teaching assistant will ultimately be determined by the degree of communication you have with your major professor. Communicating early and frequently will help ensure that you are aware of your assignments and can adequately prepare for those assignments both before as well as during the entire semester.

From the Field _____

Hernan Ramirez, a teaching assistant in the Department of Sociology at the University of Southern California, says, "My mentor [major professor] has put me completely at ease. The communication we established early on helped me feel comfortable and competent. I never felt any pressure. I could always go to him with questions or concerns. This relationship is an important part of my learning curve."

Most professors are accorded a great deal of latitude in the duties and assignments they can delegate to their teaching assistants. Thus, in your initial meetings with your assigned professor, it will be vitally important for you to discover answers to several critical questions:

◆ How often will we meet during the course of the semester or quarter?

◆ Am I expected to attend course lectures?

◆ How many section meetings will I be responsible for?

◆ What types of section meetings will I be responsible for?

◆ Will I be responsible for assigning grades on individual papers and exams?

◆ Will I be responsible for assigning final grades in a course?

◆ What are the required texts?

◆ Will I assign the readings in the required texts?

◆ How many office hours should I schedule for students?

◆ What are my instructional or teaching responsibilities?

Red Flag _____

One of the most common questions asked by teaching assistants is, "Am I responsible for repeating the professor's lecture (or presentation)?" In most every case the answer will be "No!" In consultation with your professor, your primary task will be to enhance, supplement, and augment the lecture, not duplicate it.

Flexibility

It is not uncommon for teaching assistants to be asked to tackle a wide variety of tasks and duties. While teaching will be your primary responsibility, you may be asked (sometimes at a moment's notice) to tackle other assignments.

The key is to remain flexible. Indeed, the mark of a good teacher is her or his ability to be flexible and roll with the punches. By being adequately prepared beforehand, you will be better able to deal with the last-minute assignments if and when they do arise.

From the Field

Susan Massey, a graduate assistant in the Department of Education at the University of Miami (Fla.), says, "Your advisor is there to guide and assist you. However, you have to be disciplined and well prepared for meetings and you must be flexible."

Planning a Course

Depending on the policies and practices of your institution or department, you may be called upon to plan and teach an entire course. Most of the information in this book is designed to offer you strategies and techniques to be successful. You may wish to review the other chapters well in advance of any course design.

There is one question you need answered before beginning any course design. That is, "Is the course schedule, outline, syllabus, readings, assessments, and format prescribed by the department or determined by the teaching assistant?" You may discover that much of the work has already been done for you, or that you may be required to design a course from scratch.

The opportunity to teach an entire course may present you with some interesting challenges. Following are some topics you will need to address in planning a successful course.

Course Objectives

What will students learn by the end of the course? What concepts or principles should they master? You will need to determine the basic objectives of the course and then organize the course around those objectives. Limit your objectives to three to five per course.

Organizational Plan

It will be vitally important for you to know how the course fits in with other offerings of the department. Will the course extend concepts in previous courses or will it serve as a prerequisite? You will also need to know if the course will be a *lower-division* or *upper-division course*.

def•i•ni•tion

Lower-division courses are those designed for freshmen and sophomore students. They are typically introductory courses. In many institutions they have course numbers in the 100s and 200s.

Upper-division courses are those primarily designated for juniors and seniors. They provide students with more in-depth information and sophisticated problem solving. In many institutions they have course numbers in the 300s and 400s.

Topic Plan

In consultation with your professor it would be valuable to construct an outline of the major topics to be covered in the course. You may wish to organize this list in chronological order (start of the semester to the end), or in order from simple to complex.

Textbook(s)

Find out if you will be responsible for selecting the textbook and supplemental readings, or if that is determined by your professor. Check out the resources in the campus library as well as any online resources, too.

Instructional Strategies

Review the instructional strategies detailed in Chapter 8 of this book. Be sure to plan for a variety of strategies in the design of any course. Keep in mind that variety is the spice of life ... and any college course!

Syllabus

Depending on the requirements of your institution, you may be asked to prepare a course syllabus. There are guidelines for this in this book (see Chapter 6). The advantage for you will be that it formalizes the course for students and conveys a business-like approach to the teaching-learning equation.

Schedule and Location

Find out as early as you can about when the course will be taught as well as where it will be conducted. You will need this information in planning your own schedule for the semester. You will also need to know about the configuration of the room, available resources, seating patterns, and other physical details.

Office Hours

Depending on the requirements of your institution, you may be required to schedule office hours so that students can meet with you in private. Students may need individual attention for written assignments, examination preparation, or resource materials in a specific field.

Supportive Services

Get to know the people who work in your department and how they may assist you. Find out if there is a teaching resource center on campus—specifically one for teaching assistants. What materials or resources on teaching are available in the library or online? How can you meet with other teaching assistants to share techniques and information? How can you tap into the expertise of other professors in the department?

From the Field

According to Hernan Ramirez, "It's important that students are clear about when I am available. I'm here to help them and to answer any questions. I believe that my primary responsibility is to be a good role model for students. I take that responsibility very seriously."

Discussion Sections

Most teaching assistants' primary responsibility will be to lead one or more discussion sections of an introductory course taught by a tenured professor. These discussion sections provide opportunities for students to meet in a small group setting (as opposed to the large lecture format led by the professor) to discuss ideas, opinions, and perspectives related to the information shared in the larger lecture.

These sessions are critical to students' comprehension of course material. They are equally important because they provide students with opportunities to investigate and examine elements of a topic in significantly greater detail than would be possible in the large lecture hall. These are wonderful opportunities for you to actively engage students in your excitement and passion for your discipline.

Please review Chapter 10 on effective discussions. Here are some additional ideas and suggestions that have specific applications for your role as a teaching assistant.

Plan the Objectives

Good productive discussions sometimes happen by accident. However, in an under-graduate discussion section, it is essential that you have specific objectives in mind—what do you want students to know or understand at the end of the discussion? It is vitally important that you design specific objectives for each session.

The advantage of having objectives set prior to a discussion is that they will provide you with guideposts or markers to be sure that any discussion is on track and focused. It's quite easy for students to become distracted with issues or concerns unrelated to the topic under discussion. Specific objectives provide an important and necessary structure for any discussion. Here are two possible objectives for a discussion section following a lecture on "Racism in Twentieth Century America":

Red Flag

Limit your objectives to one or two per class session. Most discussion sections are scheduled for 45 minutes to 1 hour. Two objectives is the maximum that you should pursue in any single class.

- ◆ Students will understand the historical antecedents of racism in the United States.

- ◆ Students will be able to state two laws or legal decisions that promoted racism.

Here are a few tips for your consideration:

- ◆ Develop discussion objectives as an outgrowth of a preceding lecture.

- ◆ Post the designated objectives on the chalkboard. This provides a visual reference for students.

- ◆ As each objective is discussed, check it off the list on the board.

- ◆ Use the last five minutes of class to discuss the objectives checked as well as any unchecked objectives.

- ◆ If students seem to get off track during the discussion, refer them to the listing.

Establishing Rapport

One of the most important responsibilities you have as a teaching assistant is to establish rapport with the students you teach. The challenge lies in the fact that you may be considerably closer in age to the students than your professor. This closeness presents some interesting considerations:

- Students may see you as just an older student.

- Students may not recognize or respect your authority.

- Students may question your ability or responsibility to evaluate their progress.

- Students may not take the discussion section as seriously as they would the lecture section.

While these are universal concerns of many undergraduates, you can mitigate the effects of those beliefs by working to establish a good rapport with students in each of your discussion sections. Here are a few ideas:

Never talk down to students. As a graduate student, you may have more information or background about the discipline, but it's important to remember that undergraduate students are probably being introduced to the subject for the very first time.

Talk with students about the strategies and techniques involved in good discussions (see Chapter 10). Let them know about the value of their active participation.

Come to class early and chat with students about a weekend athletic event, a new movie, or a current event. Let students see your human side as much as your academic side.

Arrange the room in a comfortable format that facilitates conversation. A circle, semicircle, or other grouping patterns in which you and all the students can face each other is highly suggested.

Make eye contact with all the students in the room. Don't concentrate solely on those who do all the talking—give visual reinforcement to every person in the class.

Consider a whole-class activity at the start to get everyone involved. For example, go around the room and ask each person to respond to the following, "One thing that I'm not clear on is …." That provides everyone with an opportunity to contribute and gives you information about potential discussion topics.

Encourage students to visit you during your office hours.

Get to know the interests, ambitions, and talents of the students. Who's on the tennis team? Is anyone planning to go to graduate school? Can someone play the bass guitar? Be sure to interject these tidbits of information into the class discussions when appropriate ("Matthew, as a halfback you need to dodge and weave through tacklers as you carry the ball downfield. How is that similar to, or different from, the way in which electrons behave?")

Recognize each student's contribution to the discussion. ("I like your thinking there, Lucy. That's something I hadn't considered before.")

Use active listening. Include some part of a student's comment in any follow-up response. ("Steph, you're saying that there can only be a finite number of steady-state AC circuit topics. Would you care to elaborate?")

Invite students to comment on the contributions of their classmates. ("Omar, what do you think about Katie's assertion that Cortez was nothing more than an opportunistic land grabber?")

Invite students to pose their own questions at the beginning of a discussion and then lead them to discover answers to their own self-initiated queries. You may wish to invite students to work together and pose three questions they would like answered in any following discussion.

Engaging Students

This book has presented various methods for engaging students throughout a course. Here are a few additional ideas specific to discussion sections that you may lead. Consider these as possibilities for any class or any topic.

Inform students that during the lecture by the professor they must record one question on a blank index card. Students are then asked to bring those cards to the discussion section. Just before class you can quickly review the cards to determine appropriate discussion topics.

Always provide students with feedback or a reaction to their contributions. Don't allow a comment or remark to just "sit there"—rather, offer a compliment, reaction, or an invitation to elaborate. Your reaction to every student contribution will either promote or inhibit further discussion.

Make sure the comments you provide students are detailed and specific. "Good," "OK," and "fine" are nonspecific and don't stimulate further discussion. "I liked the comparisons you made between Japanese cinema and Italian cinema" provides positive reinforcement and an inducement to contribute at a later time.

Move students beyond literal and comprehension-type questions (see Chapter 12). Engage them in a series of application, analysis, synthesis, and evaluative questions that stimulate higher-level thinking skills.

Be willing to admit your ignorance. Remember that you are a student, too. Acknowledge that you may not know something (but that you're willing to discover the answer for a future class). This is not the time to pontificate or make up an answer. Be willing to model good learning as well as good teaching.

From the Field

Hernan Ramirez says, "My biggest fear was that I didn't know enough and that I was unqualified for the position. However, I realized that I was a student, too. There were always things to keep learning and as I learned more material I became more comfortable. I was able to share my own experiences in my discussion groups."

Open a discussion with a timely quote, a brief anecdote, a controversial comment, or a short reading assignment. Provide students with some material to grapple with or react to.

Include a problem-solving experience in each class. Present students with a relevant problem and invite them to solve it (in small groups) using information from a previous lecture or the current discussion.

A Final Word

Most universities and colleges have information specifically directed at teaching assistants. This information, usually in the form of a handout, booklet, or brochure, details specific institutional policies and practices for teaching assistants. Also included is valuable information on how to conduct classes, seminars, labs, and other meetings with undergraduate students.

Find out if your institution has a teaching assistant handbook. Review it well in advance of any course you are assigned to teach or monitor. If your institution does not have a guidebook, you may wish to access one or both of the following websites, which offer a thorough introduction as well as loads of helpful ideas on the teaching assistant role:

From the Field

Susan Massey, a graduate assistant, offers the following recommendation: "Enjoy what you are doing, gain as much knowledge or training as possible, and be actively involved in the process."

◆ University of California, San Diego, Center for Teaching Development— Graduate Teaching Assistant Handbook (www-ctd.ucsd.edu/ resources/tahandbook.pdf)

◆ University of Georgia, Center for Teaching and Learning—Teaching Assistant Handbook (www.isd.uga.edu/teaching_assistant/ta-handbook/handbook06.pdf)

The Least You Need to Know

◆ The duties and responsibilities of your position will vary by institution and discipline.

◆ Communicate with your major professor and be clear about your responsibilities.

◆ Awareness of the elements of good course design is critical.

◆ Establish positive relationships with students.

◆ Be aware of the resources available for teaching assistants.

Chapter 21

Teaching Adult and Continuing Education Courses

In This Chapter

- ◆ The nature of adult and continuing education

- ◆ The nature of adult learners

- ◆ Designing effective courses

- ◆ Strategies appropriate for adult learners

When I was stationed with the U.S. Coast Guard in Alameda, California, in the early 1970s, I had the opportunity to work for a local community college that had established outreach courses for servicemen, particularly those about to retire from military duty. Many of the classes were designed to assist active-duty servicemen in obtaining their GED certificates, since many of them had left high school to join the service early in their lives.

Those were exciting courses to teach, for one simple reason. The students brought incredible learning experiences to every class and every discussion. They had lived the history we were studying in American History, and they had experienced the political drama we were discussing in U.S. Government. In short, the life experiences of the 40- to 60-year-old students provided a stimulus for learning unavailable to younger students. Adult learners may be a separate breed, but they are no less exciting to teach. This chapter explores ways you can make that excitement part of your work with these dynamic students.

Unlimited Learning Opportunities

I have before me the latest edition of the *Cooperative Community Education* catalog, distributed twice a year to all the residents of my county. This catalog represents eight different school districts and their various adult and continuing education courses. These courses are distributed among the following areas:

- Arts and crafts
- Computers
- Culinary
- Finance
- Health and fitness
- Home
- Special interests
- Career classes

The catalog contains over 200 separate courses for county residents. Some courses are 2 hours long (one session), while others are 10 weeks long (computer classes, for example). Here is a brief sampling of the variety and focus of selected courses from this catalog:

- Beginning Ballroom Dancing
- Wheel-Thrown Pottery
- Learn Your Computer Start to Finish
- Investment Choices in the Marketplace
- Conversational Spanish
- Basket Weaving
- Fundamentals of Natural Golf

- Introduction to Sign Language

- Reading and Telling Stories to Children

- Symphonic Literature

- Balance—A Wellness Workshop

- Sell Your Home Fast and for the Best Price

- Adult CPR

Suffice it to say, there is a wide variety of courses for all interests and all ability levels. That's the nature of *adult and continuing education*—courses are designed with the specific needs and interests of potential students in mind. They are less about satisfying the requirements or demands of an institution or licensing agency, and more about satisfying personal goals and desires.

def•i•ni•tion

Adult and continuing education is aimed at improving skills, talents, and abilities. Most of the classes are not for credit or certification.

The Nature of Adult Learners

The definition of adult learners has changed dramatically over the past 2 decades. In the past an adult learner was defined as someone who was older than the typical public school or college student. This may have been someone who had dropped out of high school and was coming back years later to obtain her or his high school diploma. It may have been a woman who had left college to have a family and was now returning to complete her degree. Or, it may have been a senior citizen looking for a recreational activity or self-improvement course.

Today, our definition of adult and continuing education students has expanded exponentially. In short, these students are individuals of any age who voluntarily elect to participate in a class or group learning situation.

In general, adult and continuing education students are looking to improve themselves in a very narrow area or specialty. They also bring different expectations, needs, perceptions, and experiences to any class or course. Let's take a look.

Social Characteristics

Most participants in adult or continuing education courses have a wealth of life experiences. They also have a depth of social experiences that far exceeds those of typical college students. The background of experiences in the real world is both extensive and personal. Here's what you need to know to use these experiences to your advantage.

Many individuals may have less than favorable memories of their days in formal school settings. Keep discussions or references to these to an absolute minimum (if at all). Focus on current experiences and how a particular course will benefit them now.

Some individuals are active participants, others prefer to be passive. Be sure to provide learning opportunities for both types. Adult learners are often shy or reluctant to discuss their weaknesses or education gaps with others. Acknowledge this, but emphasize how the class or course will provide them with new skills. ("I know you all are a little nervous about these newfangled things called computers, but I'll show you some easy ways to get started with them.")

Learn as much as you can about the past experiences of each participant in a class. Use this information in stimulating discussions or in shaping the presentation of materials. ("Helen, I recall that you were a nurse in Vietnam. How were those experiences similar to or different from the CPR techniques we're learning now?")

"Research Says"

A significant body of research has shown that when adult learners are provided with regular, systematic, and frequent opportunities to relate the course content to their backgrounds of experiences, then the learning becomes more meaningful and lasting. Adult learners want and need a connection to what they already know.

Group work should be informal and relaxed. I like to think of adult education as similar to a group of friends gathering in my living room to chat about the latest movie or discuss a current political situation. An emphasis on informality makes adult learning more productive.

Emotional Characteristics

Adult learners are frequently *afraid* of learning. That fear may come from negative school experiences, nonsupport from parents or caregivers, or the length of time since they were in a formalized educational setting. It is always important to remember that, just like students in public school or college settings, adult learners learn best in emotionally supportive environments—that is, environments in which their self-esteem or self-worth are valued and enhanced.

Here are a few tips that will help you create that positive emotional climate in an adult or continuing education course.

From the Field _____

According to William Draves, president of the Learning Resources Network, "In helping [an adult] learn, the teacher must be able to create a positive emotional climate, and the key to that state is one's self-image."

Be an active listener. Encourage students to contribute their ideas, reactions, frustrations, or insecurities. Listen to what they have to say (without interruption) and use their words in your response. ("Yes, Karl, creating a backup file does seem like a lot of extra work, but it will also save you some unnecessary aggravation down the line.")

Always provide positive feedback to learners. Don't ridicule a person's beliefs (which may have developed over many years), but acknowledge each person's contribution. ("That's an interesting perspective, Betty. Would anyone like to ask Betty a question about her views on day trading?")

Many adult learners express their inadequacies or deficiencies in learning new things. Let them know that you are their partner in the learning process. ("Stephen, I sense your frustration regarding perspective in your paintings, so let me show you a handy little trick.")

Adult learners are often sensitive about making mistakes—especially in front of their peer group. If someone is doing something wrong, discuss the situation rather than the individual. Focus on what was done, not the person who did it. ("Francis, it looks like there are too many adjectives in this sentence. Let's see what we can do to eliminate a few unnecessary ones.")

Adult learners respond better to "I" messages than comments beginning with "You." Instead of saying, "You aren't doing this right," convey an "I" message such as, "I sometimes get tripped up on this step, too. Let me show you something I've learned."

"Research Says"

The research on adult learning is unequivocal on one specific point—verbal and/or nonverbal punishment is counterproductive to learning. Adult students learn best when they feel supported and secure. Negative words or actions (directed at the individual) undermine a student's learning potential.

Use humor whenever and wherever possible. This doesn't mean that you have to be a stand-up comic, it just means you should feel comfortable lightening the mood or injecting a joke into the conversation every now and again. Humor relaxes people, especially adults; it creates a positive learning environment and stimulates discussion and enjoyment of a learning task.

Motivational Characteristics

Adult learners, just like traditional college students, need to be motivated throughout a class or course. One of the best ways to do that is to provide consistent and honest encouragement. Here's how I define encouragement, particularly as it applies to adult learners. Encouragement

◆ Recognizes the effort of the doer. ("You worked really hard on your quilt pattern.")

◆ Promotes self-evaluation. ("How do you feel about your backstroke so far?")

◆ Emphasizes effort and progress of a task. ("Look at all the improvement you've made on your PowerPoint design.")

◆ Emphasizes appreciation of contributions and assets. ("Your efforts helped us have a successful sushi party.")

Encouragement, in large quantities, can be a powerful element in any successful academic endeavor. But you must remember some major considerations if your verbal comments are to be effective.

Use encouragement consistently. Don't just use it every once in awhile, and don't just use it for the good students and not the underachieving students. Make it a regular element for every student in every learning activity.

Be honest and sincere when you give encouragement. Acknowledge the learner's true achievement, not some fake or made-up accomplishments.

Red Flag

Encouragement should be done in a casual manner, should require no more than 10 to 12 words, and last no longer than 4 to 6 seconds.

Be specific! General statements such as "Good," "Great," or "Cool" are too general to have any meaning. Provide a very specific reference for an adult student. ("You must feel very proud about the progress you're making learning Spanish verbs.")

Give immediate feedback. It has to occur soon after the event or task is completed, or it will be meaningless.

Personal Characteristics

All adults come to class with certain mental or physical needs. Here are some of the most significant and how you can provide for them:

- **Sight:** Be sure students can see any displays, chalkboards, visual aids, and each other.

- **Hearing:** Create a classroom environment in which each student can adequately hear you, any audio presentations, and other students.

- **Temperature:** Check the temperature in the classroom and make sure it is at a comfortable setting. Adjust as necessary throughout a class session.

- **Seating:** For most classes, it would be advantageous to place students in a circle or semi-circle to promote discussion. Whenever possible, stay away from traditional seating patterns (straight rows of desks).

- **Practicality:** Most adults take a course to learn something new—something that they can apply immediately. Honor this expectation by keeping theory to a minimum and offering numerous "hands-on" practical learning opportunities.

- **Problem solving:** Adults want to solve problems. Provide them with basic information; but, more important, offer them opportunities to use the new information in real-life situations.

- **Familiarity:** Choose the familiar rather than the unusual (when selecting samples or examples). Whenever possible, tap into what students already know and build on it.

- **Perspective:** Unlike children, adults want answers and they want them right now! Keep the focus of your course narrow and specific. Short-term solutions will be more readily embraced by your adult students than will long-term philosophical treatises.

- **Concreteness:** Work with the concrete rather than the abstract. Whenever possible, use three-dimensional examples rather than theoretical presentations.

- **Simplicity:** Divide your topic into small steps. Move from the simple to the more complex. Provide opportunities for students to build on previously learned steps in incremental stages.

- **Immediacy:** If you teach a course that has multiple sessions or classes, be sure students take away at least one new skill each session. Don't hold out the promise of future skills—adult learners respond best to immediate self-improvement.

Designing an Effective Course

A well-designed adult or continuing education course does not come together overnight. Just as with any college course, it requires attention to organization, content, presentation, and outcomes. Here are some tips and ideas to make your courses successful from start to finish. These suggestions are appropriate for every course—from the casual (Making a Yuletide Treat Basket) to the complex (Symphonic Literature).

Objectives

The crux of a good course—irrespective of its length or subject matter—is its objectives. Objectives are what drive a course. Everything you do, every activity, every instructional method, every teaching resource must be tied to the course's objectives.

Writing good objectives will be challenging at first. Everything in the course must revolve around the objectives, so you must construct them with care and attention to detail. A well-crafted objective has two components:

- The audience: The students for whom the objective is intended.

- The terminal behavior: The anticipated performance.

Here are a few objectives for selected continuing education courses:

- Wheel-Thrown Pottery: Participants will be able to create various forms of pottery.

- Learn Your Computer Start to Finish: Students will be able to open, size, and arrange windows.

- Fiction Writing: Participants will craft a 1,000-word short story.

- Adult Learn to Swim: Each student will be able to swim two lengths of the pool without assistance.

- Conversational Spanish: Each student will be able to carry a 3-minute conversation with the instructor.

- Tips About Going into Business: Each student will construct a Business Plan suitable for review.

As you can see, well-written objectives help you create a course that is focused, on target, and geared for the specific learning needs of your students.

Content

One of the most difficult decisions you'll have to make is the nature and amount of material or content to include. Sometimes this will be determined by the level of the course (introductory/advanced), your level of expertise (expert/novice), and the experience of the course participants (none/considerable). My rule of thumb is to prepare three levels of material for any adult or continuing education course. These include:

◆ **Critical:** This is the information students absolutely need in order to comprehend the topic and put their newfound knowledge into action.

◆ **Valuable:** This is information that provides students with broader perspectives and more depthful learning. It is, however, not essential to their overall performance.

◆ **Optional:** This is information that is not crucial; but which adds some interesting asides, personal reflections, anecdotes and stories, tidbits, and lore to the subject.

In trying to construct a course I have found the following formula helpful in deciding how much of each category (above) to include in a lesson or series of lessons.

◆ Critical: 60 percent

◆ Valuable: 30 percent

◆ Optional: 10 percent

This formula gives you lots of latitude and instructional options. If, for example, your discussion about a critical item takes more time than you had originally planned, you can eliminate the optional material without a significant loss. On the other hand, if students demonstrate an ability to quickly learn the critical material and move rapidly through the valuable material, then you always have some additional (optional) items to share with them to successfully round out a class.

Organization

Another important decision that you will need to make before students arrive at the first class meeting is how the course will be organized. Your decision at this point is critical with respect to students' eventual success in mastering the course's objectives. Basically, there are five ways you can organize your course:

◆ **Chronologically:** This would include a historical sequence or some other time frame.

◆ **Simple to complex:** Start with the most basic of concepts and work up to more challenging concepts.

◆ **Concrete to abstract:** Start with hands-on learning activities and move to theoretical or philosophical concepts.

◆ **General to specific:** Provide students with a broad overview of the topic and then get more detailed and specific.

◆ **Specific to general:** Provide students with opportunities to master very specific skills. Afterwards, offer opportunities to apply those skills in a broader learning environment.

No single organization method is better. The choice is up to you. However, please keep in mind that how well a course is initially organized will have a lot to do with how successful students will be throughout the course.

Resources

Another decision you will need to make revolves around the availability of teaching resources for your course. Effective adult and continuing education courses combine several different resources to provide for a variety of learning (and teaching) opportunities.

Consider these resources for your courses:

◆ Magazine articles

◆ Supplemental reading material

◆ Online resources

◆ Other teachers

◆ Community resources (guest speakers, printed materials)

◆ Students

◆ Computers

- Bulletin boards
- Overhead projectors
- Instructional TV
- Slide projectors
- Posters
- Newspapers
- Contributions from students

Red Flag

It is strongly suggested that no textbooks be used in an adult or continuing education course. That's simply because many working adults will not have the time (or inclination) to read through an extensive (or expensive) textbook. For any out-of-class reading assignments, use short articles instead.

Final Words

The tips, techniques, and teaching strategies suggested in the other chapters of this book are also important in the teaching of adult or continuing education courses. The methods of course design (Chapter 4), first-day icebreakers (Chapter 7), how to conduct a class (Chapter 8), effective lectures (Chapter 9), effective discussions (Chapter 10), and higher-level thinking skills (Chapter 12) are all applicable to adult learners as much as to traditional college students.

Teaching adults or continuing education students can offer you many unique opportunities to share your knowledge with a receptive and appreciative audience—an audience eager to learn and eager to grow.

The Least You Need to Know

- Teaching adult and continuing education courses provides unlimited teaching and learning opportunities.
- Adult learners are more diverse than traditional college students.
- Adult learners bring a range of emotional, motivational, and personal characteristics to class.
- Strategies for teaching adults are often similar to those appropriate for teaching college students.

Chapter 22

Evaluation of Teaching

In This Chapter

- ◆ The value of student ratings
- ◆ Student perceptions
- ◆ Rethinking the rating process
- ◆ Peer evaluations
- ◆ Self-evaluation

Peter Filene, a professor of history at the University of North Carolina at Chapel Hill, says, "Teaching is only as successful as the learning it produces." As we have discussed throughout this book, students bring a certain set of expectations, personalities, and learning dynamics to the beginning of any course. Those elements shape *how* they learn as much as *what* they will learn. As professors, we try to adapt those factors with course content and delivery to have a lasting effect on students irrespective of their major.

But how do we know if we are "making the grade"? How do we know if we have a significant impact on student learning, student growth, or student thinking? Are we getting through to students—altering or shaping their interest in our discipline? Are we, as Filene underscores, producing learning? Let's take a look at the evaluation of teaching and how we might approach it.

How Are You Doing?

Recently, my department chair sent me the summary results of the student evaluations of a course I taught:

> *"Knows all materials thoroughly and is very informative."*

> *"Interest, engagement, and excitement is embedded in every lesson."*

> *"Always excited, many details provided for every assignment."*

> *"Class is very interesting and lively."*

> *"Takes students' opinions and feelings into consideration."*

> *"Is willing to change assignments to help students."*

> *"Clear, detailed expectations from the beginning."*

> *"Very clear and descriptive syllabus is presented to the class."*

> *"Very informative and worth taking."*

(Of course, immediately after reading those evaluations, I purchased some filet mignons and a fine bottle of Cabernet with which I could celebrate the innate wisdom of my students!)

While almost anyone would be thrilled with a set of student evaluations like those, I had to put them in proper perspective.

From the Field _____

Ken Bain, director of the Center for Teaching Excellence at New York University, says that all professors need to ask themselves a critical and fundamental question: "Does the teaching help and encourage students to learn in ways that make a sustained, substantial and positive difference in the way they think, act, or feel—without doing them any major harm?"

Those statements show that my methodology, practices, and beliefs are all acceptable to students. However, these statements are really more reflective of my performance in the classroom. The students emphasized what the instructor (me) did during the course of the semester—not what they actually learned.

That's not to say that I'm dismissing these student comments (or the bottle of Cabernet). But those comments don't tell me whether those same students learned anything, whether their intellectual lives were altered in some positive way. That's certainly not the fault of the students, but may have more to do with the questions students were asked on the evaluation forms.

Student Ratings

Most colleges and universities have elaborate, end-of-the-semester evaluations in which students rate their professors. At my institution, for example, each professor can select one of four different evaluations forms and administer it to one or more classes during the last three weeks of the semester. Students complete the forms anonymously. The evaluations are then tabulated by the department secretary and distributed by each department chairperson to respective faculty members several weeks after the course is over (and all grades have been submitted).

A Sample Student Rating Form

Here is one form (Student Observation Form B) my institution makes available to faculty (students answer a yes/no question and then record a separate response in a follow-up "comments" section):

Teaching

Does the faculty member seem to exhibit a sound understanding of the range of subject matter?

Is the faculty member able to maintain interest during the class period?

Does the faculty member present material clearly and without distracting mannerisms?

Does the faculty member attempt to improve the course where problems arise?

Is the faculty member sensitive to student responses and adaptive to student needs?

Is the faculty member fair in evaluation of student work?

Did the faculty member provide an adequate syllabus for the course so you understand the operating procedures?

Do you feel that there are an adequate number of tests given during the semester?

Where do you place this faculty member among all you have had at [this institution]?

Course

Were the objectives of this course made clear to you?

Overall, was the course of value to you?

Compared to other courses you have taken at [this institution], where would you place this course?

How Did I Do?

Just like Ed Koch's perennial question to New Yorkers while he was mayor of the city, "How am I doing?", college professors want to know how they are doing, too. We can know that only if we ask our students the right questions. For example, Student Observation Form B asks questions related to the performance of the faculty member. If a faculty member considers her or his performance to be critical, then the results generated by this form will either validate strengths or expose weaknesses in the individual's performance during the semester.

In my recent student evaluation, students seemed to feel that I was a good performer because that was the focus of the questions they were asked. However, I'm equally interested in how well my students learned during that particular course. What did I do (or not do) that had an impact on them as learners?

From the Field

When I asked Terry Seip, a professor of history at the University of Southern California, for his evaluation of a good course, he said, "[It's when] they've had a real learning experience! It's when they see that history has value and that it relates to their real lives. It's less about my performance and more about their connections, or linkages, with history."

Student Perceptions

One of the factors that influence student ratings is the perceptions they bring to the evaluation process. That is to say, if a student is a *surface learner*, she or he will praise a professor who focuses on the memorization of facts and figures. On the other hand, that same student will give considerably lower ratings to a professor who emphasizes thinking at higher levels of cognition (analysis, synthesis, evaluation). By the same token, a *deep learner* will give low ratings to a professor who emphasizes memorization and regurgitation of a finite list of facts, but will provide a higher rating to a professor who emphasizes the critical explorations of topic.

def•i•ni•tion

Surface learners like to learn the facts of a topic or subject. They equate learning with the memorization and accumulation of a large body of knowledge. **Deep learners** prefer to engage in higher-level cognitive activities—analyzing material, synthesizing information from several different sources, and evaluating the worth or utility of data from a variety of viewpoints.

So, here's the bottom line: when students rate your teaching performance, they are only assessing part of the teaching equation. It is equally important that you have information relative to your teaching effectiveness. Only then will you be able to design courses that are learner-centered, intellectually stimulating, and educationally productive.

Rethinking the Student Rating Paradigm

Students need methods of assessing their own intellectual growth, within a course as it is taking place as well as its conclusion. That information is also valuable to me in terms of making necessary modifications in course design during the semester as well as in successive semesters. Here are some proven strategies:

Criterion Checks

A *criterion check* is a way of monitoring how well students understand a lesson. It is an informal evaluation technique that can be used at the end of a class or periodically throughout the length of a course. The focus is on student comprehension, not on teacher performance.

Prepare a standardized form to be passed out to students during the last 4 minutes of a class. Invite students to respond to the following questions: How well do you understand this topic? How has your thinking been changed by today's activities? What can I do to make this topic more comprehensible?

In the middle of a class, ask students to write a response to the following question on a blank index card: What did you learn so far? Collect the cards, quickly glance at them while students are engaged in a small group discussion (for example), and take a few moments to respond to the information they share.

> **"Research Says"**
>
> According to a substantial body of research, students who take a course to satisfy their general interest or as an elective tend to give the course (or professor) slightly higher ratings. Students who take a course to satisfy a major or liberal arts requirement tend to give slightly lower ratings.

def•i•ni•tion

A **criterion check** is a point in any lesson where the instructor stops and checks to see if students understand the material up to that point.

For a particularly difficult topic or complex concept, stop every 15 to 20 minutes and ask students to give you a quick rating of their level of comprehension. Ask them to give you a thumbs up, thumbs down, or thumbs sideways according to how well they understand the presentation.

At the beginning of a class, pass out blank index cards to the students. Tell them that sometime during the first half of the lesson you would like them to write down two questions about the topic that they need the answers to. Collect the cards prior to the second half of the class and take time to respond to a selection of representative questions.

End-of-Course Ratings

While performance ratings have their place, you should consider the use of instructional ratings, too. Here are two sets of questions you may wish to include on a rating sheet for your courses. Please feel free to modify or adjust these according to the dictates of your discipline or the individual design of your classes.

Circle: High–Low

1. How well are you learning the material in this course?
   7 6 5 4 3 2 1

2. How would you rate your comprehension of course concepts so far?
   7 6 5 4 3 2 1

3. How would you rate your effort in this course so far?
   7 6 5 4 3 2 1

4. How many unanswered questions do you have right now?
   7 6 5 4 3 2 1

5. How much is the instructor contributing to your learning?
   7 6 5 4 3 2 1

6. What is your overall rating of this course so far?
   7 6 5 4 3 2 1

Provide a few short sentences answering each question:

1. How well did this course influence your enjoyment of the subject?

2. How well did this course influence your comprehension of the subject?

3. In what ways did this course cause you to think or interact intellectually with the content?

4. What was the most challenging concept or principle in the course?

5. What did you do to meet that challenge?

6. Comment on how well you learned in this course.

7. How much did you contribute to the course?

You will notice that in each of the two forms above, the emphasis is placed on the students as learners, rather than on the instructor as a performer. The shift in emphasis is enormous and can provide you with valuable data, not only on a course's effectiveness, but also on the need to modify or alter a course based on student learning potential.

Peer Evaluations

Many institutions have an established peer-evaluation system—particularly for new or untenured professors. *Peer evaluation* provides you with observations, input, and suggestions from colleagues in your department or the school in general. It has proven to be an evaluation technique that yields valuable information about your teaching style as well as student performance.

What's Its Function?

Peer evaluation promotes good teaching as a community or all-department concern. Bonds between department members are strengthened when everyone works together for a common cause—the promotion of quality teaching. You also get nonjudgmental input and advice—especially from those faculty members who are long-time members of the department or institution.

Peer evaluation can alert you to behaviors or practices that may have a negative effect on student learning. These behaviors may not be evident to the professor practicing

def•i•ni•tion

Peer evaluation is when one or more of your departmental colleagues visit one or several sections of your courses. They observe you and your students and typically provide a written report of their observations. Those observations may form part of your annual review or may be used in matters related to tenure and promotion.

them, but may be visible to impartial observers. Peer evaluation can also turn up issues that students may not recognize or be familiar with, such as unprofessional communication, organizational weaknesses, inappropriate presentation methods, or lack of student attention.

Peer evaluation can assist you in attaining a balance between professor performance and student learning. It can help you focus more on helping students understand a topic rather than the simple delivery of information to students (often in a lecture format).

Steps in the Process

Peer evaluation is handled in several different ways, depending on the practices of the institution or a particular department. Here is a typical order of events:

♦ Meet with the assigned evaluator before a class (one to two days in advance is recommended).

♦ Share your syllabus with the evaluator. Discuss how the lesson fits in with the overall direction of the course.

♦ Provide the evaluator with a copy of your lesson plan—what will you be covering and how will you cover it?

♦ Make sure the evaluator is familiar with the content of the class; its importance to student learning; how it satisfies departmental, institutional, or governmental standards; and traditions of the discipline.

♦ Provide an appropriate location for the evaluator in the classroom. Typically, this will be a desk or table in the back; however, depending on the configuration of the classroom, another location may be more practical.

♦ Introduce the evaluator to the class. Students will feel more comfortable knowing that the individual is there to assist in the improvement of departmental teaching, not to evaluate their performance in the class.

♦ The evaluator will typically record notes on the various activities that take place during the class, including students' reactions to those activities.

♦ Sometimes, at the end of the class, the evaluator may talk with several students about what took place and their personal evaluations of the class

♦ Some time later, typically one to three days after the class, the evaluator will sit down with you to discuss her or his observations as well as suggestions for improvement.

Although you may find this to be an anxious time, please keep in mind that your colleague is your ally—she or he is there to assist you in becoming the best instructor possible, not to make you look bad.

Once Again, It's Learning That Counts!

You can help the people who evaluate you by giving them a list of specific behaviors or reactions to look for. For example, invite a peer evaluator (during the observation) to respond to some of the following questions:

◆ How does the instructor foster higher-level thinking by students?

◆ How does the instructor relate new material to previously learned material or to the real world?

◆ What expectations does the instructor have and how does she or he promote those expectations?

◆ How does the instructor stimulate/encourage learning?

◆ Is the quality of student participation and student work commensurate with the objectives of the lesson?

◆ Did students learn?

The success of peer evaluation is founded on several practices. Promote these as part of your own teaching and learning cycle.

Invite a peer evaluator to visit several different classes during a semester. It's like buying a new car. We typically test drive and check out several different models before we make a final decision. Encourage your colleague to watch you "drive your car" several times before they reach a conclusion.

Encourage your peer evaluator to spend time with your students. Ask them to pose some questions to the students (see the previous section) and encourage responses. And return the favor: ask if you can sit in on your peer evaluator's classes, to get a feel for her or his philosophy of teaching and how it's applied in their classroom.

Red Flag _____

There is convincing evidence that professors tend to evaluate their peers according to their individual philosophies of pedagogy. That is to say, professors will evaluate more favorably those colleagues who teach the way they do and less favorably those colleagues whose teaching style is significantly different.

Plan regular and systematic meetings with a peer evaluator over the course of the semester. Peer evaluation is not a one-shot strategy, but one that succeeds when it is done over time.

Keep the focus on student learning. Use student ratings primarily for your instructional performance. Encourage and emphasize student learning as the critical element of peer evaluations.

Self-Evaluation, Self-Reflection

Throughout this book I have tried to focus on the concept of *professor as learner*. That means a professor who *guides* rather than *leads; facilitates* rather than *assigns;* and *models* rather than *tells*. After more than 2 decades of collegiate teaching experience, I've learned that the most successful professors are willing to learn alongside their students—providing students with the processes and the supportive arena in which they can begin to make their own discoveries and pursue their own self-initiated investigations.

Throughout this book, we have looked at all the attributes and all the qualities of good professors. But I'd like to save the best for last. That is, a good professor is also a *reflective* professor. A reflective professor thinks as much as he or she acts, and is constantly searching for self-improvement.

Introspection

Professors who reflect are open to change. Reflective educators do lots of self-assessment, and in doing so they help their students grow both as scholars and as individuals. Here are some reflective qualities essential to your success as a college teacher:

◆ Be open-minded to new ideas and new possibilities.

◆ Think about the reason and rationale for every task and assignment.

◆ Be willing to take responsibility for your actions. If students aren't learning, it may not be entirely their fault.

◆ Be open to improvement on both major and minor issues.

◆ Regularly assess your teaching philosophy.

◆ Make time for regular periods of self-questioning.

The Least You Need to Know

- There is a big difference between performance ratings and what students learn.

- Student ratings of classes and professors are influenced by their self-perceptions as learners.

- Instructional ratings can yield incredibly valuable information important in course design.

- Peer evaluations can enhance one's teaching effectiveness.

Chapter 23

The Successful Professor— You!

In This Chapter

- ◆ Good college professors—who are they?
- ◆ Individual accountability
- ◆ Student orientation
- ◆ Critical learning environments
- ◆ Constructivism revisited
- ◆ Learning as a lifelong process

Throughout this book I have talked about the qualities, attributes, and dynamics of successful college teaching. Undoubtedly, you saw some of your own college professors in the pages of this book. You saw individuals who inspired you in your graduate work, people who made an indelible impact on your interest and passion for a particular field, and educators who were inspiring as well as caring. Your current position as a teacher of undergraduate or graduate students may well have been determined by the efforts of one or two significant individuals.

What did those people do that influenced your current career path? What attributes did they consistently display? In this final chapter, we'll consider those characteristics. Most important, you will learn how you can make those attributes your own and become an effective college teacher—one your students will remember long after they leave your institution.

Students Say

What makes some college professors excellent and others ... well, slightly less than memorable? That's a question I've been asking for more than 2 decades, so I decided to go to the experts—college students. As part of my periodic survey of undergraduate students, I frequently ask them about their criteria for effective college instructors. Here's a sampling of responses from the past few years.

Good college professors

- Are eager and willing to work with students.

- Are knowledgeable about their subject and can present it in an organized fashion.

- Display lots of enthusiasm for their discipline and for teaching.

- Are willing to admit their faults, shortcomings, and mistakes.

- Are able to use a variety of teaching technique to help students learn a topic.

- Have a sense of humor.

- Encourage student opinions and provide opportunities for classroom discussions.

- Have high expectations for students and work with them to achieve those standards.

- Are respectful of students' needs and honest with their opinions.

- Are able to relate the content of the course to students' lives.

- Are available outside of class to discuss course issues and/or personal concerns.

- Treat students as adults, not as children.

Each year, when I ask students for the number-one quality of a good college professor, they all say it is a passion for teaching. That characteristic holds true for tenured as well as untenured professors; it holds true irrespective of the discipline, field or department; it holds true regardless of the number of years of teaching experience;

and it holds true for full-time professors, part-time instructors, and graduate or teaching assistants. The bottom line: excitement about teaching is the single most significant quality of any college professor.

It's important to point out that your effectiveness as a college teacher is dependent on much more than your knowledge of your specific discipline. In fact, your success will be driven by characteristics and dynamics that are as much a part of who you are as they are of your classroom instruction. Conversations with scores of college instructors around the country indicate that good professors are effective because of the interaction of five distinguishing characteristics:

- Individual accountability
- Student orientation
- A critical learning environment
- Constructivist orientation
- Learning as a lifelong process

I invite you to consider these characteristics in terms of your own personality dynamics as well as in terms of your reasons for becoming a college teacher.

Individual Accountability

There are probably many reasons you are or would like to be a college instructor. Who you are as a person and your desire to share your knowledge have a lot to do with why your chose this field, and they will be significant to your success in the classroom. My own experiences with fellow teachers have taught me that personality is a predominant factor in the success of a teacher's students.

Joy to the World

Good college teachers are joyful. They relish the thrill of discovery and the natural curiosity of students. They are excited about learning and consistently transmit that excitement to their students. They are stimulated by the unknown and are amazed at what can be learned, not just at what is learned.

Students consistently rate professors high when humor is part of the classroom environment. This humor does not come from telling lots of jokes, but rather from the good-natured conversations and discussions carried on with students. Humor helps break down conversational barriers, establishes good rapport, and builds strong teaching environments.

Be passionate! Good teachers are good because they are passionate about what they teach, and students will recognize that immediately. If you're less than excited, students will determine that very quickly, too. Your passion for teaching must be evident in everything you do.

I Wonder Why ...

Effective instructors are inquisitive. They continuously ask questions, looking for new explanations and myriad new answers. They serve as positive role models for students, helping them to ask their own questions for exploration. They are driven not to find all the answers, but to develop a classroom environment in which self-initiated questioning (by both teacher and students) predominates.

Good teachers are also creative. Never sure of what lies around the corner or down the next path, they are willing to explore new dimensions and seek new possibilities, to experiment and try new approaches. Effective teachers are not afraid of change and realize that change can be a positive element in every classroom. If something is not working, these teachers are eager to strike out into new territories for exploration. They're never content with status quo—their classrooms are always evolving, always in a state of transition.

Teaching Is Evolutionary

In preparation for this book, I interviewed college teachers all over the United States, from Maine to California and from Hawaii to Florida—and a lot of places in between. I wanted to get their thoughts and impressions of good college teaching and the characteristics they felt are essential in a dynamic college classroom.

These outstanding teachers kept telling me that teaching is an evolutionary process. One just doesn't become a good teacher overnight—it's a long, steady process of examination, discovery, change, and growth. Good professors are always open to that; in fact, they embrace it as an essential part of the academic success of their students. Ineffective professors believe that knowledge (of their subject and knowledge of teaching) is finite.

"Just deliver the goods," they say, "and the good students will learn and the poor ones won't!"

However, the teacher who keeps evolving has the most impact on her or his students—not in terms of their classroom performance, but in terms of the learning that takes place. Evolutionary teachers understand that learning is always a process and never a product. That statement is as true for them as it is for their students.

From the Field

Mike McGough, an associate professor of education, says, "The biggest challenge is to keep myself and my courses constantly evolving. I need to change and grow and so do my classes. Without that evolution, both my material and I become stagnant."

Student Orientation

If you were to walk into the classroom of any outstanding college instructor, irrespective of her or his discipline or experience, one thing will become immediately clear: students are respected, trusted, and honored. These are classrooms where the professor is not lecturing from atop a marble pedestal, but rather interacting on a personal level with students.

Demonstrating Respect

Students need to know that they will never be embarrassed or ridiculed. Nor will they be intimidated or shown excessive favoritism. The best teachers have positive attitudes about everyone in the course. High expectations abound for each and every student, and successful teachers create a learning environment in which those expectations can be realized.

Good college teachers are listeners. Good teachers know that students have much to contribute to the curriculum and to each other and provide numerous opportunities for them to do so. Or as a colleague once told me, "Good teaching often means opening your ears and closing your mouth!"

Red Flag

In traditional college classrooms, two thirds of class time is taken up by teacher talk (typically lectures), and two thirds of the teacher's talk is telling rather than interacting with students. This is sometimes known as the "Rule of Two Thirds." This rule tends to inhibit student involvement and active engagement in the subject matter.

From the Field _____

Brian Furio, an associate professor of speech communication, says, "The connection between students and the teacher is what makes a good class. Professors should always be looking for relationships between events in students' lives and the course content. The event may be family, work, weekend parties, world news, or a campus function. Strive to make the connection and you can always make an impact."

Outstanding teachers know that students bring background knowledge, perceptions, preconceptions, and a certain degree of misinformation to any course. They do not see this as an intellectual deficit, but rather an opportunity to build bridges of understanding between what students know (or think they know) and the concepts of a course. This is the foundation for comprehension development irrespective of course, subject, or topic. Those bridges can be initiated with questions like the following:

- "What did you find most interesting about today's reading?"

- "What surprised you in the chapter you read for today?"

- "What do you think of when I say 'respiration' (or 'Marxism' or 'latitude,' or any other key concept or term)?"

- "In your own words, describe a cell (or 'jazz' or 'surrealism' or 'Particularism')."

- "Here are two positions on abortion (or 'existentialism' or 'global warming' or 'customer service'). Which one do you favor and why?"

- "If you could say one thing to the author of this article, what would it be?"

Higher and Higher

The finest teachers have high expectations for their students. They continually challenge their students, engaging them in higher-order thinking activities, problem solving, creative-thinking extensions, and other instructional activities that s–t–r–e–t–c–h the minds.

Good college teachers raise questions without easy answers. They ask, "How do we know? Why do we believe this? How does this relate to what we already know? When would you need to know this? How can we prove it?" These teachers join their students in an intellectual partnership—an intellectual journey of discovery with tough questions and few pat answers.

Good professors invite students to be active participants in the dynamics of a lesson by *probing*. Simply stated, probing is a series of teacher statements or questions that encourage students to elaborate on their answers to previous questions. Probing is a way of shifting an individual conversation or class discussion to a higher level.

Good teachers use some of these probing questions frequently throughout a lesson:

- **Clarification:** "What do you mean by that?"

- **Obtaining more information:** "What's another word for that?"

- **Making connections:** "Is this like anything else you're familiar with?"

- **Comparison:** "How is your idea similar to or different from _____'s?"

- **Expansion:** "Is there any other information you can add to that?"

- **Validation:** "Why do you believe your response is correct?"

def•i•ni•tion _____

Probing is the process by which students are encouraged to elaborate, expand, and clarify their responses. This is done through a series of "invitational" questions—those that invite students to provide additional information or explanations.

Using Student Ideas

Good college teachers know that they can significantly increase student engagement in the learning process by incorporating students' ideas in classroom discussions by

- Using student ideas by repeating nouns and logical connections.

- Rephrasing student ideas in teacher words.

- Using student ideas to take the next step in problem solving.

- Drawing relationships between student ideas and information shared earlier.

- Using what students say as a summary of important concepts.

 From the Field _____

Kay McAdams, an associate professor of history, says, "I can facilitate student learning best when I help them build scaffolds, or frameworks, that enhance their critical and creative thinking. By blending their ideas with course concepts I help them develop new ways of thinking. There may be less content, but there's certainly more process."

Critical Learning Environment

Good college teachers "pepper" each class with an array of higher-level questions that help students apply, analyze, synthesize, and evaluate content. They use questions to arouse curiosity, stimulate thinking, and engage students in an active model of discovery. Rather than falling into traditional models of teaching in which all the answers are provided, effective professors make good questioning their instructional priority. In short, knowledge is never static, rather it is the dynamic process coupled with knowledge that makes lessons productive and intellectually stimulating.

Good teachers provide opportunities for students to generate their own questions for discovery. However, instead of falling into the trap of providing answers to those self-initiated queries, effective teachers help students discover the answers for themselves. Self-discovery has more lasting implications and effects than simply telling students the answers.

Good teachers provide opportunities for students to relate the content to their personal lives. Having a "head full of facts" is considerably less important than the ability to use that information to solve problems in one's personal or professional life. Good teachers ask students to draw their own conclusions and to defend the choices they make with the following queries:

- "Why do you think that way?"
- "What evidence do you have?"
- "How can you defend your position?"
- "Why is your thinking or position important?"
- "What unanswered questions still remain?"

From the Field _____

Dominic Delli Carpini, an associate professor of English, says, "I like to present material as a topic of debate. For example, 'Here's information some people think is true. What do you think? Let's look at this together.' When the discussion comes out of them, it's stronger learning. Also, I'm not afraid to ask questions I don't really know the answers to."

Dynamic Lessons, Dynamic Teachers

Effective teachers know what students need and they know how to provide for those needs. That means good lesson planning. Here are some "markers" you can use to evaluate the appropriateness of your lessons:

◆ Students know the purpose of the lesson.

◆ Students' background knowledge is assessed and used to help direct the lesson.

◆ Structuring comments or advance organizers are at the beginning of the lesson.

◆ The lesson is logical, clear, and understandable.

◆ Examples, illustrations, and demonstrations are used liberally.

◆ Group and individual activities are provided.

◆ Practice and feedback is regular and systematic.

◆ Student questions and comments are incorporated into the lesson.

◆ A variety of instructional activities and instructional materials are woven throughout a lesson.

◆ Thinking skills are emphasized and higher-order questions are used.

Constructivist Orientation

Good college teachers enjoin students in a process of discovery, exploration, and inquiry. They eschew a transmission model of teaching in which students are merely vessels into which the professor pours knowledge. Rather, good teachers embrace a teaching model that provides students with responsibilities, challenges, and a measure of self-determination.

Good teachers know that learning is not simply the passive accumulation of knowledge, but rather how we make sense of knowledge. Constructivism recognizes that knowledge is created in the mind of the learner. Professors help students relate new content to the knowledge they already have. In addition, students have opportunities to process and apply that knowledge in meaningful situations (sometimes called "hands-on, minds-on" learning).

Good professors promote the idea that knowledge is never a product; rather, it is a process. How we learn is intrinsically more important than what we learn. For college students, this is a critical factor in the academic success they enjoy in a course as well as the intellectual experiences they can carry with them well after the course is over.

From the Field _____

Jessica Nolan, an associate professor of biology, says, "I design my classes with interaction. It's not so much the content—I don't jam them with vast quantities of information—but rather how we process it. I want students to know how science is done; I want them to focus on the process."

Learning as a Lifelong Process

Good teachers keep learning, continually adding to their knowledge base throughout their teaching career. My lifelong motto has always been: "Good teachers have as much to learn as they do to teach." Your education doesn't stop just because you have a terminal degree. It means that if you are to provide the best possible education for your students, then you need to provide yourself with a variety of lifelong learning opportunities, too.

Good teachers keep current, stay active, and continually seek out new answers or new questions for exploration. Your desire to find out more about effective teaching methods and dynamic new discoveries within your field can add immeasurably to your talents as a teacher, and can also add to your students' appreciation of your discipline in their own lives.

It's important that you initiate some research in your own courses—examining, exploring, and investigating the dynamics of learning and the possibilities of teaching. Many college professors (myself included) will tell you that an exploration of the *possibilities* of teaching, rather than the *absolutes*, is the surest way to keep your career fresh, motivating, and engaging. Here's another way to look at it: when you stop asking questions you stop growing, you stop learning, and eventually you stop teaching.

The point is that successful teachers are always in training. Or look at it this way: you never *become* a teacher, you are always *becoming* a teacher! Here are a few ideas to make that happen:

◆ Join or initiate a discussion group about teaching. Meet regularly and talk about issues, concerns, or new teaching strategies.

◆ Once a month, set a personal goal for improvement. Do everything you can to accomplish that goal.

◆ Confer with colleagues in the education department of your institution. What suggestions or teaching techniques can they offer you?

◆ Ask to observe veteran teachers in their classrooms. These can be colleagues within your own department or colleagues from other departments. Take time to talk with them about teaching methods and procedures they find particularly successful.

◆ If possible, visit other institutions in your area. Ask to meet with faculty members from a range of departments, sit in on their classes, and talk afterwards about strategies or teaching procedures.

◆ Obtain teaching books and periodicals from your institution's library. Read them on a regular basis and experiment with the techniques and teaching strategies enumerated in those texts.

◆ Consider taking a continuing education or adult education course on teaching techniques. Many institutions offer a wide variety of education courses for area teachers that are frequently useful for college instructors, too.

There is real value in realizing our capacity for growth and development. Growing, changing, and becoming do not end with the awarding of a terminal degree. They are part of a lifelong process to be pursued and celebrated.

It's not the destination that is important, it's the journey.

The Least You Need to Know

◆ The most important attribute of good teaching is passion.

◆ Recognize that becoming a good teacher is an evolutionary process.

◆ Respecting students has a significant impact on their learning potential.

◆ Good college teachers involve students in a process of self-discovery.

◆ Learning to teach successfully is always a lifelong process.

Glossary: Defining the Terms

active learning   When students process new information instead of committing it to memory.

adjunct professor   An individual who is hired to teach college courses on a part-time basis.

adult/continuing education   Education that is specifically geared for mature learners outside the mainstream education structure.

advance organizer   An intellectual scaffold (typically an illustration) that provides students with a way to organize and understand material.

anonymity   When a student feels a loss of identity or sense of self.

anticipatory set   A lesson opening that prepares students for the learning that will take place.

application   A level of questioning in which students take information and apply it to a new situation.

assessment   Gathering information about the level of performance of individual students.

assistant professor   An entry-level full-time college professor.

associate professor   A rank higher than assistant professor.

asynchronous distance education course   A course in which students access instruction at their convenience, rather than at a scheduled time. Teachers and students are in various locations.

brainstorming   Generating lots of ideas from many individuals.

collaborative learning   A classroom activity in which groups of students tackle a task with multiple answers.

constructivism   The way knowledge is created in the mind of a learner.

cooperative learning   Placing students into small groups and having them work together toward a common goal.

creative thinking   Generating new ways of looking at a situation.

criterion check   A point in any lesson at which the teacher stops and checks to see if students understand the material up to that point.

critical thinking   The ability to analyze information.

deep learners   Individuals who prefer to engage in higher-level thinking activities.

desk copy   A textbook that is provided free of charge to a professor (for possible adoption in a future course).

discrimination   The differential treatment of an individual due to her or his minority status.

distance education   A teaching system in which the teacher and the students are in separate locations.

ELL   English Language Learners.

ESL   English as a Second Language.

evaluation   A method of determining if students learned what they were taught. It is usually conducted at the end of a lesson.

extrinsic individuals   Those who feel that they are strongly influenced by others.

fishbowl   A small group of students who tackle a problem or question while being watched by a larger group of students.

formative evaluation   Evaluation that is utilized concurrently with instruction.

foundational knowledge   This is basic information and factual data that forms the foundation for a body of knowledge.

full professor   The highest rank of full-time work.

goals   The ideas and principles an instructor wishes to include in a course.

graduate assistant   A graduate student who is hired to assist a professor in teaching or administering a college course or courses.

graphic organizer   A chart, outline, or web of ideas or concepts visually organized into groups or categories.

internship   A work-related experience outside of regular classroom experiences.

intrinsic individuals   Those who believe that they are primarily responsible for the events that happen to them.

jigsaw   A cooperative learning strategy in which students take on specialized roles and responsibilities.

knowledge   The facts and data of a subject.

laws of learning   Basic principles (substantiated by educational research) that determine how students learn.

learning-based evaluation   When students are provided opportunities to demonstrate their understanding of important concepts by manipulating those concepts.

lecture   Presenting information to students verbally.

lecturer   Non-tenure-track faculty who teach on a part-time basis.

lesson plan   An outline of goals and objectives, activities designed to help students achieve those goals, and objectives and ways to assess whether students have actually reached those goals and objectives.

mentor   An experienced teacher who assists a new colleague.

metacognition   When an individual thinks about her or his thinking process.

methodology   The way(s) in which information is shared with students.

motivation   An emotion or psychological need that incites a person to do something.

multimedia   A combination of technologies to create an instructional program or experience for students.

objective   A statement that describes what students will be able to do upon completion of an instructional experience.

outcomes   What students will learn as a result of exposure to coarse goals.

peer evaluation   When colleagues evaluate your performance in an academic setting.

performance   The ability to effectively use new information in a productive manner.

performance-based evaluation   When students accumulate points based on the amount of knowledge they've gained.

postsecondary students   Students beyond the high school level who are pursuing a college degree.

practical thinking   The ability to engage in productive problem solving.

prior knowledge   The knowledge a learner already has about a topic or subject, and is able to bring to a new learning situation.

problem solving   The ability to identify and solve problems by applying appropriate skills systematically.

prompting   Assisting students in thinking beyond their response to a question.

rubric   A document that describes varying levels of performance (from high to low) for a specific assignment.

significant learning   Any learning that causes a lasting change in a learner's life.

simulation   An abstraction of a real-life event.

standard   A description of what students should know and be able to do.

stereotyping   The generalizing of a person while ignoring the presence of individual differences.

structured discussion   A discussion in which an instructor takes a strong leadership role.

summative evaluation   Evaluation that occurs at the end of a unit of study.

surface learners   Individuals who like to learn the facts of a subject.

syllabus   A document distributed to college students that outlines the course and the requirements for a satisfactory completion of the course.

synchronous distance education course   A course that meets at a scheduled time, but in multiple locations.

synthesis   The combination of knowledge elements that form a new whole.

taxonomy   An orderly classification of items according to various levels (low to high, small to large).

tenure track   A full-time college teaching position which may convert to a status that gives protection from summary dismissal.

textbook   A collection of the knowledge, concepts, and principles of a selected topic or course.

time on task   The amount of time allocated to successfully complete a task or assignment.

transactional model of learning   A model in which students interact with the material through a variety of interactive learning activities.

transmission model of learning   A model in which students commit large amounts of factual information to memory.

vignette   A brief story or anecdote that illustrates a specific point of view.

wait time   The time between the asking of a question and the solicitation of a response.

Professional Resources and Websites

In conducting the research for this book I came across a variety of resources on teaching college. Many were relatively new; some had been
around for a while. What I found most interesting in these resources was
the universal idea that teaching college is equal parts passion, strategies,
and a fundamental orientation to students.

First, this appendix will provide you with a wealth of written resources to
help you on this magical journey. I have attempted to list the "best of the
best"—those books that will engage, refresh, and stimulate you to become
an outstanding college professor, one students will remember with fondness
and respect.

Also included is a collection of relevant websites. Please be aware that some
websites may change and others may be eliminated. The sites listed here
were current at the writing of this book. However, the volatility of the
Internet means that you may find something different (or even unexpected)
by the time you log on to these listings.

Books

I am indebted to Mel Kulbicki for providing me with a compendium of several previously unknown resources for this list.

Bain, Ken. *What the Best College Teachers Do.* Cambridge, MA: Harvard University Press, 2004.

This book has quickly become one of the most celebrated (and practical) books about college teaching ever written. It is chock-full of practical ideas and worthy philosophies.

Beidler, Peter, ed. *Distinguished Teachers on Effective Teaching.* San Francisco: Jossey-Bass, 1986.

This is a compendium of some of the best ideas on teaching college from some of its best practitioners. It's worth your while to track it down.

Duffy, Donna and Janet Jones. *Teaching Within the Rhythms of the Semester.* San Francisco: Jossey-Bass, 1995.

For those who are just beginning their careers as college teachers, this book can't be beat. It's full of practical ideas and excellent suggestions for any novice instructor.

Filene, Peter. *The Joy of Teaching.* Chapel Hill, NC: University of North Carolina Press, 2005.

This book is an excellent compliment to Ken Bain's book (see above). It, too, is filled with lots of insights and creative perspectives for any college teacher.

Fink, L. Dee. *Creating Significant Learning Experiences.* San Francisco: Jossey-Bass, 2003.

This book provides a complete and detailed description of how a college course should be designed and structured. Fink leaves no stone unturned in this thorough guide.

Magnan, Robert. *147 Practical Tips for Teaching Professors.* Madison, WI: Atwood Publishing, 1990.

Culled from back issues of *The Teaching Professor*, Magnan provides a quick and easy compendium of tricks and tips for any college teacher.

McGlynn, Angela. *Successful Beginnings for College Teaching*. Madison, WI: Atwood Publishing, 2001.

If you're looking for an array of strategies and techniques for getting the semester off to a great start, you can't go wrong with this little guide. This is a gem for any teacher.

McKeachie, Wilbert. *McKeachie's Teaching Tips: Strategies, Research, and Theory for College and University Teachers*. New York: Houghton Mifflin, 2006.

This book is the "gold standard" of books on teaching college. Now in its 12th edition, it is a "must have" for any professor, new or experienced.

Palmer, Parker. *The Courage to Teach*. San Francisco: Jossey-Bass, 1998.

This book offers a thoughtful, inspiring, and practical meditation on the nature of teaching. It is a book to savor and discuss with colleagues over a tall cup of coffee and a jelly donut.

Pascarella, Ernest and Patrick Terenzini. *How College Affects Students*. San Francisco: Jossey-Bass, 1991.

Here is an incredibly investigative book about the impact of college in the lives of students. It's a book to ponder and share.

Rotenberg, Robert. The *Art and Craft of College Teaching: A Guide for New Professors and Graduate Students*. Chicago: Active Learning Book, 2005.

This volume of ideas and strategies provides readers with up-to-date information and lots of practical tips for a successful teaching career.

Journals

Here are several journals you may wish to check out of your campus library, access online, or initiate subscriptions to. They offer an array of up-to-date information on the teaching/learning process:

Higher Education
www.highereducation.org

The Journal of Educational Research
www.heldref.org/jer.php

Journal on Excellence in College Teaching
http://celt.muohio.edu/ject

Journal on Excellence in College Teaching
www.iats.com/publications/journal.html

Research in Higher Education
http://airweb.org/?page=89

The Teaching Professor
www.teachingprofessor.com

Websites

Arizona State University
http://clte.asu.edu

The Center for Learning and Teaching Excellence offers an array of techniques, strategies, and suggestions that can enhance your teaching prowess.

Note: Enter "Center for Teaching Excellence" into any search engine, and you will discover an unbelievable collection and incredible array of teaching resources offered by colleges and universities across the country.

Honolulu Community College
http://honolulu.hawaii.edu/intranet/committees/FacDevCom/guidebk/teachtip/
teachtip.htm

Take the time to log on to this incredible resource. Find the "Teaching Tips Index" and be prepared for one of the most thorough and complete collection of articles about teaching college that you're likely to find anywhere. This is a site not to be missed.

The National Teaching and Learning Forum
www.ntlf.com

This site provides a wealth of information on all levels of education. Be sure to check out their resources specifically geared for college teachers.

New York University
www.nyu.edu/cte

The Center for Teaching Excellence has loads of ideas, reams of valuable resources, and loads of great ideas for any college teacher.

Rutgers University
http://taproject.rutgers.edu/video.php3

Check out "Learning Effective Strategies for Teaching Undergraduates." You'll get help on developing syllabi, conducting lectures, engaging students in discussions, and a host of other topics.

Syllabus Writing 101
https://courses.worldcampus.psu.edu/public/atb3/syllabustemplate/syllabus.html

This page is designed to be a template to write a syllabus for a distance education course. Almost everything you need to craft a distance education course can be found on this site.

University of Delaware
http://cte.udel.edu

The Center for Teaching Effectiveness has a range of resources for college teachers at any stage of their profession.

University of Illinois at Urbana-Champaign
www.oir.uiuc.edu

The Center for Teaching Excellence has a wide range of resources and information for any college instructor. Check it out.

University of Maryland
www.cte.umd.edu

The Center for Teaching Excellence is designed to offer both experienced and novice college teachers with valuable resources and creative ideas to enhance their teaching effectiveness.

University of Minnesota
www1.umn.edu/ohr/teachlearn/tutorials/syllabus

At this site you can participate in a syllabus tutorial which takes you step-by-step through the construction of a well-designed syllabus. This is a great resource for new professors.

Sample Syllabi

A syllabus is the backbone of any college course. It details for students your responsibilities are as well as theirs. It clearly states your expectations and the methods students can employ to satisfactorily satisfy those standards. For that reason, syllabi should be clear, definitive, and precise.

What follows are several (slightly abbreviated) course syllabi from college teachers in a variety of disciplines. They are presented as models of what your syllabi can look like. You are encouraged to review them as examples of different designs, delivery systems, and course requirements.

History 200gm

The American Experience

Professor Terry Seip
Lecture Section: 8:00–9:30 MW
Office: XXX
Phone: XXX
Discussion Sections: 8:00 F, 9:00 F, 10:00 F
E-mail: XXX
Hours: 11:00 F, 12:00 F

HIST 200gm fulfills the General Education requirement in Category I: Western Culture and Traditions, which is designed to "introduce students to the norms and patterns of civilizations associated with the Greco-Roman and European traditions and the legacy of those traditions in North America" and to "stress concepts, values, and events in Western history that have shaped contemporary American and European civilization." As we work to satisfy the intellectual and methodological requirements of this GE category, we hope to provide you with a useful perspective on the nation's past—a central feature of any solid liberal arts education, and, with the family history project, a historical perspective on your personal past.

I. Readings

Divine, Robert, et al. *The American Story*, 2nd ed.

Nash, Roderick and Gregory Graves. *From These Beginnings*. Vol. I and II

Periodic handouts of documents to be used in discussion sessions.

II. Course Requirements

◆ Three essay exams will be given—two in-term exams and a final exam.

◆ A research paper of 15+ pages on your family's personal history over the past few generations.

◆ All students are required to enroll and participate in one of the weekly discussion sections (led by Teaching Assistants).

◆ For those interested, credit for participation in the Joint Educational Project (JEP) is an option.

◆ Each requirement of the course will contribute to your final grade as follows: First Exam: 15%; Second Exam: 20%; Final Exam: 25%; Discussion Sections: 20%; Family History Project: 20%.

III. Tentative Lecture Schedule

1. Background and Beginnings

2. Patterns of Colonial Life

3. From Colonies to Provinces; Coming of Revolution

4. The Family History Project

5. The Revolution and Constitution

6. First Hour Exam

7. Launching and Stabilizing the Early Republic

8. The Antebellum North and West

9. The Antebellum South and Slavery

10. Drift to Disunion and Civil War

11. Contours of Postwar Society and Reaction

12. Second Hour Exam

13. Imperialism and the Great War

14. "Normalcy," Depression, and the New Deal

15. War: Hot, Cold, and the "New World Order"

16. Civil and Other Rights

17. Four Decades of Revolutions and Uncertainty

18. The Nineties and into the Millennium

19. Final Exam

Marine Biology—BIO 210

Professor Jessica Nolan
Office: XXX
Phone: XXX
E-Mail: XXX
Website: XXX
Office Hours: XXX

Class Times and Locations

Lecture: M–F 8:30–10:30 or 11:00–1:00 in A200

Lab: Marine Science Consortium, Wallops Island, VA

Reading

Readings will be placed on my website or on electronic reserve in the library.

Course Description and Objectives

Marine Biology is an introductory course designed to acquaint students with the diversity and ecology of marine organisms. The main objectives of this course are to understand …

- ◆ How scientists investigate questions in marine science.

- ◆ Which organisms are found in the ocean.

- ◆ How marine organisms are adapted to the unique physical, chemical, and geological characteristics of various habitats in the ocean.

- ◆ Aspects of ecological theory as they apply to marine environments.

- ◆ How human activities are impacting the ocean.

Examinations

Lecture exams will contain a variety of questions including multiple choice, true/false, fill-in-the-blank, illustrations, short answer, essay, etc. Your exams may cover material from the lectures, readings, and field trip to the Marine Science Consortium.

Marine Science Consortium

The lab section of this course will include a multiday field trip to the Marine Science Consortium in Wallops Island, VA. We will visit sand dunes, a high-energy beach, a low-energy beach, a salt marsh, and will participate on a boat trip to trawl in nearby channels. You will be asked to determine how physical, chemical, and geological features of the environment help to determine community structure.

Lab Report

While at Wallops Island, we will perform student-designed experiments. Over the semester, you will write up the experiments in scientific paper format, including an introduction, materials and methods, results, and discussion. A detailed description of this assignment is attached to this syllabus.

Evaluation

- Exams (2 × 150 points)   300
- Marine Science Consortium Handout   100
- Lab Report   100
- Total 500 points

Grading Policy

- 4.0 = Excellent (90–100)
- 3.5 = Very Good (85–89)
- 3.0 = Good (80–84)
- 2.5 = Above Average (75–79)
- 2.0 = Average (70–74)
- 1.0 = Below Average (60–69)
- 0 = Failure (<60)

Attendance Policy

It is very important that students attend lectures. We will have several in-class activities, which will be important for the exams… [More]

Writing Standards

Students enrolled in Marine Biology are expected to use literate and effective English in their speech and in their writing. [More]

Academic Dishonesty

Academic dishonesty (including cheating, plagiarism, etc.) will not be tolerated under any circumstances. [More]

Maintaining Copies of Graded Assignments

It is the student's responsibility to save copies (hard copies or disk copies) of all assignments in the unlikely event that materials become lost, destroyed, or damaged while in my possession. [More]

Schedule

1. Introduction, Classifying living things
2. Phytoplankton
3. Invertebrates
4. Invertebrates/Introduction due
5. Fish
6. Test #1/Methods
7. Whales
8. Sea turtles/Birds
9. Marine Science Consortium
10. Coral Reefs
11. Deep Sea
12. Fishing
13. Final/Results and Discussion

Diversity and Racial Conflict

Sociology 142gm

Professor Ed Ransford
Office: XXX
Phone Number: XXX
E-Mail: XXX
Teaching Assistant: XXX

PLEASE TURN OFF ALL CELL PHONES AND BEEPERS

An Overview of the Course

What is "race?" What is "racism?" Why does race continue to matter in contemporary society? This course emphasizes the past and present relations between the white majority and the "colonized" or "kidnapped" minorities (especially, African-Americans, Latinos, Native Americans, and Asian-Americans). White ethnic immigrants and "mixed racial groups" are also discussed.

The focus is on power inequality as the most important dimension of a racial stratification order. For example, the colonized minorities not only entered into relations with whites by force and violence, but they experienced enduring systems of subordination such as the slavery institution and the control of tribal institutions by the Bureau of Indian Affairs.

I think you will find the class challenging and, hopefully, provocative. Your class attendance and participation in lectures and discussion sections are mandatory and constitute an important portion of your final grade.

Required Readings

Course Reader for Soci. 142gm, Ransford

Feagin, *Racist America*

Espiritu, *Asian American Women and Men*

Hayes-Bautista, *La Nueva California*

Course Grade

5% quiz, 26% midterm, 26% empirical paper, 26% final, 10% participation and attendance in discussion sections and 7% attendance lectures. Attendance and participation in class discussions is important and the 17% allocated to A&P can make a substantial difference in your final grade. To receive full credit for attendance and participation, you must arrive to class and discussion sections on time.

The midterm and final emphasize essay questions with a preview set of questions handed out one week before the exam. For example, I will pass out 7 or 8 questions one week before the exam. On the day of the exam, I might call out 3 essays.

Schedule

1. Introduction to the course

2. Multiple Hierarchy Stratification

3. Colonized vs. Immigrant Minorities

4. Conquest of American Indians

5. Asian-Americans

6. Bureau of Indian Affairs

7. Paternalistic race relations

8. Video: Ethnic notions

9. Research methods

10. Later competitive relations

11. "Eyes on the Prize" video

12. Latinos

13. Midterm Review

14. The social construction of race/ethnicity

15. Interracial marriage and growth of multiracial groups

16. "Color of Fear" video

17. Mexican Americans and education

18. Dual mobility patterns in Black America

19. Race, class, and health outcomes

20. Mexican immigration

21. Asian immigration

22. Final exam

Empirical Paper

The empirical paper (about 10–12 pages) is a required observation paper. It must be a current (this semester) empirical paper dealing with some area of race/ethnicity. It must not be a library report or synthesis of existing research. It must involve direct observation or field work (e.g., questionnaire surveys, in-depth interviews, diary accounts of some situation, participant observation, or an analysis of stereotypes in the media books or magazines). You must do the paper to complete the course.

There are three options for the empirical paper:

◆ Participation in the Joint Education Project

◆ Ethnic immersion in churches

◆ Research report on a race/ethnic topic

Index

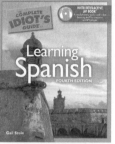